Frog Pond Philosophy

FROG POND PHILOSOPHY

Essays on the Relationship
between
Humans and Nature

STRACHAN DONNELLEY

Edited by
Ceara Donnelley and Bruce Jennings

Foreword by
Frederick L. Kirschenmann

UNIVERSITY PRESS OF KENTUCKY

Scholarly publisher for the Commonwealth,
serving Bellarmine University, Berea College, Centre College of Kentucky,
Eastern Kentucky University, The Filson Historical Society, Georgetown
College, Kentucky Historical Society, Kentucky State University, Morehead
State University, Murray State University, Northern Kentucky University,
Transylvania University, University of Kentucky, University of Louisville,
and Western Kentucky University.
All rights reserved.

Editorial and Sales Offices: The University Press of Kentucky
663 South Limestone Street, Lexington, Kentucky 40508-4008
www.kentuckypress.com

Library of Congress Cataloging-in-Publication Data

Names: Donnelley, Strachan, author.
Title: Frog pond philosophy : essays on the relationship between humans and
    nature / edited by Ceara Donnelley and Bruce Jennings.
Description: Lexington, Kentucky : University Press of Kentucky, 2018. |
    Series: Culture of the land: a series in the new agrarianism | Includes
    bibliographical references and index.
Identifiers: LCCN 2017052027| ISBN 9780813167275 (hardcover : alk. paper) |
    ISBN 9780813167282 (pdf) | ISBN 9780813167299 (epub)
Subjects: LCSH: Human ecology—Philosophy. | Nature—Effect of human
    beings on—Philosophy.
Classification: LCC GF21 .D66 2018 | DDC 304.201—dc23 LC record
    available at https://lccn.loc.gov/2017052027

ISBN 978-0-8131-7669-7 (pbk. : alk. paper)

This book is printed on acid-free paper meeting
the requirements of the American National Standard
for Permanence in Paper for Printed Library Materials.

Manufactured in the United States of America.

Member of the Association
of University Presses

To Vivian

Contents

V. Postlude

Foreword

Strachan Donnelley's *Frog Pond Philosophy* is an extremely important and timely book. We, especially in the industrial world, still seem to be locked into a culture that is focused on instant gratification and the notion that the most efficient way to achieve that objective is through the mechanistic, nature-dominating philosophy proposed by René Descartes, Isaac Newton, and others, and it is a culture that threatens the very health of the planet and the human species that is an integral part of it. As Donnelley points out so eloquently, there have been other thinkers in our history who have advanced an alternative view, including Alfred North Whitehead, Charles Darwin, and Aldo Leopold, but many of our academics have featured their perspectives only as rational academic exercises, which have failed to energize us to embrace the existential reality that we humans are part of nature and all of its emergent properties. We are still focused on how to use nature more efficiently to achieve our distorted objectives, and so we are still a long way from recognizing Leopold's vision that we need to move beyond the notion that the land is a commodity belonging to us rather than a community to which we belong.

Donnelley also used creative analogies to help us make the transition to an engagement philosophy that can move us toward a more alive embrace of nature as an engaged experience in which we are an active part. Among many other analogies, he used music to show that life is a complex interaction, constantly evolving, of "the composer; the musical score; the conductor; the orchestra and the chorus; the soloists; the members of the audience (each with different musical ears and personal concerns); the orchestral hall with its acoustics; the wider world in its present historical and cultural moment; and no doubt more" (see chapter 2). Given this complex and dynamic context, we have no choice but to become personally engaged. Objective, disengaged academic exploration will not do.

This evolving experience of life in nature gives us a radical and extremely important perspective that must become a part of our new culture if we are to evolve with a life experience that has the potential to engage us in a fruitful and sustainable life and world. I hope that this book will be read by academic professionals and business leaders, as well as by ordinary citizens, to start us on a journey toward a new culture that will be essential to our existence *within* nature and to a quality of life that currently escapes us.

Frederick L. Kirschenmann

Introduction

Editors' note: At the time of his death in 2008, Strachan Donnelley had orga-nized a number of his published and unpublished papers for publication as a book and had written this introduction. He did not finalize the sequence of chapters as presented here himself, so this introduction does not present an overview. It does, however, offer an important statement of the intent and the spirit in which Strachan hoped his work would be read. For more infor-mation, see the Editors' Afterword.

I have always believed in truth in advertising. I see no reason to stop now. It will serve me to introduce this collection of essays and articles.

Early last fall, I was diagnosed with gastric cancer, which is inexorably working its dark magic. It is time for me to get my many-roomed house in order, including bringing together these several pieces written over several years of professional philosophic and civic life.

This inconvenient truth and what I like to call "yapping puppies" (the cancer), now having bolted from the kennel, push me in a direction that I want to go in any case. I have long had a core personal and profes-sional passion for exploring nature: its innumerable landscapes, values, and goodness; the nature of earthly ecosystemic life and our own dynamic and historical implications in this incredible realm of natural existence; finally, what we can do, culturally and practically (civically), to help secure and enhance the future of both humans and nature. Humans dwell within an ultimately valuable and good nature. And nature, both abroad and internally within our living, mindful bodies, which include our individ-ual selves, is in us personally, culturally, civically, spiritually, and more. As Alfred North Whitehead would say, humans and nature are mutually and internally in each other (mutually immanent). We together constitute "nature alive." On some level, we all know this to be true, despite counter-vailing cultural and religious habits to the contrary.

The rub is not only the ingrained cultural habits that bedevil an ade-quate understanding of ourselves and our world. Despite our core, experientially well-founded conviction, not easily assailable, that we dwell within nature, we do not fully understand or know how we dwell within nature alive. Most likely, we never will. *Ignoramus:* we are ignorant.

What has this stubborn fact meant for me? At my best, I have lived the life of an explorer, most pointedly as a thinker: before college; as an undergraduate and graduate student; as a "professional thinker" (Hannah Arendt's mocking term for employed philosophers) in teaching institutions; at the Hastings Center (an independent bioethics organization); and presently at the Center for Humans and Nature, which I helped to found in 2003 and still direct. Unsurprisingly, the mission of the center is "to explore, articulate, and promote ethical and civic responsibilities for human communities and nature." We are still on the road.

Exploration and the recognition of my fundamental ignorance is really a key to all this. It accounts, at least in part, for the unconventional road that I have taken in my philosophic and civic career. More or less, I have danced to my own tune and blazed my own path. (With what success, others can judge.) Exploration also marks the character of my writings.

The essays collected in this book center on two themes, which I label now, as I look back over them, "living waters" and "magic mountains." The idea of living waters evoked, sometimes described, always felt, in these essays reflects my passion for fly-fishing, which has been a ruling force in my life and many of these essays. I am a fly-fishing philosopher. Moreover, living waters seems an apt metaphor for my view of the world, still in the making.

The idea of magic mountains expresses the central role that certain philosophers, both from the tradition and more contemporary, have played in my quest and the ongoing evolution of my thinking. I poach the term from e. e. cummings (*The Enormous Room*). As a political dissident and ambulance driver in World War I, cummings met in jail four or five individuals who were morally the most magnificent people he ever encountered. He called them "Magic Mountains." Whether borrowed or not from Thomas Mann (*The Magic Mountain*), the term seems particularly good for thinkers from the cultural, especially philosophic, tradition who have meant so much to me: Heraclitus and Spinoza; Whitehead and Hans Jonas; Nietzsche and Boris Pasternak; Darwin and Ernst Mayr; Isaiah Berlin and Aldo Leopold, among innumerable others. This is an eclectic group, but I hope to reveal, through a glass darkly, the deep, blood-brother bonds between them, and why they might so nurture my own thoughts. All are centrally and philosophically concerned with earthly life.

This has meant one bold, if imperfect, move with respect to presenting these pieces. To underscore their exploratory character, I want to speak in my own voice as far as possible, and to reveal who and what ideas were particularly animating my thinking at the time of writing. Each essay in its own way reveals (I hope) the unfolding progression or "the coming into being" of my ongoing reflections and an invitation to readers to carry farther the quest, whatever their own road or journey might be.

One problem of this approach is the appearance, or reality, of repetition. Readers will note that I take up the same thinkers again and again. However, this is usually in different contexts and in comparison with different thinkers. The different contexts and comparisons are based no doubt on the faith that further dimensions of the thinkers—and the reality and problems that they thought about—will emerge. This must be a primary motivation for this way of proceeding and embracing its imperfections.

Such a plan beyond traditional philosophical and logical argumentation is not innocent or, I think, insignificant. It reflects corresponding moves made by others, including the magic mountains themselves. Darwin's "One Long Argument," *On the Origin of Species,* with its recurrent circling back to plural and fundamental themes and hypotheses, stands in stark contrast to Spinoza's mathematic-logical approach in *The Ethics.* Mayr, in *The Growth of Biological Thought,* states that to understand the new scientific and philosophic worldview of evolutionary biology, you must know the historical evolution of ideas against which the new, trailblazing thinkers fought. This is as much a historical and cultural issue as it is a systematically logical affair. Thus Mayr begins with the pre-Socratic Greeks and historically traces his way through the Western Tradition to Darwin and beyond, following the pattern of evolution itself. Similarly, especially in *Process and Reality,* much to the consternation of many readers, Whitehead circles back again and again to his fundamental themes and philosophic proposals to reveal the plural dimensions of his systematic thought. I will not mention the cryptic aphorisms of Heraclitus and Nietzsche or ponder the significance of Spinoza's mathematical, logical approach. Are these merely eccentric, oddball thinkers? Or do the different methods of argument and presentation bespeak the different visions and realities of the world they explored? (This itself is worth exploring further.)

In the end, I can hear the final call: "Where's the beef?" Why encumber busy lives by reading Donnelley's riffs and philosophic explorations?

Why not go straight to the magic mountains themselves? A very fair question, though unfortunately the magic mountains today live on the dust-gathering shelves of libraries. If I can lead interested readers back to these primary sources and explorers, this is justification enough for this collection. In any case, we all need "guides to the naturally perplexed," to paraphrase Maimonides, the medieval theologian. I hope these essays will serve as such a guide.

I want to add to what is really a common quest: to live well in thought, action, and spirit in the reality into which we have been born and must perish. Look for recurrent themes or leitmotifs: the need to look critically on the culturally dominant, fundamental assumptions of modern sciences and market systems in fashioning "new world symphonies," or philosophic worldviews of nature and earthly life; "populational thinking and realities," "orchestral causation," and "emergence" as systemically related and fundamental dimensions of a nature alive and ourselves; and moral ecology, the troubled middle, and ethical and civic responsibility to humans and nature as a primary moral duty and a much-needed feature of a humanly full and satisfying life. With luck, readers will find more.

Finally, I come to acknowledging those who have professionally and personally so influenced my life. Honestly, given nature alive and the fundamental features of ourselves and the world, how could I acknowledge all who deserve the honor without inadvertently passing over some, clumsily being unjust, and stinging those who have meant so much to me? I choose not to take this risk. Whatever, the individuals know who they are. I hope they realize their significance in my life.

I must break this self-imposed rule and mention my major mentors and good friends: Dick Gurney and Hans Jonas from the past and, more lately, Wes Jackson and Father Francis Kline. But I am sure others have had an equal or greater influence on my life professionally and personally.

I also need explicitly to thank my wife, Vivian, and my five daughters, Inanna, Naomi, Aidan, Ceara, and Tegan. They know how much they have meant to my life and explorations. They have been an extraordinary blessing for this decidedly imperfect one. I should add my debts to the pets, dogs and cats, that have lived with us over the years. These remarkable creatures, along with wildlife, have been open windows to nature alive, its character and goodness.

New York, N.Y.
June 11, 2008

I

Two Preludes

1

Prelude

The Marginalist

Father Francis Kline, abbot of Mepkin Abbey, Moncks Corner, South Carolina, was deeply loved and respected by those who knew him: the brothers and nuns connected to the monastery, the citizens of Berkeley County, Charleston, and the Lowcountry, and well beyond, including other regions in the United States, South America, and Europe (for example, the Vatican). Father Francis was brilliant and uncommon, a graduate of the Juilliard School of Music, headed for an international career as an organist, when he had one of those days and became a Trappist monk. Slight of build, dark haired and dark eyed, with an impish smile and a wicked sense of humor, Francis was equally at home with local and ecclesiastical politics and inside gossip about the music world as he was with metaphysics and creatively updating the 700–900-year-old Cistercian theology. He could shift these gears on a dime. In sum, he was a unique moral and spiritual force and authority for many of us who came from widely disparate cultural, social, and economic backgrounds.

I came to learn that as a person and Cistercian monk, Francis considered himself a "marginalist." He used the term in a pregnant sense heretofore unknown to me. I want to explore the meaning and significance of "marginalist" and "marginalism" in the best way that I know how: by examining my time with Francis as a friend and professional colleague. I have come to recognize a way of life and being that I never fully appreciated—a way of life crucial for our time and the civic challenges that we face both here in the United States and abroad.

I first met Francis when I was at the Hastings Center, an independent bioethics organization in Garrison, New York. It was the late 1990s. I had recently stepped down as the president of the center to become a director of a Humans and Nature program, with work in South Carolina's Lowcountry, New York, and Chicago, among other places. Francis showed up one day more or less unannounced. A pink note informed me that an abbot was coming for a visit. I was taken aback and, to be honest, somewhat peeved. I had many visitors, but an abbot of a monastery? Was there no control or screening in place? Whatever, Francis arrived, and we went into my office, which offered an extraordinary commanding view of a big bend in the Hudson River and West Point. We quickly slipped into a substantive discussion about Mepkin Abbey and Francis's community and conservation work in Berkeley County. Francis immediately put me at ease and intrigued me. I took him down to lunch with my Hastings Center colleagues, and he equally captivated them.

In fact, I felt so comfortable with Abbot Francis that within two hours, I asked him bluntly, "Francis, what do you do with Darwin?" (Darwinian evolutionary biology, thanks to Ernst Mayr, a leading twentieth-century biological scientist and philosopher, had become a major interest of mine). "Darwin? I have no problem with Darwin. It's the fundamentalists in South Carolina that are my problem. You know that there is an open hunting season on Catholics in South Carolina." Francis gave what I was to learn was a characteristic giggle. He was my man, and we became friends there and then. We soon became professional colleagues, holding Humans and Nature Lowcountry meetings at Mepkin Abbey.

We held a planning session before one such meeting. The meeting was to be entitled "And God Saw It Was Good" and was intended to help "green" local churches and their congregations. (Our efforts were only mildly successful, especially with the clergy.) I was asked to speak by Bruce Coull, our codirector of Lowcountry efforts and dean of the School of the Environment at the University of South Carolina. However, he told me that I should not speak about Darwin. I paused for a moment and asked if I could speak about Aldo Leopold, the patron saint of American conservation. "Yes." That was all that I needed.

Francis was present at the session, and I again asked him in all seriousness, "What do you do with Darwin?" This time he looked me straight in the eye and said in all earnestness, "Strachan, in the Catholic Church there are two traditions, the Dogmatic and the Interpretative tradition. We Cistercians are enjoined *not* to take sacred texts literally, but to return to them again and again, to interpret and reinterpret their meaning in light of our worldly experience and existence."

This set off in me a minor epiphany. Francis was not talking just about the Catholic Church or religion in general, but about every discipline that I know, theoretical or practical. There are dogmatists, who know things with unshakable certainty, and there are interpreters who are forever exploring the inexhaustible complexity and plural dimensions of the world. Francis was a frontline explorer. He knew that he did not know but was a lover of wisdom and understanding, the old definition of a philosopher. Here was another deep bond between us.

This trait vividly displayed itself at the meeting. Denied my standard riff on Darwin and Ernst Mayr, I borrowed a page out of Leopold's *A Sand County Almanac* and told some wild trout and salmon stories, involving me, my daughters, and the deep meaning rivers and fish have for us. The audience was puzzled and hushed by these unusual stories, not the ordinary fare of monasteries or churches. I saw Francis sitting along the side of the library conference room, his head in his hands, nodding in recognition. He knew that I was speaking about experiences of the Ultimate, my participation in a wild, natural reality much wider than myself, my daughters, and the fish. In short, I was describing spiritual or religious experiences unknown to Francis, which all the more interested him. As noted, Francis was a spiritual trailblazer, ever ready for fresh, new disclosures of the Ultimate and the Sacred. Francis and I never tried to convert one another to a monastic or a wild river and fish life. We had too much mutual respect, too much to learn from one another for such clumsy misadventure.

There emerged another dimension to our relationship, which came unexpectedly. We were having a characteristically fine dinner at Mepkin, cooked by Francis's indispensable sidekick, Cecilia, who loved him dearly. After much good food and wine, I talked freely about my mother, Mimi, who was suffering from Alzheimer's disease in our old family home in Libertyville, Illinois. I was telling Francis about the good, funny moments that came with caring for my mother. I mentioned in particular Mimi's unplanned trip to a nearby hospital. I arrived from New York to find my uncle in field boots directing traffic in the emergency room. Using what diplomatic skills I could muster, plus my status as durable power of attorney, I got my distraught uncle out of the emergency room, for which the doctor thanked me profusely. The hospital staff stabilized my mother, and the crisis passed. The next day, before leaving, I told Mimi that I had to go home to New York and walk the dogs, that we lived in a Dr. Dolittle house filled with animals and children. She looked at me quizzically. "How do you know Dr. Dolittle!?" (She had read the book to me as a child some fifty or sixty years earlier.) I tried another memory experiment and mentioned Uncle Wiggily, another children's book that we read together. "How do you know Uncle Wiggily!?" She then added, "You know, you are a good-looking man."

I laughed. How often do mothers tell their sons that they are good-looking men? I went home to New York but immediately was called back to Illinois. Mimi's condition had worsened significantly. On my return, I said that I had walked the dogs, so now I was back. Mimi smiled and successfully weathered another crisis.

While I was telling my Mimi stories, Francis was silent. Then, with deep feeling, he thanked me for telling him such intimate, personal, loving details of my life. He felt privileged by such generosity. I did not think it such a significant deal, but Francis obviously meant what he said and that took me aback. Later he spoke eloquently at my mother's memorial service and officiated at my daughter Naomi's wedding, giving an extraordinary, seemingly spontaneous meditation about my family and our relationship to the surrounding Illinois farmscape. At the wedding, which cost him much effort (he was fighting cancer), we acknowledged to one another that we were like brothers, with a deep and unique brotherly love that I, for one, had never felt before.

I mention this personal side of my relation with Francis not only because it gives me pleasure, and I want to acknowledge my personal debt to him, but mainly because it crucially leads and weaves into the main focus of my interest: the nature of the marginalist, marginalism, and their human significance.

Here I skate on the thinnest of ice, for I am not a student of religion or the Trappist, Cistercian mode of monastic life. I have read a bit about what Francis has said on the subject, meant mostly for a religious, if not Catholic, audience. But I would rather give my own imagination free rein, guided by what I personally learned from Francis and his life.

If I understand Francis correctly, the marginalist leads a freely chosen, highly disciplined mode of life, meant to serve one's "home" community, whether that be a monastery, the Catholic Church or other religious institution, or a civic community (local, regional, national, global), if not more, including the ecospheric community that is the earth and includes all life.

The marginalist periodically and regularly leaves the home community so at appropriate moments to return to it, to serve it by helping to renew its foundational mores, values, or ideals. The marginalist leaves the world of everyday life to seek, explore, live, and become his or her fundamental passion. For Francis, a Cistercian monk, this journey was following the life of Christ in the truest, most personal, authentic way that he could. The fruits of this quest, carried out on the margins of the communities to which Francis belonged, account for the authority, the strength, the "gravitas" that Francis held and carried when he returned to the communal world and, when necessary, spoke truth to power.

I use Francis and his passion for following the life of Christ as a particular case study of marginalism. However, I am a philosopher and want to be true to my own origins and journey. I want to reserve the right to generalize from my particular experience of Francis. I want to hold open the possibility, if not reality, that there are many authentic forms or modes of marginalism, marginalists, ways of "speaking truth to power" for the sake of that power's and our own good. If this is true, it is a great boon. Given the state of our earthly world, both human and natural, we need all the authentic marginalists, in all their differences, that we can get. I think—no, I know—that Francis would agree.

I do feel that all marginalists share certain things in common. In following and exploring their fundamental passions and ways of life—whether it be religious, philosophical, scientific, naturalist, artistic, political, or the innumerable other forms it may take—the marginalist encounters and recognizes what he or she takes to be ultimate reality, laced with final significance, meaning, goodness (value), or sacredness—a reality that is much wider than the self and embraces all things. That what is ultimately sought can be "taken" in so many innumerable ways and that the seeker can "take" (interpret) the ultimate in equally innumerable ways speaks volumes about this fundamental reality and about our human selves, the seekers (explorers, the marginalists themselves). This has both significant theoretical and practical import that I pass over here.

Back to Francis and his marginalist ventures. I stick to events with which I was personally involved. The first concerned a Humans and Nature meeting held at Mepkin Abbey about the Santee-Cooper River. The Cooper River, emptying into Charleston Bay, is the Hudson River of Berkeley and Charleston Counties, laden with a complex natural and cultural history, intricately intertwined. Many stakeholders—fishermen, hunters, other recreationists, cultural historians, landowners, businessmen, among others—are passionately concerned with conserving the river in the face of an onslaught of development that threatens the historical culture and nature of South Carolina and the Lowcountry. The problem was that these seemingly natural allies do not like each other very much and would just as soon shoot at one another as talk and collaborate.

Francis had a simple but brilliant idea. Invite the stakeholders to a meeting on the Cooper River in the library at Mepkin Abbey. No one would fight and curse at one another in the library and in the presence of Francis, whom all knew and deeply respected. Beyond this initial assumption, we had no idea what would happen. But it was worth the risk and the fun that no doubt would follow.

The stakeholders came and behaved themselves. There were two excellent presentations on the natural and cultural history of the Cooper River, and a lively discussion ensued. Without forcing our Humans and Nature agenda on the meeting, we asked some leading questions, focusing on water flow regimes, which was a central concern of the participants. "Where does the Cooper River start?" "In North Carolina." "How many dams are there on the river?" "Eighteen." "Is there any coordination of flow regimes between the dams?" "No! We need to go to Washington and talk to Fritz Hollings [South Carolina's beloved senior senator]!" Without raising the red flag of regionalism, we had slipped into watershed thinking.

A political leader of Berkeley County went off on a private property harangue. (I voluntarily invoke Chatham's rules, revealing no names or professional affiliations.) "We do not need people, laws, and regulations to tell us what to do with our land." Without thinking, I asked the politician, "Do private property rights imply private property responsibilities?" "Yes, they do." I glanced at Francis, who looked like he was going to fall off his chair. Here was a powerful local politician making a telling moral and civic statement in public.

Whatever, the meeting continued in the same positive and constructive vein until the stakeholders asked, "You have your Lowcountry Humans and Nature Forum. Why can't we have our own Cooper River Forum?" We said they could, and we would help them set it up at another meeting. At that meeting we elected an executive committee that included a respected African American from a local Gullah community (Cainhoy) and a female forester from the nearby Marion Forest (their own idea). Consequently, the group established a Cooper River task force, and the politician became a leading local proponent for natural and cultural conservation. Francis stayed involved throughout the process.

In hindsight, we called the event "The Miracle Meeting." Who could have predicted such an outcome? Consider for yourself the role that Francis played, his very being and presence, as well as sage advice, in all this.

But this was not the end of the story. Not long after, MeadWestvaco, a major regional timber company, announced that it was selling 10,000 acres of its prime Bonneau Ferry holdings to a private developer. (Bonneau Ferry, close by Mepkin Abbey, included a conference center/guest-house complex.) Against prior practice, MeadWestvaco did not signal its intentions to the conservation community, but rather called a meeting of all parties to announce that this was a done deal. Everyone should save their breath, time, energy, and money in trying to stop it.

Francis was at the meeting in his abbot's robes. (I was not at the meeting but got reports from reliable friends.) At a crucial, appropriate moment, Francis looked the MeadeWestvaco representatives squarely in the eyes. "God damn you," he said, and turning his head to the side, added, "and that is a verb!"

MeadeWestvaco backed down and reopened the deal. Governor Mark Sanford of South Carolina got involved, as did Fritz Hollings. Senator Hollings was leaving the Senate, and he took this challenge as his last hurrah. He knew the landscape of federally appropriated but unspent money and cobbled together $50 million.

Not only was Bonneau Ferry saved and given to South Carolina's Department of Natural Resources, but another 15,000–30,000 acres of prime historical, cultural, and natural land in Berkeley County was protected from development. This land included 4,000 acres of land owned by a self-described fisherman who had been at the original Miracle Meeting at Mepkin. He was going to sell a conservation easement for $8 million–$9 million, quite a deal, I thought. However, before the deal was consummated, a developer from Georgia offered the fisherman $32 million for the 4,000 acres. The developer was told, "Get out of here. I don't want to hear about it"—so enamored had the fisherman become with conserving Berkeley County and Cooper River fishing for his grandchildren. As it turns out, the fisherman was also a timber man, land rich and cash poor thanks to the devastation wrought by Hurricane Hugo, and could afford his decision. Nevertheless, to turn away $24 million is noble and impressive under any circumstances.

What role did Francis play in this complex turn of events? The events themselves tell the story. The respect, love, and authority commanded by this consummate marginalist negated powerful political and economic interests, though other important players were obviously involved. Whatever, his contribution was the being and force of personal moral and spiritual authority and was recognized as such by everyone involved.

This was not the end of Francis's effect on ensuing events. Despite the ravages of cancer and its treatment, he tried to help create a Humans and Nature conference center at Bonneau Ferry, to be jointly sponsored by Mepkin Abbey, South Carolina's DNR, and our own Center for Humans and Nature. (Strange bedfellows indeed.) The Bonneau Ferry buildings proved to be beyond renovation, and we switched to an alliance between the three organizations to ongoingly explore at Mepkin our moral and civic responsibilities to the future of the Lowcountry's humans and nature, now forever complicated by climate (really ecospheric) change, global warming, and rising sea levels.

Francis died soon after in August 2006. Many of us refused to believe that he could be touched by such mortal business. He was too indispensable to the region's conservation work. Francis knew better. He successfully pressed to complete a conservation easement for Mepkin Abbey, which required the blessing of the Vatican. (No obstacle for Francis's political skills.) He quit a torturous cancer treatment regime at Memorial Sloan Kettering Cancer Center in New York to come home and spend his remaining days with his brothers at Mepkin and with his God and Christ. Personally, this move robbed me of wonderful lunches and dinners in New York during which we would jump back and forth between intimate matters of health; the shallow-rooted, consumerist market culture of our times; and the work still to be done in the Lowcountry. The latter conversations summoned forth all the former energy and acute judgments of the marginalist who would not, could not, quit.

During his last days at Mepkin, amidst what must have been much pain and suffering, Francis planned and orchestrated his own funeral and memorial service. (I imagine, or know, that Francis at times could be a control freak, not always a sweetie.) Whatever, with some impish delight, I am sure, he assigned me to talk at his memorial service about his contributions to conservation in the Lowcountry and elsewhere. I considered this a singular honor. However, Francis knew that this task would push me to reexplore our parallel journeys, their commonalities and differences, and their significance. I imagine that this gave him one of his last impish chuckles.

At the service, I concluded my remarks and returned to my seat on the podium. I was met by a large, workman-like hand, which I soon learned belonged to the bishop of Charleston, the leader of the local diocese that included Mepkin Abbey. There were tears on his fleshy, aging face. "Thank you. You caught Francis perfectly. That was eloquent, eloquent words that can only come from the heart."

The bishop's words moved me a great deal, especially coming from someone with whom Francis, the marginalist, must have often "spoke truth to power." He, too, obviously loved and respected Francis deeply.

That day, I think, it finally hit me. I, too, and many of my colleagues involved with the Center for Humans and Nature are and have been marginalists, each individually an explorer of the Ultimate, with an urge to return home to speak truth to power. Moreover, this is the moral and civic role that we ought to play in the world. We need to spawn more and more marginalists, a whole next generation, with civic communities, local, regional, national, and global, that genuinely come to welcome and cherish their marginalist critics. This may be the only way that we can realistically hope to protect the imperfect but wildly valuable and good realm of earthly being to which we inextricably, perhaps without reminder, belong. Ultimate matters are at stake.

What would my life have been if Francis, the marginalist, had not showed up at the Hastings Center in the late 1990s? What would I have missed? Certainly some of the blessings of my existence, including the unspoken encouragement to stay the course of an exploring philosophic and conservation marginalist.

2

Prelude

The Roots of a Philosophic Vocation—
Prairie Ball Fields and
Louisville Slugger Ideas

In 2007, Al Gore, former vice president of the United States and Nobel Prize winner, made us realize that we have come to the time of "inconvenient truths." Calving Greenland glaciers and melting Arctic ice, perhaps more than Gore's film itself, are driving home the sobering realities of global warming, rapid climate change, indeed long-term ecospheric change in which we humans are inextricably enmeshed. We are stunned and disheartened by the ongoing political and civic failure to prepare for and respond to adequately the manifestations of these changes that are already apparent (such as Hurricane Katrina and its aftermath). We witness an ecologically ill-advised rush into biofuels, especially corn ethanol, which will only exacerbate Midwestern industrial agriculture's pillaging of soils, freshwater, wildlife, and rural communities, not to mention vain, desperate attempts to extract the last quantum of remaining fossil carbon energy: coal, natural gas, dirty oil from tar sands—entrepreneurial dreams (or nightmares) all promising future environmental and ecological disasters.

Further, we are living through a paralysis of governments at all levels. We are amidst presidential primary races that seem more like American Idol than genuine, democratic processes. Our political and cultural, if not civic, lives run to the tune of, or are run by, a free-enterprise market economy that characteristically knows no moral oughts or civic responsibilities. And as they say on NPR's *Market Place*, "the market giveth, and the market taketh away." The glib biblical allusion is telling. What god does present American civic society worship? Which god or ultimate should we the people worship? Given that the state of the union is more or less in disarray, this is a serious moral and civic question. These too are inconvenient truths with which we must grapple; less tangible than severe weather, drought, or melting glaciers and ice caps, perhaps, but no less important.

And speaking of inconvenient truths, in 2007, at the Vernal Equinox, I turned sixty-five, once the mandatory retirement age, and still a psychic threshold in one's identity. On my birthday, I woke up Grumpy Gramps, but thanks to my family, which includes five daughters and five grandchildren, the dark cloud soon passed. However, a week later we lost a good, old friend. We had to turf, put down, our thirteen-year-old black Labrador, Snorri. No, Snorri was not named after one of Snow White's seven dwarfs, but after the great poet-historian of the legendary Icelandic Sagas, stories of times long past. As I gently stroked Snorri's head for the last time, I told him that I soon enough would follow, a remark that unnerved the young attending veterinarian.

Memento mori, perhaps inevitably provoking stock taking and mortal reflections. How did I get to where I am today? Indeed, where *am* I now? And where will I be going in the future? For how many years? For how many good, productive years? I am amidst my own climate of concern and change. These questions are worth pondering, at least for me. Here they serve as the backdrop for a philosophic riff on prairie ball fields, Louisville Slugger ideas, and conservation philosophy and ethics.

I

I was born in 1942 during World War II. After my father returned from the navy in 1945, we soon left the Chicago suburban town of Lake Forest and moved to a nearby rural farming community, Libertyville (population 5,000). This was a fateful move for me and my family.

We first lived in an old house adjacent to a dairy farm that my father rented to a farm family with over twenty children. Our house was on the corner of Casey and Almond, both gravel roads. In 1952, we moved to a new house built atop a former alfalfa field. We called our new homestead, which included a small barn and dog kennel, Windblown Hill. Though I and my own family have lived in New York City since 1969 and both of my parents are gone, we still hold on to Windblown Hill, now only for sentimental reasons and the beauty of the Midwestern farmscape.

Over the last forty-five years, Libertyville has radically changed (its present population is more than 30,000), and it is now a full-blown suburb of Chicago. Windblown Hill lies in the heart of Liberty Prairie Preserve, some 2,000 acres of mostly protected farmland, woods, marshes and wetlands, remnants of native prairie, even a 3,000-year-old archeological site. The preserve is a challenging community effort aimed at protecting the traditional farmscapes from encroaching housing developments and wildfire sprawl emanating from Chicago and its older suburbs. The dairy cows are gone. Casey and Almond are now paved roads, with morning and evening rush hours and traffic jams.

Back to the late 1940s and 1950s. Though I continued to attend school in nearby Lake Forest, it was Libertyville, Windblown Hill, and the rural farming landscape that importantly shaped my life and emerging self. I spent much of my time bicycling up and down the gravel roads, fishing for bullheads in the nearby Des Plaines River, hanging around the dairy farm and helping with seasonal haying, as well as practicing sports by myself, inside or outside our barn, on the driveway or the lawn, or in the surrounding fields, anywhere and any sport: football, basketball, ice hockey, baseball, not to mention fishing, hunting, and more. I was a sports nut. Here the wider world of Libertyville comes into play.

Libertyville was a typical rural Midwestern town, crazed by baseball. Out of the population of 5,000 individuals, 500 boys and girls played on various teams, all in uniforms. Knowing no one save kids from Sunday school at the Presbyterian Church, I tried out for Little League baseball. (In passing I should mention that my Sunday school experience was a mixed blessing. I was the new kid in the pew, and all there was not brotherly love. I later came to consider that I had run into a particularly virulent form of Northern Illinois Presbyterianism, which eventually drove me into trout streams and salmon rivers for spiritual and religious nourishment. That was an unmixed, decided blessing.)

Well over 100 boys vied for four Little League teams. At age eleven, this was my first encounter with open competition. I made the cut and was assigned to play first base for a team sponsored by the Sparkler Manufacturing Company. I had a double my first time at bat and a good season. The next year I was sent to an expansion team in a nearby rural town, playing for the Mundelein Businessmen's Association. (We had blue hats with red bills, just like the then Milwaukee Braves.) After Little League, I played on Pony League and American Legion teams until my Midwestern career ended in my later teens.

I will not dwell on my baseball exploits, successes or failures. (Early on, I passionately wanted to play in the major leagues and with the Chicago Cubs in particular, which, given their prowess and talent, did not seem beyond the realm of imagination.) Rather, I want to fasten upon two facets of my Midwestern baseball years that vividly live on in the depths of my being: prairie baseball fields and Louisville Slugger bats.

Old prairie ball fields are indeed memorable. Our Little League field had fences 255 feet from home plate; stands for 400 or so spectators (mostly parents and family); a loudspeaker and an announcer; and lights for night games. (We were well ahead of the Cubs and Wrigley Field.) However, it was in later years that the prairie ball fields really came into play. In the town of Half Day, the ball park had a cow pasture in right field, a cemetery in center field, and a trailer park in left field. Where to hit? We chose right field, but not out of respect for the living or the dead. The right fielder moved about gingerly, trying to avoid cow pies. There was also the baseball field in Volo, with a swamp in left center. To my and everybody else's surprise, I lined a pitch into the swamp and chugged around the bases for a home run. Nature had come to my aid. Finally, there was a flat, featureless ball park (only a backstop) in Gurnee. As the sun set and evening twilight approached, I was playing center field, and our pitcher was protecting a 1–0 lead with a no-hitter. The batter hit a ball toward deep right center. I ran over as fast as I could and thrust my glove over my head into the air. The ball struck and stuck in the glove's webbing. (Did I catch the ball, or did the ball catch me?) Our loyal fans went wild. The game and the no-hitter were saved. Horns blasted from fifteen or more cars, the time-honored way to celebrate on prairie baseball fields. I ran into the bench amidst a cacophony of honks, a triumphant moment.

But what about the Louisville Slugger bats? There were no metal bats back then, with their tinny ping when the bat strikes a ball. This was the real thing, wooden bats. (We used to be off and running at the crack of the bat. What do runners do now—listen for pings?) My first Louisville Slugger was a 32-inch, big-barreled, Johnny Mize model, used in Little League. Parents of opposing teams grumbled. The bat, they claimed, exceeded Little League regulations. No matter, I got seven hits over two games before I broke the bat, or it was taken out of my hands. Choosing the right Louisville Slugger was always a fundamental ritual. Just to swing those straw-colored, shiny varnished bats, with the oval Hillerich & Bradsby trademark, was magical. I remember my last Louisville Slugger, a 35-inch Ernie Banks model. I have it to this day, unmarred by baseball marks. It proved too heavy for me to use in games. I did not have Ernie's powerful wrists, which propelled him into baseball's Hall of Fame, despite having played for the Cubs.

II

Enough of the past: literal prairie baseball fields and Louisville Slugger bats. I now find myself in different arenas, wielding different tools. As a conservation philosopher, I now ply my wares in natural ecosystems and landscapes, including their human communities. I use what skills I have as a thinker, which fundamentally involves ideas, inherited from the past or brewed up anew. Some people traffic in drugs. I traffic in ideas. Whatever, these new arenas and tools have deep experiential and metaphorical roots in my Libertyville youth and baseball past.

I am fortunate to have had graduate school, doctoral training in the history of philosophy, going back to the pre-Socratic Greeks. (I studied at the University in Exile, home of mostly Jewish scholars fleeing Hitler's Europe: the Graduate Faculty at the New School for Social Research in New York City.) Even for a student of philosophy, this was a rare opportunity. (Academic philosophy, to its own impoverishment, usually spurns its own history.) I have always been drawn to big, bold thinkers with truly big ideas, the Magic Mountains of philosophy's history, to borrow a phrase from e. e. cummings. In short, I have been primarily drawn to cosmological thinkers—those interested in understanding the universe or cosmos and our human place within it, big picture philosophy. Louisville Slugger ideas lighting up the cosmic playing field. Here is where my past experientially and metaphorically undergirds my present. The young one in me refuses to grow up and stop swinging for the fences or the swamp.

Many "enlightened" modern philosophers believe that we are well beyond the age of such heroic, big picture thinking. They are wrong. Human individuals and communities endemically and necessarily need some form of cosmogonic myth, some basic philosophic, moral, and spiritual orientation. Such thinking is inevitable, as well as necessary and good, if done critically and with awareness of what we are doing: pursuing philosophic, speculative *understanding* and *meaning*. This is not the same as scientific *knowledge*, testable by recurrence to natural or empirical phenomena. Such understanding and meaning are necessary for us to gain a fundamental orientation in the world and, moreover, to discern our fundamental moral and civic responsibilities to the earthly world of humans and nature. In short, the heights and depths of philosophic speculation have decided and important practical implications.

That is to say that traditional and venerable philosophic terms and inquiries, ontology, cosmology, and cosmogony, *matter*. Ontology is the study of the fundamental character of reality or "being": for example, whether reality is essentially permanent, unchanging, and eternal; or always in a state of becoming, change, flux, and process; or some intermingling of permanence and change. Cosmology is the study of the structure (permanent or achieved) of the universe or cosmos. On the other hand, cosmogony is the study of the genesis or coming-into-being of the (structured) universe or cosmos. Among many others, the Greeks, starting with the pre-Socratic philosophers, such as Heraclitus, and later Plato had much to say on these issues.

These seemingly esoteric, though actually fundamental, questions and explorations are relevant to us because they are all deeply value laden, have moral import, and form the backbone of cultural and ethical worldviews. For example, the cosmogonic myths ("true stories") of traditional societies provided a fundamental and socially crucial cultural and moral orientation to members of their communities (Eliade 1985). The myths related where the world and humans came from, who the community members were, their role and significance in the wider scheme of things, and what their fundamental moral duties were to themselves and wider reality.

Over my philosophic career, my concern has been the importance of such fundamental ideas in discerning the landscape of conservation ethics and our attendant moral and civic responsibilities. Here I present a few relevant examples of such ruling ideas. I want particularly to keep our eye on the philosophic interpretation of humans' relation to nature.

For many, the term "cosmogony" is esoteric. We have never heard of it. (My philosophic mentor, Hans Jonas, once quipped that we Americans are allergic to metaphysics, the critical consideration of our deepest big ideas.) Yet cosmogonic stories or creation myths are central to our cultural lives, as they have been to all human societies. A dominant cosmogonic myth (or myths) of the Western tradition is expressed in the Bible's Book of Genesis. God created the world in six days; set its existential, including human, dramas in motion for all time; and saw or declared His creation was good. (There is a Louisville Slugger, world-orienting idea if ever there was one.)

But we should note at once that this is not the only cosmogonic myth the world has known and that it may not capture the "whole truth" that we practically and morally need. There have been innumerable cosmogonic myths, reflecting their times, places, and worldly settings. For example, pre-Socratic philosopher Heraclitus, who lived in the fifth century BCE, claimed that it is wise to know that all things are one: the Logos or Everliving Fire, kindling and extinguishing in measures. When duly elaborated, this fundamental idea explains all things as dynamically and essentially intertwined and mutually dependent on each other and the underlying Logos for their very being or existence. This dynamic, living cosmic web includes the "fiery" philosopher Heraclitus himself. The knower, knowing, and the known are radically, fundamentally one and the same (aspects of the Everliving Fire). This powerful idea and worldview remains importantly suggestive to me, and others, to this day.

Or take the much later scientific and philosophic revolution of the sixteenth and seventeenth centuries in Europe, which involved a significant shift in fundamental, world-orienting ideas. Descartes and his philosophic and scientific cohorts elaborated a new kind of "substance" philosophy, defining substance "as that which requires nothing else in order to exist" (Descartes 1969: 323). Descartes posited three kinds of substance: God, Mind (*res cogitans*), and Matter (*res extensa*). Here is Descartes's famous dualism of mind and body, his radical split of humans and nature, which haunts us to this day. Arguably, he was most interested in fashioning a fundamental new conception of nature: a merely material nature—no minds, no values—that is ruled by deterministic, billiard-balls-in-motion causation. This conception served the new mathematical-mechanistic science of the day, which was interested in discovering the universal and timeless laws of nature (for example, the laws of gravitation, thermodynamics, and more). All this led to a new Deistic conception of the universe. God created matter *ex nihilo*, set it in motion guided by divinely instituted laws of nature, and exited the natural cosmic scene. Scientists and philosophers were left free to use their rational wits (*res cogitans*) to discover the laws and workings of this "naturally necessitated" world. Note the radical change in worldview from traditional Greek and Christian conceptions. This change was effected by a shift in fundamental ideas and presuppositions. (Averting their gaze from this history, the more hard-nosed, practical, and pragmatic among us still vigorously proclaim that ideas do not matter!) Moreover, we should note that many other philosophers and theologians powerfully challenged Descartes and questioned the coherence of his novel dualistic thinking and philosophic meditations. For me the most interesting challenge, and the one with enduring significance for conservation philosophy, came from Spinoza.

Spinoza claimed that in truth there is only *one* substance, God or Nature (*Deus sive Natura*): an infinite substance with infinite attributes, acting out of the necessity of its own being (no choice, no free will). Everything else consists of modifications or modes of this one substance, sharing in the attributes of which we know only two: body and mind (or the idea of the body). Each finite mode has, as its essence, a *conatus,* an active endeavor to preserve in its own individual being. All modes are systemically and causally interlocked with one another in their individual endeavors to persevere in their being. Spinoza as a philosopher conceives himself as integrally interwoven in this cosmic realm of natural, dynamic necessity. He nevertheless points the way to freedom through rational (scientific and philosophic) knowledge and to high blessedness (the intellectual love of God or Nature). In Spinoza's monistic thinking we can discern shades of Heraclitus and a whole new rack of Louisville Slugger ideas that may yet serve us well, especially considering that, with Spinoza, nature is alive (animated) and value laden, and not dead and valueless, as with Descartes and more orthodox and positivist materialists and physicalists.

How can we swing these ideas for the fences and put them to use? I believe that it is fundamental, world-orienting ideas such as these that are required in order to establish a comprehensive and persuasive conservation ethic; an ethic that will help us discern our complex civic and moral responsibilities to humans and nature, both in the present and long into the future.

One key connecting link between cosmology and conservation ethics resides in the work of Charles Darwin and in the fields of evolutionary and ecological biology. Ernst Mayr, perhaps the leading twentieth-century evolutionary biologist and philosopher, has claimed that Darwin inaugurates *the* most profound revolution in Western scientific and philosophic thought—a revolution that most of our intellectual culture, to say nothing of our political culture, has yet to grasp. To follow our guiding metaphor, in the aftermath of Darwinian, evolutionary, and ecological thinking, there has been a radical change of profound Louisville Slugger ideas that, for the most part, has escaped notice. Yet, according to Mayr, unless we digest and assimilate this fundamental conceptual shift, this new framework of thinking, we will never appreciate and understand evolutionary and ecological realities and our responsibilities to nature and ourselves.

Evolutionary theory holds that there is a common descent of all life (including our own) from a single earthly origin via an evolutionary two-step: genetic and organismal (bodily and behavioral) variation and natural (and sexual) selection or elimination. So far, so good. But, according to Mayr, to understand the theory of evolution, we must consider this definition outside the conceptual framework of thought inherited from Newton and Descartes, with its attendant and outmoded fundamental ideas and assumptions. Mayr, born in Europe, was historically oriented, philosophically as well as scientifically well trained, and adept, indeed masterful, at critically dealing with fundamental ideas. He argues that there are numerous traditional assumptions that we must philosophically discard and get over if we are going to understand Darwinism. He fastens upon three in particular: (1) cosmic teleology or purposiveness; (2) physicalist (material) determinism; and (3) typological or essentialist thinking. Cosmic teleology gets all the popular press and attention, but the other two ideas are equally as important. All three together must be left behind in the dust of old ball parks as characterizing outmoded worldviews.

Cosmic teleology is the notion that the natural universe and earthly life are fashioned by a Divine intelligence and purposive or goal-directed Designer or Watchmaker. Darwinism holds that there is no such designer, as traditionally conceived. Nature, and animate (organic) nature in particular, creates its own forms, capacities, and structures in passing. The realm of evolutionary life is undergirded by a Blind Tinkerer, not an Intelligent Designer. Though this does not rule out all possibilities of theology, it does call for a more or less radical revision of certain traditional theistic worldviews.

Physicalist determinism holds that all material "consequents" are strictly causally determined by their physical "antecedents," with no brooking interferences from mind or supernatural forces. It is this underlying idea that crucially allows for the conception of abiding "laws of nature," which are essentially unchanging and atemporal in character. They hold always and everywhere and thus have no essential reference to any particular time and place. Thus, according to this view, "natural history" is almost an oxymoron. Nature has no real history, only the eternal or everlasting play of natural laws working over and through physical matter. (Spinoza himself held a similar conviction.)

However, natural history and its changing realities are at the heart and soul of the nature studied by evolutionary biology and ecology. Time (temporality) and historical becoming, contingencies, and chance really count. In particular, with organic individuals, populations, and species, genomes (with all their causal effects) are historically brewed up via variation and selection. In brief, though the realm of life may presuppose physical laws of nature, it is not solely constituted or determined by them. Indeed, evolutionary biology and ecology have no (are not ruled by) atemporal laws of nature. If we insist on looking at the world through Newtonian and Cartesian eyes, Mayr claims that we will never see and comprehend the world of animate, living nature, including our human selves.

Typological or essentialist thinking, which traces its roots back to Plato and the Pythagoreans, if not beyond, holds that all individuals of any species (rose, dog, human being) are essentially alike. Any variation among individuals is merely accidental or adventitious and does not count in reality or in understanding the nature of things. (Note in passing how well the conception of typological thinking, with unchanging essences, ideas, or forms [eide], goes with the worldview of laws of nature and a rational cosmic designer.)

But such thinking is fundamentally anathema to evolutionary thought. It is precisely the variations among individuals within a population—almost without exception, all organic individuals have their variations or differences—that allows natural selection to blindly work its wonders: ongoing adaptations to changing worldly environments, and indeed the very diversification of animate life into new species, the engendering of biodiversity. None of this grand historical, worldly, natural drama can be captured by essentialist thinking and thinkers.

Out with the old and outmoded, in with the new fundamental ideas and assumptions. But what are they? Following Mayr, we can identify three: "populational thinking," interactive or "orchestral causation," and "emergent properties," which lead to a fundamentally new conception of what a biological species really is.

Populational thinking flips essentialist thinking on its head. It is the variation, not sameness, among individuals in a biological population that is important. Variation accounts for one half of the evolutionary two-step. Species are now not defined by their timeless forms or essences, but by actual or potentially interbreeding individuals living in populations—by those who can share genetic variations among themselves and thus allow evolutionary and adaptive processes to engender themselves.

Moreover, the fundamental conception of an interbreeding population living within a wider, causally efficacious historical and changing environment cries out for a fundamental, new conception of causation. And here interaction, not one-directional relations of cause and effect, is the key to understanding. Biology requires that we grasp the reciprocal influences among and between all abiotic and biotic levels, including genomes, cells and organs, individual organisms, populations and species, natural communities and ecosystems, indeed the global ecosphere itself. Interactive causation simultaneously works upward and downward; as Heraclitus said, "The way up is the way down."

How can we best conceive this grand new fundamental idea? Imagine a musical, orchestral performance, say Verdi's *Requiem*. What factors are at play? There is Verdi, the composer; the musical score; the conductor; the orchestra and the chorus; the soloists; the members of the audience (each with different musical ears and personal concerns); the orchestral hall with its acoustics; the wider world in its present historical and cultural moment; and no doubt more. Who or what is the cause of the performance? No one single thing or factor. Rather the performance *emerges* out of the *interactions* of all these factors. Change one or more factors, the interactions change, and a qualitatively different performance emerges. Without stretching the metaphor too far, we can call such systemic interaction "orchestral causation." Here is a Louisville Slugger idea to replace Newtonian, physicalist causation and determinism.

"Emergence," in fact, is another such fundamental, new idea. Emergence is a concept central to evolutionary and ecological thinking. The idea coheres with the concept of a hierarchy of nested natural systems—systems including, or included within, one another. Interactions on one systemic level produce natural properties or entities on the next higher level that are in principal unpredictable. The simplest illustration is water, H_2O. Who could have predicted that the interaction between hydrogen and oxygen atoms would produce "aqueousness"? Similarly, who could have predicted that the interactions of abiotic elements would produce biotic entities (organic molecules), and the interactions of the abiotic and biotic still further natural phenomena: genomes within cells within organs within organisms within populations within ecosystems within the ecosphere, all no doubt influenced by their wider cosmic, natural setting? Such unplanned and unpredictable spatiotemporal, historical, dynamic emergence makes little or no sense within the ahistorical, deterministic, "laws of nature" worldview of Newton and Descartes.

To emphasize the significance of this new rack or system of fundamental ideas—populational thinking, orchestral causation, and emergent properties and entities—I want to reconsider briefly the age-old philosophic quandary over the nature of the human self and human communities. Given the rack of Darwinian ideas—we have considered only a few of them—new notions of the human self and human communities suggest themselves. We humans are complex, bodily organisms living within natural and cultural populations amidst historical, orchestral causation and emergent properties above and below our individual organismic selves and communities. The suggestion is that we too are emergent ones, selves emerging out of worldly (natural and cultural) interactions, and are so until we die. (Heraclitus and Spinoza would understand and concur.) As selves, human beings are not separate "atoms," or particles, requiring nothing else (save God) in order to exist, essentially isolated from and unrelated to the world, natural and cultural. Quite the opposite. We are interactively involved with the world up to our ears. (I include our minds, our souls, and the full reaches of our experience.) Moreover, our human communities and cultures, in all their diversities, seem to fit well in this Darwinian framework of ideas. They too are emergences, influenced and influencing, "unpredictable" properties or entities emerging from the interconnections of humanly organic selves interacting with each other and the wider historical world of animate and inanimate becoming. Again, the Heraclituses and the Spinozas, I think, were in their own ways clued into these natural and cultural realities. Descartes and all predominantly essentialist thinkers are not.

But what does this new rack of Darwinian ideas have to do with ethics and, specifically, our moral obligations to human communities and nature? A great deal, I think. The cosmos and our earth in particular are and have been a protean realm of historical becoming, engendering all sorts of natural and cultural capacities, forms, and patterns that characteristically strike us human, organic ones as good, significant, important, and valuable, if not strictly morally good in character. But all alike—and we know this most vividly and straightforwardly from our own human lives—are mortal, finite, and vulnerable to harm. We also know that we humans have become all-too-significant actors on the earthly, if not cosmic, scene.

With our circumscribed powers of freedom and action, we affect earthly things, including our human, multicultural selves, for better or worse. At present, we have become nature's great harmers and degraders. In short, we carry a heavy moral burden and responsibility for what ongoingly happens on the earth, and not only in our human communities. We have decided responsibilities to natural processes, structures, and nonhuman forms of animate life.

Recognition of these responsibilities is not new. It, no doubt, goes back for centuries. Certainly, our responsibilities were explicitly articulated by Aldo Leopold, among many others. In *A Sand County Almanac,* some sixty years ago, Leopold exhorted us to uphold the integrity, stability, and beauty of the biotic community, or the Land, the complex admixture and interaction of the abiotic and the biotic that includes our humanly communal and cultural selves—humans *within* nature (Meine 1987). Yet, as witnessed by a whole host of natural and human crises mentioned at the outset—the degradation of soils, water, air, wild flora and fauna, with climate change and global warming grabbing our latest immediate attention—we seem mired in a rut of moral and civic irresponsibility with respect to both our human selves and the rest of nature. Why? What is our particularly human problem? To be honest, this question baffles the best of minds. But beyond all questions of greed and parochial self-interest, among innumerable other factors, how much depends on our having the wrong set or rack of fundamental ideas in our heads?

Ideas matter, and truly big ideas truly matter. Why are Darwinian ideas and worldviews still marginalized in our cultural communities? The United States is an especially striking example. Why are we ruled by old, outmoded ideas, inherited unthinkingly from the Western cultural past—scientific, philosophic, and theological? If, as Hans Jonas claimed, Americans are allergic to deep, systematic thinking, we are indeed in deep cultural trouble. We remain on an old nineteenth-century, coal-fired, smoke-belching, Newtonian locomotive train, headed for a mountain tunnel that has no exit. By not comprehending nature and our complex responsibilities to it, we ignore our complex responsibilities to ourselves. Nature and humanity will be degraded, fail, or prosper together. Such is the message of everyday experience and Darwinian philosophic and scientific thinking. It is time to bring out our new Louisville Slugger ideas, rap ourselves upside the head, and engender the climate of worldview concern and change that we so sorely need.

This is the work I have set myself to do, on prairie fields where I continue to play.

II

A Guide for the
Naturally Perplexed

3

Frog Pond Philosophy

Several years ago, after fishing an evening mayfly hatch for wild brook and brown trout, I sat by a northern Wisconsin pond, Brock Pond, sipping Old Grand-Dad whiskey, smoking a cigarette, croaking along with the frogs—all good subversive behavior according to civilized, urban standards. Suddenly a philosophic lightning bolt shuddered through my body. The universe burst forth into sound with the croak of a frog. Before, there had been a vast, meaningless silence of whirling forces. Now there was sound, a sounder, and an audience appreciative of the character and quality of the sound, which was laced with subtle meanings and significance. Before a soundless universe; now a soundful universe, a cosmological frog leap forward.

No doubt my memory of the details is selective. Probably there were pre-frog murmurings to be overheard. But the basic philosophic insight of the cosmological emergence of sound (as well as life) seems right, and Brock Pond ever since has been for me a sacred time and place for philosophic reflection.

Actually, I have lately been thinking about our world and its evolutionary life as one vast, temporally deep frog pond, serving as the wider natural context of our humanly cultural adventures. I think back to the sixteenth and seventeenth centuries and the modern ontological and scientific revolution—a job left only half finished. Perhaps the New Science of the sixteenth century moved the sun and earth away from the center of the universe, but thanks to personal gods, universal reason, language, and other cultural talents, we humans still consider ourselves at the center of all things significant and meaningful, right in the middle of the frog pond. Despite Darwin, little has changed. We "central ones" take all the natural resources that we need for ourselves (billions of us), leaving what is left over for the rest of the pond's creatures, present and future. We industriously pursue our economies and technologies, spewing our wastes into the pond, recycling some of these wastes, but not enough. Few seem to care or even to know what we are doing, and all of us, like it or not, live more or less in the middle of the pond.

A few individuals, Aldo Leopold among others, have digested the Darwinian message and are morally and practically anxious to move us humans off-center, to find a seemly and right lily pad upon which to live and croak, morally moved by a central concern for the overall and indefinite well-being of the frog pond as a whole. This is only a frog pond version of Leopold's land ethic, but neither has penetrated our urban centers and minds, where so much fateful human action and decision making take place.

Let me take one more philosophic turn around the pond in hope that it might somehow help. Prompted by the notions of orchestral causation and emergent individuals, I have begun to think of genomes, human or other, as scores of music, say a symphonic poem or Mozart's *Requiem*. Imagine the score in the hands respectively of elementary school, high school, college, and professional orchestras, soloists, and choruses. Given the differing contexts, we would expect to emerge different phenotypical results, more or less artfully expressed. So it is with uniquely diverse genomes in their uniquely different contexts.

But is not this the realm of life, the frog pond, itself? There are billions upon billions of organisms with their innumerable genomes, a vast realm of historical interaction provoking the expressions of scores of natural music, some bursting into sound, some taking other naturally artful forms. What an incredible realm of historically engendered existence! So much value ongoingly bursting forth into being.

But then there is this problem at the center of the frog pond, that small section of the natural orchestra that refuses artfully and harmoniously to blend in with the others, risking discordant cacophony in following its own tune. In fact, by its misadventures, it is destroying or degrading the genomic scores of other individuals and species of life. (We are told we are amidst a "human extinction" event.) The grand symphony of life and its future is being seriously marred and degraded. If we humans do not tune in, the pond literally might become frogless, humanless, and soundless. Such a lapse into disvalue and lifelessness is a potential ontological and cosmological evil that vastly overshadows the pleasures, pains, life plans, and deaths of individual organisms, human or other. The wonderful and complex interplay of the bounded, boundaries, and the boundless threatens to become unraveled, leaving insignificant life or animate being, if any at all. Relatively or absolutely, there might be only the soundless, the valueless, the boundless. We would then need to replace the Benedictus of Mozart's *Requiem* with a contrite Ignoramus.

Urban philosophers and ethicists of mainstream utilitarian or deontological persuasions will be of little help here. They remain at the center of the pond, all too humanly bound and concerned. We need more measured reflections. We will need bullfrog philosophers who somehow can forcibly express the pond's natural music and the complexly intertwined and interactive symphonies that need to be protected and reinforced. Perhaps it will only be by such philosophic and moral music, or other value expression, that we will be able to penetrate and awaken urban ears, including our own. How else are we going to save nature's protean but vulnerable sacred time and space, our earthly frog pond? This is urgent business that knows no bounds.

4

Intelligent Design and the Matter of Matter

I cannot leave well enough alone. I have another philosophic itch that demands attention. This irritation is provoked by the most recent outbreak of the interminable, mostly befogging, debate between evolutionary biologists and creationists, a.k.a. intelligent designers. Those in Kansas know the story well.

In typical, all-too-human fashion, the proponents of science and religion choose sides and take shots at one another across the ball field. The Daniel Dennetts, Richard Dawkinses, and Jerry Coynes of the biological world are quick to point out that intelligent design is not a scientific theory at all. The contemporary version of intelligent design is based on a negative argument from complexity—we know that natural structures exist that seem too complex to be explained by natural variation and selection alone, therefore they must have been produced by an intentional, creative force outside of the evolutionary process as we understand it. But this is not a theory or hypothesis that could be tested by empirical experiment or observation. Moreover, if such natural complexities require an Intelligent Designer, it (she or he) would need to be more complex than its creation. (That the complex cannot emerge from the simpler is the putative potency of the designer's argument.) But then how are we to explain the complexity of the Designer? "Aha!" exclaims the chorus from the religionist ballpark, "that has been our point all along. The Designer is beyond the knowing capacities of our feeble human minds and flawed scientific theories."

"Not so fast," retorts the scientific crowd. "Just look at the design of the natural world, including your individual human bodies. Note the innumerable flaws and imperfections. Some Designer!"

I do think the scientific biologists have a point here. My own body attests to it, but I will spare you the details. However, I think the Dennetts and the Dawkinses are all too harsh, if not haughty.

So it goes back and forth, a sound and fury signifying little. This is a shouting match with no end, unless we can lure the protagonists out of their entrenched sides and stances. I have a modest suggestion. Instead of reinforcing these entrenched positions, let's move everyone to a new field, which is actually an old ball field with some modest renovations as needed.

As you will guess, the ball field that I suggest is venerable old philosophy. However, each team must abide by some rules. In philosophy, no dogmatists or dogmatic arguments are allowed. Commit the cardinal sin of dogmatism and you are immediately ejected from the contest. Intolerance is not to be tolerated.

From within the confines of philosophy's ball field, then, let us briefly look at the debate again. A fundamental bone of contention is the origin, fundamental character, and diversity of organic life, human included. Alfred North Whitehead, early in the twentieth century, searingly critiqued modern materialist, physicalist science and the dead, inorganic nature of the so-called New Physics. He found them seriously wanting. Since their early beginnings in the sixteenth and seventeenth centuries, the physical sciences had progressed to the point of providing what Whitehead referred to as "a mystical chant over an unintelligible universe" (Whitehead [1938] 1968: 136). Moreover, life cannot issue from death. Whitehead proposed a philosophic cosmology, a philosophic interpretation of nature alive, which he felt more adequately explained the full reaches of our human experience. (For Whitehead, organic life is characterized by an experiential emotional enjoyment of the world, creative and self-creative activity, and aim, as well as the hierarchal systems and emergent properties of nature known to contemporary naturalists and biologists.) In his philosophic scheme, Whitehead employed a Deity, conceptually much transformed from Christian traditions, which participates in co-creating "the process and reality" of the universe. However, this is speculative philosophy and not science, with no guarantees of certainty or truth. Whitehead knew it, and everyone else knew it. No one tries to teach Whitehead's systematic speculations in science classes, important as his critiques of science's limitations might be.

Similarly, Hans Jonas, an ethicist and philosopher of organic life, critiqued early modern scientific and philosophic traditions that led themselves into philosophic absurdity and incoherence. He too claimed life could not issue from the dead and that life was a fundamental or ontological revolution in the history of matter. The origin of life, he claimed, was beyond our philosophic ken or ability to know. But once organic life is on the scene, which it manifestly is, it is there to be philosophically interpreted in its full reaches, up to and including human beings and their capacities for moral responsibility. Jonas skillfully followed through on this philosophic project. Moreover, he conjectured a religious myth about a god giving itself over to the world that organic life might be. But he hastened to add that he would only *like* to believe that this myth is true. It has no legitimate place in philosophic argument, let alone scientific explanation or truth, verifiable or falsifiable.

Let us look at the rival interpretation that life can emerge out of the dead: organic matter, entities, and processes out of the inorganic realm. Ernst Mayr, the eminent biologist-philosopher, was an avowed naturalist, materialist, and atheist, though he was equally as critical of the tradition as Whitehead and Jonas. However, Mayr was much impressed by the complex, multileveled causation that characterizes organic and ecosystemic interactions, systems, and individual organic entities. Out of this "orchestral causation" historically emerge all the phenomena and realities of earthly life. Mayr speculates that organic life primordially emerged out of the complex interactions of the inorganic in a similar fashion. Some form of matter! Well worth our philosophic pondering, if not also our genuine respect and reverence. But again, this is philosophic speculation, not proven, and perhaps not testable, science. Mayr knew this. Science is not the only important game in town. Philosophy—good, honest, explorative philosophy—is also eminently worth pursuing.

Why am I so exercised by the debate? Because it seemingly matters so much, theoretically and practically. Note that Whitehead, Jonas, and Mayr can challenge one another and us with rival interpretations without rancor. They move in the same ball field, philosophy, which at its rare best is a civilized place. They can awaken us from the dogmatic slumber of old habitual thoughts and unreflective opinions or prejudices. They do not summon us to culture wars, but to cultural explorations into ultimate, perhaps finally unanswerable, yet all-important questions and issues, for example, the origin, nature, and significance or worth of organic life.

Why does this practically matter? Why should we be philosophically awake and explorative rather than content with cultural slumber and sideshow bickering among dogmatists? Consider a possible answer. If we were intellectually, morally, and civically wide awake, perhaps we would be less tolerant and accepting of human and natural tragedies, or the cultural and natural mess spawned by modern industrial agriculture (Jackson 1980, 2011). I want to get back to fishing and its Leopoldian wildness.

A pox on all culturally bound dogmatists, of whatever stripe. Theoretically and practically, they are stealing the wild world out from under us. Rather let us have wild men and women, naturally wild thinkers and actors. We would be better off—practically, morally, civically, and spiritually.

5

Kansas on My Mind

I have recently enjoyed a rare treat—a summer sabbatical. As a fly-fishing philosopher concerned with the long-term moral responsibilities to human communities and nature (ecosystems and landscapes), I took the opportunity for primary fieldwork. I explored streams and rivers, as a participant observer of the ethology of trout and salmon, and reread two eminent thinkers, Ernst Mayr, an evolutionary biologist and Darwin scholar, and Isaiah Berlin, a political philosopher and historian of ideas. In brief, I went fishing, literally and intellectually. I know of no better way to fire up the soul and the philosophical imagination than rubbing together the sticks of Mayr, Berlin, and primary reality (rivers and fish).

The sabbatical started in sandy-bottomed northern Wisconsin streams, surrounded by wild brook and brown trout, and with evening mayfly hatches on an evergreen-bordered pond, fishing with my daughters for the stream's big brothers and sisters. In addition, there were eagles, whip-poor-wills, loons, deer, snapping turtles, a black bear, and more—a good ten days.

We shifted our venue to a new region and ecosystem, far from streams and trout. We visited my wife's family in Kansas. There were the old prairie flatlands, thunderstorms, tornado watches, blistering heat, family picnics, and basketball games.

There were other regional features as well. We read in a local paper of a municipal official wanting to hold daily prayer meetings in a public, governmental building. Christians only. Responding to constitutional objections, the official relented and welcomed everyone to the meeting, though only Christians could actively participate. Everyone has the right to follow their own religious practices, but not to pray to false gods. (This logic escaped me.)

Then there was my annual "blood-boiler"—a Sunday church service patriotically celebrating the Fourth of July. This year's sermon concerned the separation of church and state. Contrary to popular understanding, we were told, our forefathers did not mean to protect the state and democratic processes from religious fanaticism or dogma, but the freedom of religious practice from state intervention. It was fine, indeed important, to have religious influences in political life (which religion? which church?), and the state in denying prayer in schools and presumably municipal buildings had become the de facto enemy of organized religion. (I had not noticed any police cars, lights whirling, in the church's parking lot before, after, or during the service.) All the while, my family, immediate and extended, glanced at my shoulders and hands, the barometers of my blood-boil. At the end of the service, I mentioned to the minister that I was reading Berlin's *The Proper Study of Mankind* and that he might like it. (Berlin, had he heard the sermon, would not have liked it.)

We left Kansas with these clouds rumbling overhead, but they were soon dispelled. We were off to Wyoming and Montana, back to rivers, streams, and trout. We traveled through the Bighorn Mountains and stopped by various strata of exposed rock, parts of it 3.6 billion years old. (Life on earth had already begun.) I fished a mountain stream filled with lightning-quick but eager wild rainbow, brook, and brown trout—a fortuitous gift for an aging fly-fisherman. The following day, in a back eddy of the Big Horn River (Montana), a brute of a brown trout (possibly around eight pounds) swam slowly and disdainfully by me, as if I should fear him, given that I was in his home waters, rather than the other way around.

A few days later, my wife, Vivian, our ten-year-old daughter, Tegan, and I went on a week's horse backpack trip into Yellowstone Park and the Absaroka-Beartooth Wilderness. Mountain thunderstorms, grizzly bears, and wolves hovered in the background. (We met the rain but never encountered the bears or wolves.) We faced inner fears and rode over a 10,000-foot summit, with a 360-degree panorama of mountain ranges. (When and how were they formed?) We fished Slough Creek in Yellowstone Park for magnificent native cutthroat trout, endemic to this region for countless thousands of years. What a privilege to be in the water close by these recent descendants of times immemorial, observing their long-evolved ecological habits. At the end of the trip, Tegan, weeping at saying good-bye, hugged and kissed the neck of her horse, Whiskey. The trip was a roaring success. Tegan had been hooked on fishing, wildness, and the wilds. She would never again be the same.

We returned to New York, my spirits in high gear. Then it hit. Kansas, again. The state's Board of Education offered local school boards and districts the opportunity to strike Darwinian evolutionary biology from their science and other curricula. (Darwinian thought would be dropped from state tests.) Evolution is an unproven scientific thesis that need not be taken seriously, especially when compared to biblical creation stories.*

Here was a real blood-boiler, dwarfing the municipal bureaucrat and Lutheran minister. To borrow from John Lee Hooker, the blues singer, "I am mad, I am bad, like Jessie James." The board's decision goes beyond national bemusement, humiliation, or embarrassment. (What is the rest of the world to think of us?) This is serious, reprehensible moral and civic irresponsibility. The Kansas Board of Education would allow the state's children and future citizens to be maimed personally, spiritually, and civically.

If I had come under the tutelage of Kansan fundamentalists/creationists or their ilk, who now would I be personally, intellectually, emotionally, spiritually, and philosophically? What intellectual sticks—philosophic, scientific—would I have to rub together in pursuit of a good and responsible human life? I might be able to limp along, but I would be decidedly impoverished. Without the perspective of Darwinian biology and its accompanying worldview, I would not get so fired up and overwhelmed by mountains, rivers, fish, the nurturing of my daughters, or worldly human life in general. The grand and dramatic story about my, our, and the biosphere's interwoven origin and history would be missing. I would be stunted intellectually, aesthetically, emotionally, and spiritually.

Nor is this all. The students of Kansas are the state's next generation of citizens, with important civic responsibilities ahead. As I have learned again and again from my work in Chicago and elsewhere, the problem is not that there is too much Darwinian understanding in the world, but that there is far too little (Donnelley 1998b). Most of us are ecologically illiterate. We do not adequately grasp the basic tenets of evolutionary biology and ecology, which mutually imply each other, and how we human beings are intricately implicated in the larger texture of things, as crucial ecological and evolutionary actors. (Humankind is presently perpetrating a major biological extinction event, which largely goes unnoticed.) We fail to grasp ultimate moral and civic responsibilities to human communities and the natural systems that sustain them and within which they are nestled. In the face of this dangerous public and civic ignorance, the Kansas Board would encourage us to return to a pre-1859, pre-Darwinian dogmatic darkness, a cognitive midnight that would obliterate the all-too-little that we actually do know scientifically about nature and our biological and cultural selves.

For the sake of the future of both humans and nature, each of us individually, professionally, and civically must have our feet put to the moral fire of human and civic responsibility. Real lives and achieved values, human and natural, are at stake and hang in the balance. How we act and think, morally and practically, really does matter. Hopefully the many good citizens, educators, politicians, and religious leaders of Kansas will courageously rise up and rebuke their Board of Education's "scorched foot" policy, if not turn this dark farce into an opportunity to further deepen the Darwinian dimensions of their schools' curricula and the educational lives of their students. That is what is truly needed. That would really get Kansas off my mind and relieve my distemper.

Actually, later in the summer my spirits were lifted, if my moral outrage not abated. At the Margaree River in Nova Scotia, a twenty-pound salmon leaped twice into the air and flipped my fly back in my face. I had seen the fish emerge from the dark depths of the river to take the dry fly. This rarely witnessed act of natural grace transformed the salmon pool into naturally sacred time and space. The salmon was on for an eternity and off in no time at all. We were both the winners, firmly reconnected to the deep historical drama of humans and nature. A nice ending. Would things fare so well for the good citizens and students of Kansas?

Note

*Editors' note: Between 1999 and 2007 the Kansas Board of Education shifted back and forth between evolutionists and creationists, and the state's curriculum rules concerning the teaching of evolution changed five times. Since 2007 evolution has been included in the state science curriculum. In 2013 the state adopted the national Next Generation Science Standards, which make the teaching of evolution a core science standard (see Klein 2013; Pearce 2012).

6

Scientists' Public Responsibilities

As someone with a professional life in philosophy and practical ethics, I often find myself at conferences with an impressive array of scientific experts and hundreds of attendees. We have come together to discuss what we know, and do not know, about the present state of the earth's living nature and what we humans ought to do about the threats to its and our long-term viability. We are explicitly recognizing public or citizen responsibilities for the present and future of nature and our human communities. This is truly significant, at least as a first step.

What can I usefully add? As a philosopher amidst a sea of accomplished scientists, I am unsure whether I feel more like a spotted owl or a zebra mussel, an endangered species or an exotic species, resigned to insignificance or to causing havoc. I prefer to play the gadfly and concentrate on the broad theme of ignorance, which we philosophers are professionally bound to profess.

I have been struck by the philosophic tone of scientists' confessions of ignorance about what they still do not know about the diversity of biological species and their roles in evolutionary and ecological processes. There have been recurrent calls for more and better science, aimed to help us in deciding and acting upon crucial public policy issues. Who could quarrel with the practical importance of such pleas?

Yet I am equally struck by a silent, *sotto voce* indictment of scientists: their failure to dispel the ignorance of the public, to educate their fellow citizens about nature and science, and to address how we should meet our ethical responsibilities to ourselves and nature. Granted this is a difficult and complex problem, but so far the scientific community has failed us. Too many scientists have considered ordinary citizens uneducable, not worth the effort. Their rather self-serving notion is that citizens need only recognize and accept the authority of scientists' expert findings. This is a fateful mistake. It leaves even civic-minded and concerned citizens dangerously unmoored and in a public moral darkness.

For example, scientists fail to educate us about the nature of science—that science is an ongoing exploration of nature and human life, with empirical findings and concepts always incomplete, tentative, or open to revision. We tend to take the latest science as definitive, complete, or ready to plug into our technological and progressivist dreams, ignoring possible distortions of human or natural life that might await us. Specifically, scientists have failed to help us to face human ignorance with respect to the effects of large-scale corporate, economic, and public policy initiatives. In the main, the scientific community has fed our economic and technological boosterism and left us bulls in the china shop of nature.

Here evolutionary biologists and ecologists should particularly feel the moral sting. They have failed effectively to grab citizens by the throat and forcibly make them understand and take to heart that human communities and their activities, economic and otherwise, are nestled within wider and vulnerable living systems. We citizens still do not get it and blunder about with an all-too-clear conscience. We remain ignorant of basic principles of evolutionary biology and ecology, a general ignorance that really matters. Our global economies bulldoze rain forests, gulp down our fresh waters, erode our soils, pollute our air, and plunder our fisheries and ocean depths. More than human necessity and moral indifference are here at work. The ignorance of citizens and their communities play a decisive role.

More and better scientific knowledge will not suffice. The White Papers and Proceedings will not be enough. How many will read them, take them to heart, and actively heed their recommendations? Scientists will have done their public duty and fulfilled their own citizen responsibilities when environmental conferences are held not only at museums of natural history but in the atrium of the World Financial Center, the auditoriums of our teaching hospitals, and the halls of Congress and other legislative bodies—with portfolio managers and leverage buy-out artists, surgical cowboys and medical biotechnologists, and contractors on America and our natural habitats as much in attendance as scientists and the environmental chorus.

At bottom, whatever our professions, we are all ordinary citizens. Now and henceforth we must assume extraordinary responsibilities. Can we do it? Are we scientifically and morally educable? That is the question that challenges scientists, ethicists, and all of us alike. No doubt it will take all of us working together to pull it off. Yet if significant numbers of citizens can fathom the *Wall Street Journal* and the *New York Times* business section, laser technologies and transgenic knock-out strategies, and arcane bureaucracies and regulations, surely they can grasp the principles and practical implications of evolutionary biology and ecology.

There is no inherent reason why scientists should leave the rest of us in the dark as dangerous bumblers. Scientists—especially those in the life sciences—do have a professional responsibility to press for more and better science to help inform practical policy. But equally they have a professional and human responsibility to educate us citizens, to help us get our heads screwed on right and meet our long-term responsibility to humans and nature. The latter task in public education may prove as formidable, challenging, and practically important as scientific exploration itself.

The gauntlet of public education is thrown and ought not to be ignored. Our citizen ignorance is an integral part of the crisis our living planet now faces.

7

Bottom Lines and the Earth's Future

For those of us who live in market economy cultures, such as the United States, we have long become accustomed to "bottom lines," the economic or business bottom line in particular. The bottom line for the economy and business is profitability, usually by economic growth. Failure to grow or be profitable means trouble, if not going out of business altogether.

What we often fail to realize is that the economic bottom line as the ultimate standard by which we humans live and judge our success is a matter of philosophic, moral, cultural, indeed pragmatic choice. There is nothing inevitable about the economic bottom line. There have been and are other bottom lines that human communities have chosen for the ultimate standard by which they live and judge themselves, with more or less rigor and compromise. Communist states or countries were (are) predominantly motivated, officially at least, by equality and community well-being as a whole. Some religious communities, past and present, judge their conduct on how well their individual and communal lives are conducive to individual salvation, getting their community members or communicants into heaven and an eternal afterlife. One can readily imagine some individuals and communities ultimately committed to beauty, the divine right of kings, the flourishing of God's nature, or some other ultimate value that has historically presented itself to the human imagination. By "ultimate value," I here mean a humanly important value underived, and underivable, from some other important value. It "stands alone," though we are moved by many such ultimate values (freedom, equality, justice, security, etc.), which in some circumstances are compatible with one another but in other circumstances clash. Thus the complexity of our value-laden lives, personal, civic, and political.

I want to question and challenge the tendency of these ultimate values as standards or "bottom lines" to totalize themselves and to grow into full-fledged worldviews by which we live. We become dominantly *homo economicus, communicus,* or *theologicus.* All other values or ultimates are to be sacrificed, or adjusted, to the dominant value, the ultimate standard or bottom line. Witness the hegemonic tendency of our reigning economic bottom line and worldview. Things tend to get judged by, or reduced to, their monetary or economic value, even if such valuation seems awkward, if not ludicrous or downright nihilistic (eclipsing the characteristic significance of other values). Think of art, communal events, family life, and nature, including our innumerable interactions with nature. How significant are they to us, how much are they worth? A great deal. But how much are they worth to us in monetary or economic terms? Despite some economists' efforts at "shadow pricing," reducing noneconomic values to monetary terms (which may have limited legitimate uses, for example, ecosystem services), the question and the effort often strike us as absurd. For example, is my stream fishing for native wild brook trout worth $99.99 to me, not a penny more? We actually find this absurdity and embarrassment begrudgingly recognized at the center of the market economy's own armor. As the television commercial goes, "Some things are priceless [a father playing with his son; a mother giving birth to a daughter; hiking through mountains or forests; kicking a winning field goal in a football game, and more]; for the rest, there is MasterCard." (Or is it Visa?)

I do not bring up these philosophic musings idly. Something very interesting is beginning to happen in our lives that should capture the attention of those centrally interested in the environment, conservation, and the multiple "ultimate" values of both humans and nature. The economic market, private capital, and their bottom line and worldview have recently discovered the environment, if not nature in its fullness. There is money (profits) to be made in cleaning up the environment, green technologies, wetlands mitigation, capping and trading greenhouse gas emissions, producing new biofuels and other sources of clean energy (wind, solar, hydro), and more. All this is fine and good given the proper natural, social, and political contexts. But beware the creeping economic bottom line and worldview. Unless critically checked, it knows no limits. It is inherently a "totalizer," a Leviathan, sweeping away all that lies in its path.

If you doubt the cogency of this warning, let me give you a few examples, culled from various meetings and conferences I have attended recently. One such meeting explicitly addressed the issue of market solutions to environmental problems. One session concerned rapid climate change (global warming) and greenhouse gas emissions. No one seriously doubted the problem, but all the talk was about regional and global caps on emissions and trades of pollution credits, a great way for prudent and innovative companies and investors to make money at the expense of less nimble or responsible industries or companies. In over an hour of presentations and discussions, never once mentioned were moral responsibilities to the present and future of either humans or nature, both of which will be mightily affected by climate change and global warming. The philosopher-ethicist in me boiled over, and I questioned this oversight. A panelist from a market-oriented NGO looked me straight in the eye and claimed that of course she was morally concerned about people starving around the world. End of response. I, my question, and nature were stonewalled, apparently not worth serious consideration. Was this panelist tone deaf to nature and ultimate moral responsibilities?

Things only got worse. In a session on scarce water resources, those whom I (disparagingly, perhaps unfairly) call Mickey Marketeers were bolstered by Private Property Righters, especially a panelist who championed private water rights and market trades, with or without caps on water use. Again the conservationist-philosopher in me boiled up and over. I asked the panelist to consider a hypothetical situation. Imagine T. Boone Pickens on his ranch in Texas selling his water to the highest bidder in California. What would happen to the rest of the creatures and the ecosystems on his ranch? The panelist glibly laughed and said that the imagined scenario was not so far-fetched. (Pickens apparently had contemplated such a move.) Perhaps, the panelist responded, we should restrict the sale of water to those living or operating in regional watersheds. What kind of answer was that? How would that help nature on Pickens's ranch?

Another example. There is an effort to reclaim floodplains and restore wetlands along the Illinois River, a boon to wildlife, as well as a proposed natural solution to a serious human problem: polluted (toxically contaminated and nutrient overloaded) water coming downriver from Chicago and its surroundings. Here, according to a major proponent of wetland restoration, is a terrific opportunity. Municipal authorities in Chicago are mandated to clean up their water, an enormously expensive proposition if water filtration plants must be built. But if the municipality of Chicago would pay farmers to return their floodplain agricultural fields to wetlands, which would presumably naturally filter the water, there would be an irresistibly attractive win-win situation: more money for struggling farmers, less expense for Chicago and surrounding municipalities. What could be more simple, straightforward, and attractive? But only, we were told, if we adequately paid the farmers, who would without hesitation convert to wetland managers. Perhaps. But would this solution truly be naturally viable? Would it really solve Chicago's water pollution problems? More pointedly, would it be culturally acceptable or viable for the farmers and farming communities, whose cultural and personal identities have long included plowing Midwestern prairie soils? Do (or can) people so readily make such abrupt cultural shifts? The wetland proponent, a friend and a lover of nature—for example, he is enamored with beavers, a passion I do not share—just blinked and smiled at my "naive" question. "The farmers want money. [Of course, they do.] That will take care of the problem." Will it? Or does my friend suffer from economic bottom line and worldview creep? We will see.

One final example of economic bottom line–ism in service of environmental problems. I recently attended a conference in Charleston, South Carolina, on climate change and rising sea levels. As the name implies, the Lowcountry of South Carolina, perhaps inevitably, will suffer human and natural disasters spawned by climate change and global warming, arguably *the* long-term moral and civic challenge of our times. Indeed, the conference was about what we could do proactively to mitigate future human and natural disasters and suffering. We quickly learned that the looming crisis was already being recognized, if not adequately addressed.

A spokeswoman representing the perspective of insurance companies was miffed by fuzzy talk of "oughts" and "shoulds" that she was hearing at the meeting. People will be moved to action only when they get hit, not in their consciences, but in their pocket books. Insurance companies will come to the rescue. Insurance rates for homes and businesses along the vulnerable South Carolina coasts are already doubling or tripling, if insurance coverage is attainable at all. People, perhaps sooner than later, will quit barrier islands, beach properties, coastal marshlands, and other places where, by nature's standards, they should not be living. Private markets, the insurance industry in particular, can and will do what public defenders of the human and natural common good—moral and civic "do-gooders"—cannot. Indeed, this intelligent and accomplished woman felt rather awkward even being at the meeting. She did not consider herself an environmentalist, which presumably implies being soft-headed and weak-hearted, rather than realistic and hard-nosed. Perhaps, in coming to the meeting, she felt it her duty to straighten us out.

However that may be, here was economic bottom line–ism, with its attendant worldview and philosophical anthropology, in all its unequivocal, if not shameless, robustness. Some of us in the audience, given the magnitude and the complexity of the problem that we were considering, were dumbfounded and rendered speechless. Are we really going to privatize, and marketize, the earthly commons (ecospheric nature, including ourselves)?

The Bottom Line: Nature Alive

For the moment, I want to rest my case for the reality and threats of creeping bottom line–ism of the economic variety. Its proponents notwithstanding, it is not adequately going to help us face, articulate, and act upon our long-term moral and civic responsibilities to the human and natural future. It gives us a too pinched and distorted view or simplified edition of human and natural reality. But given its present cultural and political dominance, what can we do? What alternatives do we have?

I have a modest suggestion, but one that is bold enough. What if we try to engage the bottom liners on their home turf and beat them at their own game? As mentioned earlier, the choice of a bottom line is a philosophic, moral, and cultural decision, with no implication of inevitability. At least as a thought experiment, why not change the bottom line, the norm and standard by which we measure our activities and enterprises? What if we take earthly life, or "nature alive"—to use Whitehead's happy term (which he opposed to "nature lifeless," nature as conceived by modern physicalist materialism)—to be our bottom line, our guiding norm and standard? How might things look then?

For most of us, this move would constitute a decided shift in worldview: a moral, cultural, and philosophic sea change not easily effected. However, we need not start from scratch. There have been philosophic, scientific, and other cultural explorers at the task since the early pre-Socratics, if not before—Heraclitus, Aristotle, Spinoza, Whitehead, Hans Jonas, Aldo Leopold, Boris Pasternak, among innumerable others. Despite their many differences, they were all enamored by the character, values, and significance of living nature, nature alive, including our humanly organic selves and cultural communities.

This is not the place to explore the several versions and worldview visions of nature alive [see part IV], but we can briefly reflect upon themes discussed earlier in conjunction with the economic bottom line. We can see how things would look different and perhaps more adequate.

First of all, we would turn our primary attention not to the human economic realm, but to nature alive, including its inherent significance, values, and goodness. We would attend carefully to natural history: to geological, evolutionary, ecological, ecospheric time and becoming. We would try to understand, the best we can, how things biotic and abiotic are complexly interconnected and interactive. We would consider with care how human communities and the rest of earthly nature are dynamically and historically interwoven: how we fit, and ought to fit, into nature. We would note carefully the diverse ways that we interact with nature and the equally diverse experiences and values that arise or are disclosed in these interactions. We would readily discover that Nature Alive is Nature Valuable, Significant, and Good; it is the locus of ultimate moral and civic responsibilities.

Nature alive would emphatically emerge, directly or indirectly, as an important, if not our most important, bottom line, standard, and norm—an ultimate among ultimates, if you will. We would not ask which natural resources are profitable or unprofitable to our economies. We would ask how we could carry out our economic and other humanly cultural activities so as not seriously to harm or degrade natural processes and historical achievements (genomes; individual organisms; populations, communities, and species of organisms; ecosystems and landscapes; and indeed the ecosphere) upon which we ourselves, in so many ways, utterly depend. We would ask how we could realize social justice and other moral and cultural imperatives and goals (education, art, religion, recreation, etc.) without impairing the ongoing viability and resilience of nature alive. Indeed, we must always strive to discover what truly constitutes the ongoing viability of nature and human communities. No dogmatists allowed in this bottom line.

Note other salutary aspects of this new bottom line and its attendant worldview. Remember the economists' shadow pricing, their attempts to reduce our activities and value or valuable experiences to the lingua franca of monetary or economic value. Given this new philosophic context, we can re-ask all the questions. (We could take a snow day, a holiday, from our present cultural regime.) How much do we value our children and our family lives; hiking over or skiing down mountains; time spent fishing in rivers and streams for wild trout and salmon; artistic activity and going to museums and concerts? This list goes on endlessly. We can say that we value them a great deal, some perhaps more than others. But we decidedly do not need "to price them out." We can make priority decisions, both individually and collectively, without having to resort to numerical, let alone monetary, weighting. We do it all the time. We have been equipped by nature, culture, and our long evolutionary history to make such judgments among diverse values and value experiences—not always easily or without conflicts, but we do, and thus can, make such judgments (Midgley 1993). *Many* things are priceless. Perhaps the rest can be left to our credit cards. But this commercial slogan has a very different valence and meaning under the umbrella of the nature alive worldview and bottom line.

What if we put this nature alive worldview and bottom line before our Mickey Marketeers, Private Property Righters, and Economic Bottom Liners? In all honesty and moral seriousness, how would they respond? How *should* they respond? As we have intimated, we humans live by many, perhaps innumerable, ultimate values, nature alive being only one, though by its inherent, internal complexity and comprehensiveness, it may have pride of place as an ultimate of ultimates. Nevertheless, it may well be that there is no one bottom line (standard, norm) adequate for discerning our ultimate responsibilities to humans and earthly nature. We may have to exercise an art of nimbly jumping back and forth between important but different (including economic) bottom lines and attendant worldviews to make mature and informed moral, civic, and practical judgments. Such is the pluralism, the many-sided values and needs of human and natural life. Yet, contra current practice, we always should take as central nature alive, its bottom line and worldview. Perhaps this is the only way that we can straighten out our heads and truly become responsible "plain citizens of the biotic community," as Aldo Leopold put it.

Transgenic Animals and Wild Nature

A Landscape of Moral Ecology

Animal biotechnology and the fashioning of transgenic animals, along with biotechnology in general, are potent new tools in the arsenal of modern, postindustrial societies. They promise to transform scientific and biomedical research, medical therapies and health care, economic markets and agribusiness, if not the rest of our lives. They augur a new era of human existence and well-being. Yet, animal bioengineering in particular confronts a curious cultural stumbling block. It faces a cacophony of ethically ardent supporters and passionate opponents alike, animated by equal moral zeal (Dresser 1988; Krimsky 1991).

We do not live in a morally harmonious world, undergirded by one or a few coherently ethical values that neatly organize our moral life and coordinate our practical activities. Rather, the opposite seems to be true. With respect to humans, animals, and nature, we confront an ineradicable moral plurality: a bewildering variety of values and ethical obligations, each claiming attention and not readily coordinated with the others (Brennan 1992). How can we make philosophic sense of this moral disjointedness? And how ethically and practically do we deal with this plurality with respect to animal biotechnology?

Historically and logically, there seem to be two basic strategies for dealing with the pull of opposing values or obligations. One is to subsume the moral many under some grand monistic scheme: to establish a hierarchy of values and obligations under the hegemony of one ultimate value. The other possible strategy is to face the plural values and obligations squarely and somehow attempt to give each its proper due in conjunction with the others.

The monistic strategy may serve the peace of the soul by reducing internal moral conflict. Perhaps it is possible in relatively small and homogenous communities, but it is not an option for us. In any case, it invariably is bought at the price of the variety and richness of human experience and significant cultural activity. In this sense, it impoverishes the soul.

To effectively face plural obligations, we need to recognize that there are several relatively autonomous yet mutually interacting spheres of human activity. This means that there are always specific or "provincial" contexts of human activity. Thus, the coordination of obligations must always be contextual. Moreover, given that the many spheres of human activity can and do influence one another, there must be a coordination of values both within and among particular spheres of activity (Norton 1991). Contextually coordinating our plural obligations requires a decision-making art of moral ecology, applying judicious mutual weighting of the several obligations in the various contexts at hand, be they narrower or wider.

Philosophic and Ethical Challenges

From the early days of biotechnology and the fashioning of transgenic organisms, a major ethical concern has been the purposeful introduction or unintended escape of bioengineered organisms into natural habitats and ecosystems (Krimsky 1991). Will the novel organisms wreak ecological havoc, threaten the dynamic stability of habitats, and set off destructive chain reactions throughout resident populations of animals and other organisms? The fear is of negative systemic effects that would undermine the well-being of both humans and the natural world.

The immediately relevant critical questions are: Do we know the effects of such introductions? Can we predict them? Can we control them? Reasonable doubt on any of these questions counsels practical and ethical caution. Only the most weighty obligations to humans would justify countering this caution, if the risks are truly considerable and systemic. The Achilles' heel of ethical decision making is our endemic ignorance of causes and effects when it comes to the flourishing of natural ecosystems. Yet, in this context, the ethical weight decidedly should be with concerns for nature and the multiple significance of nature for humans, rather than more parochial and marginal human interests.

Take the case of experimentally designing transgenic fish—for example, carp, trout, and salmon. The motives for such interventions might be complex: economic, recreational, or preservationist. The practice might serve fish farming (faster-growing fish, with a better and more standard quality of meat). Beyond entrepreneurial aspirations, the technology might answer the pressing nutritional requirements of local human communities or the protection of rapidly dwindling, if not endangered wild fish stocks. (This is a worldwide crisis already upon us.) Or, the transgenesis might produce fish better adapted to polluted or regional aquatic habitats than their wild counterparts and with qualities attractive to sport fishermen (gullibility, size, or fighting ability).

Here, long-range, morally ecological thinking is crucial. We may easily dismiss the putative "needs" of sport fishermen and entrepreneurs. It is less easy to counter genuine nutritional requirements of human populations and the protection of wild fish stocks and aquatic food chains. Yet, issues of escape and exotic species introduction haunt the moral ecology. The genetic or behavioral qualities of transgenic fish introduced or escaped into the wild might undermine the very wild stocks and habitats that they were meant to preserve, to the long-term detriment or impoverishment of both humans and nature (Allen and Flecker 1993). This is not to mention the problems of environmental pollution engendered by fish farming.

But this is not all. There is the more elusive, less urgently practical, but fundamental cultural issue for which we need the ethical reservations of natural preservationists, philosophers, and theologians. By practicing transgenesis in the wild, do we or do we not break into natural processes that are goods in themselves and that hold an ultimate significance (cultural, religious, ethical) for many, if not most of us? This is nature engendering its own, more or less well-adapted biological creations—individuals, species, and ecosystems—the animate and animal issue of evolutionary and ecological processes. How important is it for us humanly, culturally, and ethically to protect, within the overall mandates of plural moral obligations, original nature and its creative dynamism (Ralston 1989)? All these pragmatic and moral factors, human and natural, must be relatively weighted in deciding the role that animal biotechnology ought to play in the wild.

Transgenic Animals, Biomedicine, and Scientific Research

The plural values and obligations relating to humans, animals, and nature that arise in ethically considering animal biotechnology in the wild also surface in scientific and biomedical laboratory settings. But in shifting the scene of scrutiny, the constellation and relative weightings of the values and obligations may change significantly as well. Typically, practical ethical concerns for nature—for wild animal populations, habitats, and ecosystems—fade into the moral background. We may still be seriously concerned with the genetic (genomic), bodily, and behavioral intactness of individual animals, but these concerns are now dominantly conjoined with issues of animals' experiential welfare and the possible benefits of the biotechnological interventions for basic science and fundamental human welfare, particularly the alleviation of suffering.

All things considered, we might allow biotechnological interventions in "controlled" laboratory settings that we would deny in the wild. This shift, beyond pragmatically determined considerations, is due to the dominant values and moral imperatives of scientific and biomedical activity: human (and animal) welfare, the relief of suffering and physiological distress, and the pursuit of basic knowledge about ourselves and the natural world. Thus, we might ethically condone the transgenic production of Oncomouse, Cystic Fibrosis mouse, and Memory mouse (undertaken to facilitate the study of fundamental memory and learning processes). The decision would depend on the importance of the scientific project's purpose, amidst all other things that need to be considered.

Further considerations involve the legitimate stakes of the other realms of human activity, with their own ethical mandates, in biomedical and scientific research. From our participation in private life and webs of intimate personal relations involving both humans and animals comes an insistence on attention to the welfare of individual animals, with a minimization of suffering in research protocols and care settings as is appropriate to legitimate scientific goals. From public political ethics comes the ethical demand that there be a just and fair proportion between the overall benefits to be gained and the harms (especially suffering) to be inflicted, with a maximization of the former relative to a minimization of the latter. From the cultural and natural preservationists and others responsible for protecting ultimate values comes a serious questioning of the admissibility of intervention and research: whether it is ethically out of bounds with regard to violating the animal's individual or species integrity or inflicting significant suffering, no matter what the benefits envisioned (Donnelley and Nolan 1990).

These are the characteristic demands that are placed on animal care and use committees in their review of research and educational protocols.

The scrutiny is only exacerbated by animal biotechnological innovations. The chief "novel" issues concern animal welfare and animal integrity. How can researchers, laboratory technicians, and animal caretakers know their animals and promote their well-being or welfare if a new strain or species of animal has been created with altered and perhaps unprecedented behavioral habits? And how is animal integrity—that which might be inadmissibly violated—to be understood? Is it the intactness of the animals' genetic or genomic structure and functionings, or bodily structure and functionings, or behavioral, social, and "worldly" habits? Or are these all dimensions of animal integrity, however difficult to define adequately?

These particular hazards of animal research ethics and protocol review are only highlighted by animal biotechnology and transgenic innovations. They do not change the fundamental nature of an ethical decision making that must be contextual. In particular, no ethical value or obligation can have an absolute or final precedence over the others. Given the plurality of ultimate and fundamental values, there can be no principled "trumping" of one value over the others. Rather, there must be a contextually defined and proportionate coordination of obligations.

For example, religious objections to tampering with natural creation cannot by themselves block the creation of Oncomouse or CF mouse, with the anticipated benefits to human welfare and scientific knowledge. On the other hand, given deeply ingrained cultural or religious habits (which themselves may change over time), what might be ethically tolerable or even mandated in one local human community with respect to science and biomedicine may be inadmissible in another. Presumably one would not transgenically manipulate a sacred animal or plant of an indigenous culture, for example, cows in the more traditionally Hindu regions of India. This only underscores the cultural and social embeddedness of all scientific research and medicine, and the fact that human welfare concerns and a thirst for knowledge do not always take precedence over other humanly or naturally important values.

Animal Biotechnology, Economic Markets, and Agribusiness

The domains of scientific and biotechnological research, biomedicine, and economic activity increasingly overlap and shade off into one another. The creation of mice, goats, and other animals that produce easily retrievable pharmaceutical products such as human insulin or tissue plasminogen activator (tPA) at once serve significant human welfare needs and economic entrepreneurial goals. We move away from such immediate health care concerns and attendant ethical obligations when we come to potentially lucrative bovine somatotropin (BST)–boosted cows, growth hormone–primed pigs, and the aquatic factory farming of transgenic fish (Evans and Hollaender 1986). As we traverse this spectrum, pressing human welfare obligations often recede, and the morally ecological analyses of animal biotechnological practices significantly change. Animal welfare and human social/cultural factors come more to the fore.

The Beltsville pig, genetically fashioned for cost-efficient growth rates and feed consumption and for the leaner quality of its meat, proved to be severely compromised by arthritis and multiple other diseases. All parties, including the scientific animal production community, consider this an unfortunate ethical misadventure. There remains, however, the biotechnologists' expectant hope that the animal welfare issues can be overcome and that a new generation of engineered "food animals" will be more socially acceptable (but at what ethical harm?). Similarly there are animal welfare concerns for the BST cows, although immediate animal suffering or harm seems much less acute, and ethical attention is more on the effects of intensifying factory-farming practices.

Beyond heightened concern for animal welfare and unjustifiable suffering, the economic boosters of animal biotechnology, whether from agribusiness or pharmaceutical industries, meet an interesting and complex social and cultural resistance. Small dairy farmers complain that the "big business" of BST-boosted cows will hasten the demise of family farms and local rural traditions. Others object to the pollution of milk with the bovine growth hormone. Still others challenge the patenting and economic commodification of animals: the conceptual reduction of their status as genuine living beings, aboriginally the creation of nature and unowned by humans, to mere configurations of living matter instrumentally at the disposal of humans for their own self-interested purposes, economic or other (Dresser 1988; Verhoog 1992).

Obviously, whatever the actual saliency of these ethical charges and critiques, fundamental social, cultural, and religious values are at stake, arising out of broad cultural traditions and interests. Animal biotechnology, coupled with the engines of corporate economics, is felt to threaten fundamental and traditional moral, religious, and cultural orientations.

Again this poses an important challenge to a morally ecological analysis of animal biotechnologies, in the context of economic activity and elsewhere. There may be certain human communities or cultures in which animal biotechnological practices, even for the best human welfare reasons, are considered morally inadmissible. This raises important social or cultural justice issues on an international scale as biotechnology's province becomes increasingly global. Arguably, local cultural communities ought to decide whether they wish to participate in the enterprise and benefits of animal and wider biotechnology, regardless of the insistent pressures of global economic markets and more narrowly defined international issues of economic justice. (For example, who should benefit economically from the genetic resources, natural or "artificed," that are swept up into international biotechnological-economic activity?)

On the other hand, what should the moral ecology be when cultural or religious objections come from a minority within a wider and culturally diverse community, such as the United States and many other countries? Granted, social, cultural, and community considerations ought to receive serious attention, especially in relation to optional or peripheral economic practices. But again, with a plurality of moral obligations, no sphere of human activity and no ethical interest group can be allowed to override the legitimate ethical interests of the plural others. What then should be done? How do we reach an ethically adequate accommodation between rival values and ethical obligations and their human advocates? This question remains at the core of moral ecology's unfinished business.

Moral Ecology's Landscape: The Outstanding Issues

I have been arguing that the ethical consideration of animal biotechnologies defies any easy solution or subsuming under a "mono-valued" ethical system. There are too many different interventions in too many different contexts involving too many different motives, values, and ethical obligations. Yet the call for a contextual consideration of plural obligations and moral ecology decidedly implies a coordination of disparate and perhaps conflicting values and obligations within and between specific contexts. We require systematic ethical responses that genuinely recognize the plural value and ethical dimensions of our worldly existence. How do we square this circle, which is demanded by our overall responsibilities to humans, animals, and nature? How should such practical decisions be substantively guided? This is an outstanding and unsettled issue.

Yet we may begin to see our way. The first clues come from the sheer plurality of practices, contexts, values, and obligations themselves. This constitutes concrete and experientially incontestable evidence of the plural and complex goodness of human existence. Moreover, the goodness of both humans and nature is vulnerable to change and various harms. We must become ethically committed, as an overarching and fundamental moral duty, to this plurality itself: to upholding and promoting the various abiding and culturally significant spheres of human activity amidst the ecosystemic life and animate world in which they are embedded.

Herein is the second set of clues: The spheres or domains of human activity interpenetrate one another, and there are contexts within wider contexts within still wider contexts of activity and moral significance. Ethical atomism or provincialism is practically impossible and ethically irresponsible. Rather, we must concurrently pursue the human, animal, and natural good. We must fashion an ethically and publicly responsible life that is broadly ecological.

Such an ecological ethics cannot be rationalist or universalist in a traditional sense, that is, they cannot involve principled logical arguments from first moral premises. Rather, its "reasonable connections" must be more ethical-aesthetic. Its modes of thought must be more in keeping with the informal reasoning and moral art of the private realm of intimate relations, which must take in whole webs of life and multiple moral considerations at once. In short, moral ecology deals with complex wholes.

Even if we could adequately see our way through the methodological and epistemological problems of establishing priorities of ethical concern and obligation, we face another problem. Is this commitment to the coordination of plural activities, values, and obligations practically realistic or an impossible dream, given the aggressive disharmony inherently spawned by ethical and political pluralism itself and the dynamic nature of humans' worldly life? History is sobering. Yet the world's dynamic becoming, which will not be rationally, technologically, politically, or ethically subdued, presents a way out of such impasses. Different cultures and different domains of human activity can over time grow together, at least in understanding if not also in practice. This requires both mutual appreciation and mutual criticism as a way of moving toward a more adequate and ethical flourishing within and between particular spheres of activity and human cultures.

The Goodness and Significance of Nature and Animal Life

Given our newly emerging and insistent responsibilities for biological life, ecosystems, and the environment, nowhere is mutual appreciation and criticism more globally and regionally needed than in trying to ferret out the meaning, significance, and goodness of animate life and evolutionary and ecological processes. (As we have seen, this is crucial to the various contextual ethical analyses of animal biotechnologies.) For such an understanding, we need to bring together thinkers from various spheres of scientific and cultural activity: evolutionary biologists, animal researchers, anthropologists, philosophers, theologians, and others with a central stake in the multileveled significance of nature. A serious mutual confrontation of these plural areas of disciplined thought and activity promises philosophical and ethical advances.

For example, more traditional philosophers or theologians, committed to long-dominant modes of essentialist thinking, might see the significance of nature and animal species as arising from (or grounded in) atemporal and unchanging Platonic ideas (for example, the archetypal form "horse"). Or they might appeal to Aristotelian substantial forms (the "formal plan" of development into an adult horse, perhaps an unintended adumbration of genomic information) or a once-and-for-all creation ex nihilo by a transcendent deity. This is how traditional modes of thinking typically account for the definite character, integrity, and goodness of nature's animate beings. Such traditional Western perspectives might (or might not) ethically counsel against modern forms of genetic tinkering, transgenesis, and the confounding of the eternal order of creation.

But contemporary molecular and evolutionary biologists would unite in contending that an essentialist explanation and interpretation of the animal and animate world is fundamentally flawed. Biological species arise and pass in dynamic evolutionary and ecological processes. Thanks to random genetic variation (via genetic mutation and sexual reproduction) and natural selection, species diversify and evolve out of their biological predecessors, sharing and reconfiguring genetic information. Moreover, nature is no realm of essentialist perfection. Rather, our biosphere is an extraordinary, historically particular, and "chaotically orderly" realm of dynamic and systematically related "imperfections": individual organisms more or less well adapted to worldly life; populational species of such individuals more or less well adapted to ever-changing ecological niches; and ecosystems themselves more or less internally robust and dynamically viable, while changing in evolutionary/ecological time.

This by now well-founded and incontestable general evolutionary and ecological perspective does not annihilate the questions of natural goodness and integrity posed by philosophers and theologians. It only defeats and renders obsolete essentialist modes of naturalistic thinking and philosophic interpretation. The natural goodness and integrity of biological individuals and species, as well as ecosystems, only need a new and more philosophically nuanced interpretation. Individual organisms still present themselves as having a lively integrity, intactness, or "oneness" that encompasses bodily, subjective, behavioral, and outwardly social functionings that are more or less flexibly adapted to an active, if vulnerable, life in the world. Species as populations of biological individuals exhibit a spatiotemporally bounded and flexible integrity relative to some ecological niche, also changing. Moreover, species evolve in a creative, though orderly, fashion, according to relatively few generic organic or bodily Bauplans. Finally, the habitats and ecosystems themselves evidence a flexible and dynamic intactness with respect to internal stability and species diversification, more or less vulnerable to outside, wider ecosystemic processes or forces (Ralston 1989).

No doubt these several senses of integrity—individual, species, and ecosystemic—require further and careful conceptual and philosophic articulation and systematic coordination. Moreover, we will need further collaborative efforts in appreciating the full significance and goodness of the individuals, species, and ecosystems of the animate realm. But such an enterprise should only ethically and practically serve us well. It would further and more clearly reveal the complex meanings of "nature natural" for us humans. It would help us discern what the limits of our biotechnological and other human interventions in the wild ought to be and what needs to be ethically protected in scientific and biomedical research and economic activity.

Moreover, we would better understand ourselves and our embedded existence in an animate nature that is ultimately significant yet imperfectly good: that we and animate nature are not to be perfected, but that the world's evolving complex and finite goodness—the various dimensions of activity and value realized by humans and other organisms—is to be unequivocally affirmed and ethically protected.

In conclusion, a speculative, disciplined advance in our understanding and assessment of the multileveled worth of nature would help us in the ethical coordinations required by our contextual plural obligations. Although, in themselves, such an understanding and assessment do not uniquely determine the outcome (positive or negative) of moral deliberations in different contexts, they would better inform us when it is ethically appropriate to move forward biotechnologically and when it is appropriate to take ethically protective stands. We would better know how to integrate our cultural, technological, and natural selves and how practically to fit our human communities within the wider natural and animate world.

III

Variations on Aldo Leopold

9

Nature's Wildness

I am keenly interested in wildness, its complex reality, significance, and importance. Some people can live without wild things and some cannot. I cannot. Why? And why am I so captured and captivated by water wildness?

Following the wise example of *A Sand County Almanac,* I begin with stories, as a prelude to any philosophic reflections and explorations.

Each June I go fishing during a mayfly hatch on a remote pond in northern Wisconsin. Other actors in this annual event, a natural high holiday, include my daughters Inanna and Tegan, red-wing blackbirds and swallows, brown trout, and the mayflies. Typically the pond is still, or there is a slight breeze. It is dusk with a red-orange sun setting behind a blackening forest of evergreen trees. The air is cool, and there are sounds only of birds and mosquitoes. A swallow leaves its perch on a dead stump in the middle of the pond and dives through the air. Immediately it is joined by other birds. We quickly row over to the birds. On the water's surface emerges a host of dun-colored mayflies. The surface is broken by a swirl, and a mayfly disappears.

The dusk deepens, with only the faint light of the horizon. Inanna, Tegan, and I hear slurps of feeding trout all around us. We cast our flies to the sounds. Occasionally there is a decent cast, and we dimly see the dry fly riding high on the water. There is a swirl and a sudden, strong pull on the rod. We fight the fish in the dark, trying to keep it away from submerged logs. The fish is lost, or we land it—a cool, smooth, fat-bellied brown trout. We throw it back or put it in the boat's live-box and, along with the blackbirds and swallows, go home, leaving the pond's other trout to continue their feast well into the night, hoping that enough mayflies make it to the trees and mate to ensure next year's hatch. We drive the sandy roads back to the cabin in silence, mesmerized by the moths and mayflies drawn by the car's headlights.

There are several things to note about this human involvement in a mayfly hatch. For one thing, it is the natural and animal world that importantly sets the terms of the human experience and determines reflections on its meanings and values. The concerns and preoccupations of the human city are left far behind. Moreover, a human being enters the realm of action as only one among several actors, and the actors are in a fundamental sense on equal terms. All are interlocked in a single dynamic realm, involved in characteristic living activities, whether seeking prey, avoiding predators, preparing for mating, or whatever. All this takes place within a community of interaction.

Being a participant-actor within, rather than a spectator-observer without, decisively transforms the human experience. The animals are experienced in a complex and compelling way. The swallow in this context is a living individual, an animal subject actively involved in its own world. The swallow patiently and attentively awaits the anticipated mayflies, an unwitting lookout for the parasitic human fishermen. The brown trout are wily animate others lurking in the depths, strangely beautiful, intricately patterned and colored. It takes the mayflies to bring the trout to the surface and to cast their natural caution to the winds. The mayflies themselves are shapely and delicate emissaries from the mysterious insect kingdom, the focus of this complex natural drama, even while they are having their one day in the sun, after a year as nymphs in the muddy bottom of the pond.

In short, these animals are not mere objects of scientific inquiry or disinterested curiosity. They are living, individual, and interconnected wild presences, emerging out of, while remaining in, nature. By dint of their own wild otherness and our firsthand interactions with them, they vividly confront us with our own existence as living organisms and shock us back from the provinces of the human city to our place within the wider natural scheme of things. By their own animate being, they force us to probe radically the nature of our own organic being and to question thoughtfully the natural world and its ultimate meaning, values, and goodness—why we, animals, and nature matter and matter together.

Two things stand out forcibly: the dynamic interconnection and interaction of animate beings and organisms' own individual liveliness. We are well on our way to Leopoldian wildness. But let us not prematurely bog down in abstractions. Let us explore more concrete examples and personal experiences. I want to shift to Atlantic salmon, which, as we know, are endangered and perhaps threatened with extinction, thanks to our own human blundering and lack of foresight.

I had been fishing for salmon in a Nova Scotia river, the St. Mary's, for four days without luck. In the bright noon sunshine, I absent-mindedly watched my dry fly float over a nearby riffle. A grey-silver salmon suddenly appeared, made a quick, complete circle around the fly, batted the fly with its tail, and disappeared. The fly went bobbing down the river. After making four or five casts in another direction, I came back to the riffle. This time the salmon struck, and minutes later I was on my knees on the hot stones along the river's edge taking the fly out of the mouth of a silvery grilse (a small salmon) fresh from the ocean, still covered with sea lice.

Another example. I hooked a salmon in a broad, swift-flowing Icelandic river, just opposite an imposing escarpment. The salmon made a long, determined run across and up the river, returned closer to where I was standing on the bank, and hunkered down on the river's bottom. I could neither see the fish nor move it. Some twenty minutes later, the salmon rolled up to the surface, showed its silvery side, and swam straight for a narrows, two hundred yards downriver. The salmon had recently come through the narrows on its way upriver to spawn. With no success, I tried to stop its run. I ran along the bank, tripped, fell to my knees, and scrambled up, all along keeping my line taut. When I got to the narrows, the salmon had stopped. I held tight. After several minutes of no movement, I dipped the tip of my rod into the water and came up with my fly, moss hanging from the hook. The salmon had rubbed the fly off on a moss covered rock and was gone.

Yet another salmon story. A few years ago, I traveled to Newfoundland to fish Portland Creek and the River of Ponds, both storied North Atlantic salmon rivers. I was guided by Gideon House, a local senior citizen with a brogue that seemed to echo down Dublin streets: "Yes, Strachan, me boy, the River of Ponds is the river for salmon. For salmon, it's the River of Ponds." There followed a tuneless, "La de da de da," which over the week we came to tolerate, if not love. One evening on the River of Ponds, following a frustrating day of rising salmon toying with my fly, Gideon reached into his vest and took out a black salmon fly with a yellow butt. "Yes, Strachan, me boy, the Lemon Tip is the fly for the River of Ponds. For the River of Ponds, it is the Lemon Tip."

Gideon tied the Lemon Tip onto my leader, and at the end of the pool, just before dark, sure enough, a salmon broke the water's surface and took the fly. This was no ordinary salmon, but a real Smokin' Joe Frazier, with a game plan from the start. The salmon raced to the far side of the pool, leaped high into the air, and swam straight back toward me, leaving a wide loop of slack line (a great opportunity for losing a salmon). It charged upstream, back down to the bottom of the pool, and then allowed me to reel it in closely. It slowly rose to the surface, gave me the eye, and returned to the river's bottom. Soon after, it made a sudden, backward leap six feet into the air. Snap. My line and leader went slack. The salmon and the Lemon Tip were gone.

Wonderful. I had hooked up with a wild one in its native home river, surrounded by evergreen forests. An area of clear-cut logging was nearby, but out of sight.

A few days later, our fishing trip over, we visited Newfoundland's Humber River and its Big Falls to watch salmon jumping the falls on their way upriver to spawn. It had been raining heavily all week, and the volume of water transformed Big Falls into a mini Niagara. We saw countless salmon trying to leap up, through, and over the falls. None made it. They would have to wait for the river's water to go down.

This was an awesome scene, in the old and genuine sense of the term. I was humbled, overwhelmed with respect. Compared with Atlantic salmon and their naturally rigorous lives, spent traveling from natal rivers to Greenland and back, we humans (at least many of us) are couch potatoes, leading cushy lives in cultural enclaves. We usually miss life's stark, challenging reality and the natural world that spawns and fosters it.

I want to tell one more story, this time not about wild trout and salmon, but about wild ducks. In the Lowcountry of South Carolina, there is a coastal island, Fenwick Island, with five duck ponds, all with poetical names—Long, Back, North, Middle, and South Ponds. Middle Pond has not been hunted for five years or more. Wild ducks are smarter than we think. Each fall, after running the hunter's gauntlet from Canada down the Atlantic Seaboard, the ducks pour into Middle Pond. By best SWAG calculations (scientific wild-ass guesses), there are 15,000 to 25,000 ducks on the pond.

Each evening, joined by the ducks from the nearby ponds, the ducks flock together and leave the pond to roost elsewhere for the night. Their flight always commences ten to fifteen minutes before dusk—rafts and rafts, species by species, taking off into the sky. Middle Pond is transformed into a natural smokestack, with dark, billowing clouds of wild ducks emerging from the water and rising into the air, trailing far off into the northern horizon. The show is over in ten minutes.

The next morning at dawn, the ducks return—widgeon, teal, gadwall, mallards, and more, especially pintail. From 2,000 to 3,000 feet high in the sky, pintail set their wings and carve their way down into the pond, without fear or their usual caution. Other times, returning ducks look like thick swarms of mosquitoes overhead.

These evening and morning events are one of Mother Nature's great wild *son et lumière* (sound and light) shows. It stirs the depths of spectator birds, me, and human others.

Wildness is nature's wildness, a character or value that does not fly in from some anatural elsewhere. Wildness is of this earth, if not also of the natural universe as a whole. It is ingredient in the earth's beauty and goodness, which themselves are generated in and by evolutionary, ecological, and geological processes. We encounter innumerable organic capacities and forms of order and innumerable instances of individual lives interconnected in the rigors of earthly existence—births, matings, life cycles, deaths; predator-prey relations, competition and symbiosis, extinction events; and explosions of new ecological niches and biological diversity. The list, and life, goes on.

Such natural wildness, beauty, and goodness may be ultimate values, not to be finally captured in words or definitions, but only encountered, experienced, and wordlessly enjoyed. Yet the values are ingredient in the concrete facts of our world, and about the concreteness of the world many things can be said.

In a certain sense, the wildness, beauty, and goodness of our earthly home is out there, generated by a protean nature that transcends the human realm and is beyond human comprehension. Yet I dwell in this nature and can appreciate its wildness, beauty, and goodness, as do we all. How can this incredible fact of our human existence be? For me, the only plausible speculative answer is that we are also wild ones, organisms living within a nature that has aboriginally developed the capacities of feeling, emotion, thought, and action to capture, however imperfectly, its own self-engendered wildness, beauty, and goodness, which by now we emphatically must realize to include ourselves. If we breathe, metabolize, move about, feel— do what natural organisms have been evolved to do—we are wild ones, whether we live in the wilds, on farms, in rivers, or in cities. Oddly, this most basic of worldly facts comes as a stunning revelation to many of us, who have been taught to live in denial of our natural and evolutionary origins. I live in a city of eight million wild ones, and few seem to know it.

What a shame this denial is. What natural riches are missed. What a grand, historical, worldly drama that includes ourselves is hidden from view. This was Darwin's unspoken judgment, and this regret very much underlies Leopold's indictment of modern culture and of those who can live without wild things and wildness, and who cannot find wildness within the deepest recesses of themselves.

Yet this cultural eclipse of wildness is not merely sad or to be regretted. It is dangerous and pernicious. Those well acquainted with the wildness, goodness, and beauty of earthly nature are also actively aware of the finitude, mortality, and vulnerability to harm that pervade the animate realm and all its creatures. Of course, this too is natural fact, but it is equally an ethical issue that inescapably confronts us. Responsibility to act well within the natural world is given with our very being as wild ones, who are born into a world laced with value—wildness, goodness, beauty, and other. We can either face our responsibilities for upholding and promoting the earth's values and goodness, including our own, or we can choose to be irresponsible. The one thing we cannot choose is not to choose.

Leopold's land ethic explicitly recognizes our moral situation and responsibilities to and for the wider natural world. Leopold knew that we were wild ones living in a wild and wonderful home. He also knew that moral responsibility was more than pragmatic, practical expedience. For example, we and other creatures need good water not only to survive as bodily, metabolizing organisms. We need good and abundant water in order that the earth's wildness, goodness, and beauty may continue to be.

Could it be that vivid recognition of our own wildness, the wildness of our earthly home, and the wildness of our waters and all creatures that dwelleth therein is the key to saving ourselves and our world, which will stand or fall together? If so, it is time to listen again, appreciatively and critically, to the prophetic voice of Leopold and, more importantly, to the wild world that he champions.

10

Wild Turkeys and Old Gobblers

As I turned off South Carolina Route 17 onto Bennetts Point Road and toward home, I entered a transition zone, full of complexities. I had been driving for two hours from Mepkin Abbey, a Trappist monastery, in Moncks Corner, South Carolina, where a daylong meeting, held in conjunction with Mepkin Abbey, the Center for Humans and Nature, and the South Carolina Department of Natural Resources, concerned the reimpoundment of traditional rice fields along the Cooper-Santee River.

The prospect of rice field reimpoundments is a complex and controversial issue, with multiple humans and nature dimensions. The topic inevitably raises the cultural-historical question of the enslavement of black Africans, as well as their traditional knowledge and capacities for growing rice and other crops. (These facts should be forthrightly acknowledged and also honored.) Breached rice fields also raise the question of public and private property, the right of private landowners and the public alike. The state owns navigable waters, which the public has access to for recreational purposes (fishing, hunting, bird watching, and more). Navigable waters include breached rice fields. Yet private property owners must pay property taxes on rice field land. What happens when the fields are reimpounded for managing wildfowl, fishing, or even new forms of farming? How should tensions between private rights and public access be balanced or adjudicated? Finally, to complicate things even more, there are the regulatory regimes of the Environmental Protection Agency and state water-control agencies, not always in sync or flexible. An earlier effort on the issue ended in a standoff and was abandoned. Our meeting at least ended civilly, and discussions continue.

The Mepkin meeting was only the latest in a series of meetings I had attended in Chicago, New York, and South Carolina during January, February, and March of 2007. This spate of meetings was finally over and behind me. This is the back end of my transition. I should also mention that a week earlier I turned sixty-five, an age at which many retire. What's more, around the same time we had to put down our aging black Labrador, Snorri, named after the poet-historian of the Icelandic Sagas. For me, these were both unsettling events, *memento mori*.

But to what was I transitioning? What lay ahead? I was driving to Ashepoo, a family home in Green Pond, South Carolina, which is in the heart of the ACE Basin, an area southwest of Charleston drained by three rivers: the Ashepoo, the Combahee, and the Edisto. The ACE Basin is an extraordinary conservation effort, protecting some 170,000 acres of land, including brackish coastal marshlands, teeming with wildlife: wild ducks, countless other birds, fish, alligators, and more. Further south lie the menacing threats of spreading golfing and retirement communities, emanating from Hilton Head and Beaufort County. Thus the ACE Basin and the proactive, protective efforts of a coalition of private landowners, conservation NGOs, and governmental agencies local, state, and federal. To date, this is a singular humans and nature success story.

At Ashepoo were my wife, Vivian, and my elder brother, Elliott, a lifelong hunter and fisherman, now compromised by poor health. For Vivian and me, this was new territory, time spent alone together in South Carolina without immediate family or friends. (We have five grown daughters and five young grandchildren.) After over thirty-eight years of marriage, what would this new, scaled-down arrangement—our being alone together—be like? As it turned out, we enjoyed our quiet time together very much. We easily slipped into Ashepoo's natural rhythms.

However, this is not the end of the transition. Besides being a conservation philosopher-ethicist, father, and husband, I too am a fisherman and hunter. Ahead of me was a much-anticipated five days of Ashepoo's extraordinary nature, including wild turkey hunting and spottail bass (redfish) fishing. As I turned off Bennetts Point Road onto the sandy drive to the house at Ashepoo, out of the depths of my transitioning body and soul emerged the "wild one" in me, the hunter and the fisherman, all too long suppressed by professional and family matters.

A short way down the drive, I was shocked out of my reflective, pensive mood. There along the road was a flock of seven wild turkeys, including a large jake (a first- or second-year male) and an old gobbler with his tail fanned. (Five hens seemed unconcerned and unmoved by his show.) The turkeys crossed the road into a nearby field. I stopped the car no more than thirty or forty yards from the birds. If I had had a shotgun, this would have been my chance to shoot a turkey, and, as I well knew, this might be the only chance that I would get on the trip. As it was, I was armed with only my Parker ballpoint pen, my favorite weapon of choice these days. No matter, it was a great privilege just to see the turkeys at such a close range.

The birds moved out of the field into the woods, and I drove on to the house. Vivian and I had drinks and dinner, and after talking briefly about the Mepkin meetings, we went to bed.

At 5:30 the next morning, I got up, put on a camouflage suit, drank a cup of coffee, and headed to a field not far from where I had seen the flock the evening before. As I got into a turkey blind—it was still dark—John Miley, the manager of Ashepoo, put out a hen turkey decoy and left the field in his pickup truck.

Ritualistically, I got everything in order. I pulled a gauze camouflage mask over my face, loaded my shotgun, and gave a few practice "tuts" on a turkey call. I am a novice at calling turkeys and am better off keeping silent. But the call is part of the ritual.

I sat in silence and awaited dawn, listening to the first early-morning birds. As the sky lightened, I heard two gobblers in the distance. My body tensed, and I focused on the surrounding landscape, which slowly appeared in the morning light. The turkeys gobbled again but seemed no closer. Then they were silent.

By now, I could clearly see the turkey decoy in front of me, and I settled down for a long wait. Some twenty or thirty minutes later, it happened. Over a small rise, along a field road, came the flock of seven turkeys, slowly walking into the field. The hens came first, indifferent to the decoy. The gobbler and the jake showed characteristic caution. They moved along the far edge of the field across from me, some forty yards away.

They walked deliberately and were not going to stop. If I were to take a shot, it would have to be now. Slowly, I poked my gun through a hole in the blind and fired, breaking the morning silence. The turkeys bolted out of the field through the woods opposite me.

I scrambled out of the blind and, favoring a knee injured long ago, followed them through the woods into an open field. I saw the jake fly off into the woods across the field. With a sense of emptiness at a rare opportunity missed, I scanned the field that was boarded by a hedgerow of thick brambles. Unexpectedly, I caught sight of the fanned tail of the old gobbler, pressed hard against the brambles. I had hit him in the neck, the only way you can wound or kill a turkey. Buckshot bounce off turkeys' heavily feathered bodies. I hobbled across the field as fast as my balky knee would take me. The turkey disappeared into the thicket. When I got to the hedgerow, I peered into terra incognita, the heart of South Carolina's darkness. There was the gobbler, standing on the other side of a big drainage ditch. I shot again, but he just moved farther into the thicket.

I faced a moment of existential decision. Prudence would say, let the old gobbler go and save my body and knee for another day. Something deep in me decided otherwise. Forsaking caution, I plunged into the brambles and fought my way to the ditch, which, to my knowledge, no human had ever crossed on foot. How deep was it? I took the fateful step. Water came up to mid-thigh, well over my boots. I scrambled up the far bank.

I discovered that the gobbler had recrossed the ditch and was crouching in brambles on the opposite bank. I shot at the bird with my last two shells, but to no avail. He again moved off.

I found a small otter or beaver dam and crossed back over the ditch and made my way around a small tree surrounded by bushes. I saw the turkey crouching under a thicket of thorns, and I slowly made my way to the bird, which did not move. Putting my foot on his neck, I tried to figure out how finally to dispatch him, now that my ammunition was gone. I tried hitting his head with the butt of my shotgun. It did not work. Then I considered waiting until he died and took my boot off his neck. Instead, he revived and crept under the thorns back into the ditch.

I followed him into the water and grabbed him by his long tail feathers. (He was unable to swim across the ditch.) I pulled him toward me and grasped his neck, keeping well away from his powerful wings and the spurs of his legs.

It was only then that I noticed that I had broken the stock of my double-barreled shotgun, which I had had since 1960, my first year in college. There I was, broken shotgun in one hand, turkey in the other, standing thigh deep in the ditch. What to do? Trying unsuccessfully to break his neck, I considered an alternative option. I would drown him. I squeezed his neck and shoved the head of the gobbler under the water's surface. I watched his wings flap until they were still.

I dragged myself and the turkey out of the ditch and, holding the bird high in front of me, fought my way through the thorn patch back to the road. My hand, ungloved, was covered with blood and embedded thorns. I put the gobbler down, picked him up by his legs, and carried him back to the field where we started. I left him by the side of the road and went back into the blind, for want of anything better to do.

Some minutes later, a hen turkey came into the field, scratching the dirt, pecking for seeds and tubers. After a time, she raised her head, warily scanned the field, and spotted the dead gobbler. Giving a "chuck," she strode out of the field.

Around 9 a.m., I heard Johnny's pickup truck. He drove into the field, stuck his head out the window, and stared at the dead gobbler. "Damn." He got out of the truck and picked up the bird. "Heavy."

On the way home, I told him my saga, wondering whether this might make Ashepoo's Hall of Fame for turkey retrieves. His eyes lit up, and he chuckled over and over. "Damn." As far as he knew, no one had ever gone into the dense briar patch and crossed the ditch. I later talked with Porky Rhodes, the former manager of Ashepoo, and told him the gobbler story. Again, a deep, uncontrollable chuckle. He thought my pursuit of the turkey might indeed make our Hall of Fame (or Infamy), perhaps topping the list. I have since learned that the story of "Donnelley and the Old Gobbler" has been traveling around the Lowcountry.

I am not sure what this tale is doing for my reputation as a conservation philosopher and ethicist. However this has not been the primary question for me. Rather, what possessed me to go into the bramble patch and the ditch in the first place? Some character flaw or strength? Something from my personal past? Something deeper, more primordial and aboriginal, brewed up in evolutionary, ecological time and space? Or some deep, almost personal affinity between me and the old gobbler, each acting out inevitable stages in our lives? After all, in the thicket of thorns and the ditch, we did get to know one other intimately. Who was the wild turkey and who the old gobbler: him, me, or both of us?

Ignoramus. I do not know the answers to my own questions. I will continue to ponder them in my heart, without really expecting to happen upon any final insights. Yet, I am glad that I did spot the fanned tail up against the brambles across the open field. For better or worse, the ensuing wild dance of death has become an ongoing, if not permanent, part of myself.

11

Big Little Snake

Metaphor Mongers
and Mountain Rainbows

I founded the Center for Humans and Nature in 2003 to explore and promote long-term moral and civic responsibilities to human communities
and natural ecosystems and landscapes. Three years later, the center and
its colleagues inaugurated a series of multidisciplinary meetings on concepts of ecosystems and their theoretical, practical, and moral implications. As would be expected, we immediately found ourselves in trouble,
skating on thin ice. We examined the historical and continuing contro-
versy over the concept of ecosystems: its nature, character, and usefulness.
Since I am trained as a philosopher, this was for me *déjà vu* all over again,
a reflection of fundamental battles that have raged through the history of
philosophy, still unsettled. We found a continuum of fundamental convictions, with a complex mix of issues concerning reality, knowing, and
value: ontology, epistemology, and axiology, in the jargon of professional
philosophers.

Most agree, in some fashion or other, that the concept of ecosystems
connotes the notion of complex, natural wholes that involve interdependent, dynamically interrelated, and interactive parts, biotic and abiotic.
But then the philosophic battles begin. Are ecosystems realities unto
themselves involving their interrelated, constituent parts, or are they mere
aggregates of interacting parts, with no real wholeness or reality of their
own (an "empty container" conception of ecosystems)? Indeed are ecosystems any kind of reality at all other than an abstract conception in our
minds, either totally useless regarding practical issues (for example, conservation of human and natural communities) or of limited pragmatic use
for particular projects? Here there is no claim of comprehending natu-

ral reality in any scientifically or philosophically adequate fashion. As you might guess, there are intermediate positions along the ecosystem concept spectrum. Some of us are convinced that there are real natural ecosystems, with real, if permeable, boundaries and ultimate value with respect to the being and becoming (genesis) of animate, organic (including human) life. However, we do not have, and perhaps will never have, the capacities of perception and conceptual discernment finally and adequately to understand ecosystemic and ecospheric reality. At best, we will always see more or less through a glass darkly, though we gaze upon the natural, earthly, value-laden real.

All this is enough to make heads swim and jolt us out of philosophic slumber. Once again we should realize that we know that we do not know and that there is plenty, perhaps unending, philosophic exploration ahead.

Amidst the heated back-and-forth discussions, one parenthetical remark particularly struck me and stopped me in my tracks, kindling a small philosophic fire. We were reminded that all human language and thought are ultimately metaphorical. This is not an original remark, but it got me buzzing. We have one foot in natural reality—we are, after all, biological organisms—and the other foot in the domain of metaphor, symbol, conceptual thought, and whatever else attends conscious human experience. (As an old song goes, we have one eye on the pot, the other up the chimney.)

This dual-leggedness, this straddling natural reality and a human conscious experience that is importantly constituted or undergirded by metaphors, raises a host of questions. First and foremost, what is the relation or connection between our status as biological organisms living in evolutionary, ecological, ecosystemic nature and our being "metaphor mongers," inveterately engendering and trafficking in metaphors? What accounts for the meaning and value of metaphors, their felt power over our thinking and practical, active lives? What are the genetic, constitutive relations between metaphors (powerfully fundamental and other) and concepts and conceptual thinking, up to and including various sciences and philosophic (and religious) worldviews? In short, what are the concrete relations between nature, organism, metaphor making, and human existence in all its complexity and fullness?

These are mind-bending, speculative questions that enduringly cry out for serious and systematic philosophic exploration. They require a Heraclitus, Plato, Aristotle, Spinoza, or Whitehead, or similar philosophically bold lights. Setting aside all questions of competence, this is not a task that can be seriously undertaken here. But we can make a modest, first-step beginning. That is what I intend to do here. I want to return to and reflect upon firsthand experiences of myself and the world.

Mountain Rainbows

Fortunately for my philosophic quandary over organisms and metaphors, I recently found myself in a western mountain river, the Little Snake River, which borders Colorado and Wyoming. I was fly-fishing for wild trout, a longtime and primary passion of mine. It was a hot, sunny day (not good for catching fish); I had already had a modestly successful morning of fishing and was working my way back upriver toward the car that would take us home. I stopped at a pool that I had previously fished. A young guide tied a dropper on my dry fly, a Parachute Adams, and left. (A dropper is a short bit of clear leader material with a small nymph fly tied at the end, giving me one fly on the surface, one underwater. I am not a fan of casting "double flies," but, when on the Little Snake, do as the little snakes do.)

As I waded into the pool, I saw a flash of silver deep in the current ahead. The sun had reflected off a slashing rainbow trout, no doubt pursuing some insect. For me, the river and pool came alive and were transformed into sacred time and space. Such is the magic that a slashing, flashing wild trout works on me. There was a promise of *bonheur,* good fishing, ahead. This turned out to be the case. But something truly arresting happened. As my dry fly floated nearby on the inner edge of the current, a rainbow slowly arced underwater into the middle of the river. It touched either fly, but was, or seemed to be, an order of magnitude bigger than any trout previously encountered that day. Here was one of the fabled monster rainbows of the Little Snake, about which I had heard so much. What a privilege just to see such a fish.

I thought little more of the red-striped, silver-sided rainbow, "Big Little Snake," and went back to fishing the current. Then there was Big Little Snake again, resting in front of me under the water's surface, its broad back brown with black speckles, my nymph in its mouth. I carefully but firmly pulled up on the rod. The rod arched against the fish's weight.

Big Little Snake was solidly hooked. It shook its head, rested a moment, then bolted upstream into the current. I could see flashing silvery sides as the fish worked back and forth across the river. I silently exhorted myself,

"Be careful. This one is worth landing." I coaxed the fish up into shallow water, a good place, as I have learned from salmon fishing. (In the shallows, fish tire more easily from the lack of oxygen.) I tried to keep the big rainbow in the shallow water, but it knew its home hole, its aquatic habitat and landscape. Sensing my presence and its danger, it again bolted out into the current, heading for a fallen tree in the water on the other bank, a promise of freedom. (It would wrap my leader around a dead limb and bust off my fly.) I tried to hold the fish back from the tree trunk. Snap. The line went slack. Big Little Snake and its red-striped silver sides were gone. A knot in the leader had broken. Thus ends the saga of the Little Snake River and sacred time and space.

I was not particularly upset. The fish was probably too big for my fishing tackle. I would have returned it to the water in any case. Part of me would have liked to know how big it was: twenty to twenty-two inches, four pounds? More? But I always remember the fish I lose more than the ones that I land. Actually it was a win-win situation. We both got what we wanted: Big Little Snake its freedom; I the natural encounter and enduring memory.

So far there has been no hint of metaphor, just straightforward experienced reality: my hooking up with a big wild rainbow trout in a mountain river. But metamorphosis, or metaphorizing, soon set in. It has yet to abate. Big Little Snake had been at its feeding station, no doubt previously won through struggles with other wild trout, awaiting what was coming downriver. It was living its regular, if rigorous, existence in a natural, familiar setting. Suddenly it was wrenched out of its feeding lane and regular routine by an unanticipated and unwelcome intrusion into its life. Its existence was thrown off-balance, and it was compelled to struggle mightily to regain its normal worldly, rainbow trout, Big Little Snake self.

How do I know all this? Because, like Big Little Snake, I too am an organism living in the world, struggling recurrently to keep my bodily self together and functioning well. (Spinoza would say that we share a similar essence: a *conatus,* an endeavor to persevere in our own individual being.) The rhythm of both our lives moves back and forth from being conatively lost and found. "I once was lost, but now am found," as the old hymn "Amazing Grace" goes.

I think that we can glimpse a crucial key for the transition from reality and firsthand worldly experience (one leg of our knowing) to metaphor (the other leg). The key precisely is our being natural, "conative" organisms, with the evolved, complexly dimensioned capacity for engendering meta-

phors and metaphorical experience, an act of meaning making and valuation. My encounter with Big Little Snake and its world can stand in for,
or symbolize, me and my world. My real experience creatively transmuted
into metaphoric experience has real significance for me. It is how I can get a
hold, a purchase, on my own self and my world, how I can orient and recurrently reorient myself. I vividly comprehend that I gain, lose, and regain my
balance within a dynamic world and existence in which I must recurrently
and actively struggle to maintain an individual integrity or integral oneness. There is nothing abnormal about this existential wobbling or recurrent rebalancing act. (In the above sentences, substitute "we," "our," and "us"
for "I," "my," and "me" and recognize fundamental commonalities of our
human existence, shared in significant part with nonhuman organisms.)

Thus it makes sense that we naturally are metaphor mongers (metaphor
makers) and that fundamental metaphors have such a strong, meaningful
hold over us. They play crucial and effective roles in our lives. "Metaphorizing"
and metaphors are endemic to our human mode of organic, earthly existence.

Metaphors and Concepts: Science, Philosophy, and Other Modes of Thought

We need not leave things with such "close to the bone" metaphors as Big Little
Snake's encounter with me and my nymph. We can move from such worldly
particularity to more advanced levels of generality or abstractness, which are
emptied of the initial particulars of firsthand experience without ever (perhaps) fully transcending them. (In short, conceptual experience and activity
presuppose organic and primary metaphoric experience and activity.)

Let me try to give a persuasive example. I have long been philosophically interested in the interrelations of nature, organism, individual selfhood, and value experience. Thanks to such thinkers as Heraclitus, Spinoza,
Whitehead, and Hans Jonas, among numerous others, I have increasingly
become a convinced philosophic naturalist, forsaking any form of anatural
explanation (for example, recourse to otherworldly, supersensible platonic
forms or ideas, or supernatural interventions into the scheme of things.)
No doubt, my philosophic journey has been fed by numerous metaphors—
"Everliving Fires" (Heraclitus), "Conative Organisms" (Spinoza), "Nature
Alive" (Whitehead), "Needful Freedom" (Jonas), and more.

Lately, I have been much interested in the Darwinian, evolutionary
biological reflections of Ernst Mayr. I have been particularly taken by

notions of "emergence" and "emergent properties" (a natural metaphor turned concept) and "orchestral causation" (another metaphor seeking the status of concept). Orchestral causation is meant to replace the outmoded notion of Newtonian determinism, physical "billiard-balls-in-motion" antecedents strictly determining physical consequents. Evolutionary biology relies on ideas of causal influence working "up and down" among many levels of natural existence and interactors (for example, genomes, organisms, ecosystems, and the ecosphere), with a real role given to chance and historical contingency. Thus the metaphor of an orchestral performance, which involves innumerable concrete actors and factors interacting with one another, no one to be singled out as the cause, let alone the sufficient cause, of the performance.

In sum, I have come to think of human selves as inextricably bound to their organic bodies and the dynamically evolving natural and cultural world. I think of us as "emergent ones" engendered by the orchestral causation of the world (including past personal selves) and ongoingly so until we die. Lately, I have entertained adding the metaphor of "watersheds" into the mix of conceptualizing the self, especially if we conceive of watersheds in their temporal, as well as spatial, dimensions. Think of all the streaming influences that have entered into and helped constitute our ever-becoming selves, an augmented (or depleted) river flowing into a future still in the making.

My encounter with Big Little Snake can help strengthen and amend this watershed metaphor or conception of the self. Whitehead claims that the universe (and the self) is a creative advance into novelty, that worldly becoming moves out of the past into the future. This insight may strike us as fundamentally true. But think of Big Little Snake in his feeding lane, facing upstream, awaiting what comes down the river, whether a natural mayfly, my nymph, or some other misfortune. Don't we similarly face an (unpredictable) unfolding present and near-term, as well as long-term, future? The self, in terms of its necessary existential concerns, emerges out of the present and near- and long-term future, as well as the past. Both Whitehead and Nietzsche recognized this fact. (For Nietzsche, time flows from the future, through the present, into the past.) If Big Little Snake serves adequately as a metaphor, leading to a conception of the self, this fundamental anticipatory, "forward-looking" aspect of organic existence must be woven into our metaphors and conceptions of "emergence," "orchestral causation," "watershed," and more.

Enough said about the metaphor-based conception of the self. There are other equally important and more general lessons to be learned from the primary experiential encounter with Big Little Snake. The primary encounter was organically existential and experiential, not conceptual or reflectively rational. Rather, I have argued that fundamentally the "natural progression" is from primary worldly experience, to metaphorical experience, to conceptual, rational experience, irrespective of whatever interfusions of the different realms or levels of experience there might be and that often, if not invariably, take place. The message seems clear. Rational, conceptual experience and truth do not lie at the foundations of our existence, certain philosophic and theological traditions notwithstanding. (Beware of Pythagoras, Plato, Descartes, and their cohorts.) Quite the opposite. Science, philosophy, theology, and whatever other rational, conceptual disciplines there might be (including mathematics) must be creatively fashioned out of the "arational" bases of organic and metaphoric existence and experience. This insight is important, if not new or original. (Darwinian evolution lends its crucial support.) There is no basis whatsoever for any claim to dogmatic, final, rational truth. Our human experience and existence, including our thinking, is as open-ended and unfinished as Big Little Snake facing upstream in his feeding lane. We may be able critically to check and recheck our metaphors and concepts for their accuracy and adequacy to primary worldly encounters and experience. Yet seemingly we can do this only by the use of other metaphors and concepts that in principle are themselves suspect, finite, or "uncertain," for all have been woven out of our worldly organic and metaphoric existence. Rational certainty, versus experiential and existential conviction, is a ruse. (So claimed the mathematician-physicist-philosopher Whitehead, who should know about such matters.) Our solace and strength are that we, thanks to being natural organisms, have one foot in nature's reality, and nature has its own definite features and character, even if they change. Again, we experience and consciously grasp reality, if only through a glass darkly.

Organism, Metaphor, and Morality

We have spoken much about natural reality and organisms, as well as knowing, whether metaphorical and existential or conceptual and theoretical. Questions of value have been lurking in the background. Once again we can return to the primary experiential encounter with Big Little Snake.

Things matter to (have value for) Big Little Snake and ourselves, and for fundamentally the same reasons. Fish and humans are alike organisms, endeavoring to maintain a good, satisfying, unharried, balanced, conative existence amidst the inescapable vicissitudes of earthly life. As we saw, a primary motivation for engendering metaphoric experience and existence is to get a better grip on ourselves and our world, so that our selves and our values may effectively continue to be. At the base of this value and valuing is our existential status as biological, animate, living organisms, carried into new dimensions of existence and experience by the evolutionary, ecological, and cultural engendering of human capacities—capacities of thought, feeling, and action; capacities for creating metaphors, science, philosophy, art, theology, and cultural existence in its fullest sweep. But we should not be duped or fooled by what we might take to be unique human capacities and dimensions of existence and experience.

We are not aworldly creatures, individually or communally. We live *in* the world, natural and cultural. In the end, we need robust and resilient natural settings, and not only to serve basic bodily, organic needs. In striving to gain and regain a grip on ourselves, individually and collectively, we need an abundant and varied nature with which to interact. We need a plethora of primary resources for metaphoric activity and existence. (As we should realize by now, our status as human, moral, and cultural agents rests on our status as metaphoric agents.) We need to foster both our human capacities and the world upon which their exercise depends. This primarily means the world of nature.

Let the encounter with Big Little Snake stand as a metaphor for a rich and abundant nature. Beyond all practical, bodily necessity, we need nature and our fellow living creatures and the metaphoric opportunities that they afford us. To impoverish the "biodiverse," natural world is primordially to impoverish ourselves, perhaps robbing us of our very humanity. I do not here speak of the emphatic goodness—ontological (being), cosmological (order)—of ecospheric nature and life itself, irrespective of human beings. To consider ourselves the source of all "order, beauty, and goodness" is sheer and shameless hubris.

Given the present natural states of things—ecological crises, biodiversity loss, global warming, and more—striving to uphold nature's resilience, complexity, and dynamic integrity is extremely serious business, masked by a pervasive cultural crisis within which we find ourselves. For various complex historical reasons, we refuse to consider ourselves as natural organisms vulnerably dependent on nature for all dimensions of our lives. In the long run, this cultural attitude amounts to nihilism, the willful destruction of value, human and natural.

Ecospheric nature may be in an ever-increasing and irreversible crisis, yet we seem incapable of taking this possibility or probability seriously. What are we to do? We need a new form of Pascal's wager. Three centuries ago Pascal exhorted his readers to believe in God and the afterlife even though God's existence is uncertain. If God does not exist and we believe, then we have nothing to lose anyway. But if we don't believe and He does exist, we are in trouble. Today the wager must not be about God, but about our earthly world. Wager that the worst might happen, so to provoke whatever remedial measures that we might still make to promote the resilience of the natural world. If sober but dire warnings prove false, so much the better. We will have lost nothing, for we will have laid the foundations for a better and more enduring human and natural world.

This to me seems an eminently sensible and morally responsible wager. I owe these reflections, at least in part, to my hooking up with Big Little Snake. May the fish be resting comfortably and confidently in its home pool, feeding lane, awaiting whatever comes down his mountain river of becoming.

I firmly believe in the reality of the ecosphere, all its ecosystemic, biotic, and abiotic constituents, and their ultimate goodness, value, or worth. I also believe that our metaphoric and conceptual experience and existence are motivated by innumerable organically natural and humanly cultural interests. These interests provide many perspectives on the world, each with its own strengths and limitations. This makes me, I think, a critical realist with respect to natural and cultural being and value (ontology and axiology), while a pluralist with respect to knowing (epistemology). I like this middle position. I can emphatically champion our ultimate responsibilities to nature and ourselves, while being skeptically and critically chary of any proposed solutions to practical long-term, earthly problems of humans and nature. This dual position challenges us to be morally bold and courageous while being humble and practically cautious. This seems about right to me. I think that Big Little Snake, representing the rest of nature, would approve, if only the mountain rainbow could.

12

Hunting Hennepin's Windblown Bottom

Aldo Leopold enjoins us to become members and plain citizens, rather than conquerors, of the land. By land and biotic community, he means much the same thing: the abiotic and biotic elements, including flora and fauna (above and below ground), of the ecosphere and the ecosystems in which we humans inescapably live. This natural biotic community home involves its own temporally deep, evolutionary past and future.

Leopold realized that the land ethic is a further extension and broadening of human ethics as it has culturally and historically evolved. The land ethic as a practical ethic of human communities was for the mid-twentieth century a civic ethics of the future. In our early twenty-first century, it still is. Few, if any, of us recognize the full reaches of our biotic responsibilities to ourselves and our earthly home. This is a major cultural and moral problem of our times.

Why has it been so difficult to recognize ourselves as full-blown, charter members of the biotic community, with all the innumerable benefits, burdens, and attendant moral obligations that go along with such membership? (We, along with all natural organisms, are undeniably "wild ones," born of evolutionary and ecological processes.) Why do we characteristically consider ourselves at bottom anatural or outside of nature? Further, why was Leopold himself so prescient and farsighted about our fundamental status in the scheme of things? Others knew their Darwin and evolutionary biology as well as or better than he, yet few saw as clearly or as far.

I think a clue to Leopold's moral pioneering and originality can be found precisely in those passages of *A Sand County Almanac* that trouble so many of his readers and sympathetic critics. Leopold unapologetically tells several stories of hunting and fishing. There is not only the shooting of the she-wolf (discussed in chapter 13), but also other stories such as the ones in which Leopold describes killing his first wild (black) duck; his crafty luring, hooking, and landing of a large wild brook trout; and his love of autumn woodcock hunting, as well as his delight in their springtime mating dance. (He learned to take only so many woodcock in the fall as to allow enough dancers in ensuing springs—a fundamental insight for any adequate conservation ethics.) Despite the robust moral demands of the land ethic, Leopold never condemns hunting and fishing, though he does claim them to be atavistic sport. Why this silence? It is not as though the ethics of hunting were not being discussed in his day. Is this a sign of his own moral immaturity or lack of insight? Or rather, is there not something deeper and more nuanced afoot, something that escapes the critics of Leopold's sensibility and stance?

I will not defend Leopold by quoting, explicating, or interpreting chapter and verse from his writings or letters. Such a critical, academic enterprise would not get to the heart of the matter. Rather, I will heed Leopold's example and tell my own stories. Here, I revisit my own youth and early days of duck hunting near Hennepin, Illinois, which is in a historical, storied duck-hunting and decoy-carving area along the Illinois River—the home of the Illinois River carvers Robert Elliston, Charles Perdew, and others who served duck hunters of the late nineteenth and early twentieth centuries. Nearby Hennepin are Henry, LaSalle, Peru, and other rural towns, which, like Cairo farther south, have their own uniquely Illinoisan and Midwestern pronunciations. My father owned a farm with two small lakes in Hennepin, meant for fall duck hunting. The farm was named Windblown Bottom.

My early duck hunting had its distinctly human hues. I started hunting when I was eight, ten, or twelve—I cannot remember exactly—under the rigorous tutelage of my father. I was given a single-barreled, 20-gauge shotgun with a hammer cock. I was to learn gun safety and the art of shooting before moving on to double-barreled or pump shotguns, which everyone else used.

Family weekend trips to Hennepin included my mother, several dogs (Labrador retrievers), friends of my parents, and occasionally my brother, Elliott, four years older and already an accomplished hunter. We always stayed at the widow Isa Turner's house in Hennepin, which, though the county seat, was a small town, everyone knowing—and watching—everyone else. For dinner, we invariably went to the Ranch House, the local supper club, where we were joined by Paul, a local contractor, and Buttons, the local police chief, and their families. Paul and Buttons were our hunting guides, both seasoned duck callers. The dinners were lively, jovial, if not ribald, and there were many Isa Turner house stories, including guests peeing out upstairs windows because it was too cold to go downstairs to the bathroom. There was also a weekend with an eccentric cousin, Thorne, who bought a new car every six months (he had a Lancia sports car at the time), driving with his head out the window as we left for Windblown Bottom in the pre-dawn darkness, cursing his windshield wipers for not working. I mentioned that the windows were merely fogged on the inside, wiped my side, and looked at the road ahead. Cousin Thorne would have none of my youthful suggestion and braved the six-mile ride in a cold morning wind.

We always had breakfast at 5 a.m., were assigned a black lunch pail with coffee and sandwiches, each painted with a name of a dog (my favorite was "Joe"), and proceeded to the farm and the modest Windblown Bottoms club house. We were guided along the way by the blinking red lights of a nearby coal power plant.

Once at the farm, we quickly put on hip boots. Day was coming, and we needed to be in the duck blinds before dawn. We drove in the darkness past the power plant, which was next to the river, to duck boats and then headed for the blinds along shallow channels.

Often, it was cold, Midwestern cold, with ice on the lake, which we occasionally had to break to get to the blinds. In the dark, just ahead of us, flocks and flocks of wild ducks—mallards, black ducks, teal, pintail, and more—would take off into the dark sky, thousands of birds. The landscape was all wildness and sounds of silence. We humans were but shadowy creatures. We would break a hole in the ice in front of the blind, put out the duck decoys, climb into the blind, and await the light of dawn and returning ducks.

After dawn and the early-morning return flight of ducks (if there was one), we would sit back in the blinds and scan the lake for flocks of mallards, black ducks, and the swift-moving blue-winged teal. On rare occasions, flying high, pintail would come over the lake. Mere specks in the sky, the pintail would set and cup their wings, masterfully carving and slicing their way down to the water. Their commanding performance transformed the natural landscape of the lake and its surroundings into a background stage for their art. (No matter how many times you see them, such pintail shows never cease to be magical.) Other times, we settled for watching butterflies and small song birds.

I remember well the first duck that I shot. I was hunting with my father. It was bitterly cold, 8 degrees Fahrenheit, with a 40 mph wind. A single duck came in from the right side of the blind, flying downwind. I stuck my gun out the left side and shot. The bird dropped dead in the water and floated against the ice. It was an American goldeneye. (In all my duck hunting, I have never seen another goldeneye since.) I looked at my father. As I remember, neither of us said a thing.

Another time, I was shooting with my mother, Mimi. She was always more interested in the dogs—especially petting her favorite female Labrador, Widgeon—than in shooting. A flock of teal landed in the decoys. I got up, the birds flushed, and I shot. Three teal fell into the water. Looking up from Widgeon, Mimi shouted, "Great shot!" and sent Widgeon out to retrieve the birds. I looked around the lake, then back at the teal in the water, filled with an adolescent son's pride.

A curious thing characteristically would happen as the days warmed up. I would leave the blind in my hip boots and wander alone, wading amidst the willows, looking for potholes and wounded ducks. Often I found them. They would flush, and, with luck, I would shoot them and tuck them into my hunting coat.

On one such excursion, I wandered over to the nearby smaller lake and climbed into an empty blind. I was alone, with no decoys, but I did have a duck call. (I was very much the rookie duck caller.) A flight of forty or so mallards flew over. I called. They turned. I kept calling, and, after a number of swings over the lake, they lit in the water in front of me. I cannot remember whether I shot or not. No matter. I, all by myself, had decoyed wild birds on their home turf, a solitary bottomlands lake along the Illinois River. I was visited by a feeling of excitement never before experienced.

What relation do these youthful memories and stories have to recognizing our membership in Leopold's biotic community? A lot, I think. Were these hunting trips introductions to nature and its wildness (here wild ducks)? Yes. Were these trips further bondings with my family, with a new, enhanced familial status? Yes. Now I could bring something of my own to the table. Did I feel remorse and pangs of guilt when I shot the ducks and looked at their unimaginably beautiful feathered forms lifeless on the floor of the blind? Yes. (Hunters' emotions are decidedly not simple.)

But why is it that duck hunting, including killing the birds, did not morally repel me, and does not to this day, though I have lost all youthful trigger itch? In particular, why did pothole hunting and especially calling the ducks to the blind so deeply stir me?

At the time, the experiences were emotionally, if not spiritually, deep, though more or less mindless. But that was over fifty years ago. For me, they were pre-Darwin and pre-Leopold. Now, I can hazard a guess at what was happening to me. I was experiencing deep-time, well-honed predator instincts, interests, and satisfactions. I was implicated in predator-prey relations that psychologically and behaviorally bound me to natural landscapes, to evolutionary and ecological time and space. Never again could I deny an aboriginal membership in historically deep, biotic communities.

Leopold could not live without wild things. Neither can I. Perhaps for both of us hunting and fishing afforded an explicit, specific, and decisive entry into the biotic community and prompted life-long philosophical and moral reflections. In one sense, the biotic community and predator-prey relations are amoral, natural realities and processes spawned by the Crafty Blind Tinkerer (Darwin's nature). However, for us humans, biotic communities and natural processes have come to hold a deep, complex cultural and moral significance. We know, however imperfectly, that these communities and processes are how earthly life, including human life, comes into being—an earthly life laced with innumerable values moral and other (aesthetic and spiritual, centrally concerning life's innumerable and incredible forms, capacities, and interactions). This amounts to stunning, bedrock philosophic and spiritual revelation. We also know that all these values, forms, capacities, and interactions are mortal, finite, and vulnerable to harm, especially now to our own human activities.

Why might recognition of our aboriginal status in nature, our membership in the biotic community—prompted by hunting, fishing, or whatever other means—matter so much? Precisely because the recognition so radically underscores our moral situation and demands squarely facing ultimate responsibilities. There are several forms of stewardship or caretaker ethics that enjoin us to care for the earth and all the creatures that dwelleth therein. But if we do not explicitly and emphatically count ourselves among the earth's creatures, and as integral participants in earthly communities, we all too easily let ourselves off the moral hook. We value nature as not essentially mattering to us humans. (An externalist, instrumental attitude toward nature seems dominantly to pervade present moral and civic practice.) However, if we own up to our biotic community membership, we must recognize that we are a central and significant factor in immediate and future threats to nature and ultimately ourselves.

For example, there are too many of us human ones in the earth's biotic communities, taking too many of its material resources, wreaking too much havoc to ongoing evolutionary and ecological processes (Owen 2005). What are we going to do about this daunting human overreaching and natural injustice? No doubt the earth and evolutionary, ecological processes will survive our human onslaught, perhaps with a new abundance of biological species life. But at what cost? What goodness and values, including those of human life, painstakingly evolved over natural (evolutionary, ecological, geological) and cultural time, will be lost? Ought we to collectively condone such moral and spiritual guilt, such sins against earthly life and being?

If deep, existential recognition of our charter membership in the biotic community would help to stem this disastrous moral slide, then we must morally educate, or reeducate, ourselves in a hurry. If hunting and fishing, among other means, are effective avenues to explicit recognition of biotic community membership and attendant moral responsibilities, then readers of Leopold should move past their ethical puzzlement and ponder anew Leopold's and other's hunting and fishing in their widest, biotic community contexts. Nature's complex, dynamic, and uncontrollable interconnectedness and interactions defy moral simplicity, easily drawn bright lines between the good and bad, the right and wrong. If we are morally going to return to our native home and community, we need culturally and morally to grow up.

Biotic Communities and Large Predator Responsibilities

In marginalizing our membership in biotic communities, and specifically our implication in predator-prey relations, we marginalize central, fundamental moral issues that already confront us. Let me be more specific, at risk of repetition.

In the United States and elsewhere, whether by intentional design or not, we have extirpated large predators from their native landscapes and ecosystems, with real, usually negative consequences. Consider metropolitan areas—Chicago, New York, and others—with newly engendered species and ecosystem problems: for example, an overabundance of deer, Canada geese, and even wild turkeys. This overabundance threatens regional flora and fauna, as well as human well-being (causing Lyme disease, car accidents, and more). What should we do in the absence of former large predators, who were a natural check to species overabundance? Arguably, we must take over their large predator roles in keeping regional ecosystems healthy and resilient. For the sake of the biotic community as a whole, we should cull the superabundance by whatever means we deem most morally appropriate and acceptable. Their large predator roles have become our moral responsibilities.

But this is only the beginning of biotic community responsibilities. Actually, it is not the deer, geese, or turkeys that are the greatest threats to regional landscapes and ecosystems. That prize emphatically goes to ourselves. Again, despite the significance and innumerable distinctive values of human existence, what are we going to do about our own superabundance and overpopulation of biotic communities, our overuse of their life-giving resources; our pollution and disturbance of natural structures and processes? As members of biotic communities, from the regional to the global, as in fact the community's most effective large predators, we cannot in good conscience evade these facts and attendant responsibilities. Of course, this is exactly what we are doing. Whether out of ignorance, neglect, or willful amoral intention, the reigning large predators (ourselves) are undeniably and inexcusably irresponsible. Here is an issue that we must not duck, but resolve humanly, that is, responsibly.

Consider further ramifications of our present irresponsibility. Given our status in evolutionary, ecological nature and biotic communities, to undermine biotic communities is to undermine and threaten the future of humanity, its very bodily being, the quality of its life, and whatever important capacities and values—from the bodily, psychic, and mental to the moral, artistic, aesthetic, spiritual, and others—that it harbors. Robust, biologically and culturally diverse communities are as necessary to our inner selfhood and well-being as they are to our metabolizing and physically active bodies. We, our whole selves, emerge out of the world, natural and cultural, and ongoingly do so until we die. To impoverish biological and cultural communities is to impoverish ourselves.

In short, to continue in our present cultural, political, economic, and moral ways—not to recognize ourselves as predatory organisms with a long evolutionary, ecological, earthly past, that is, as members of biotic communities—amounts to a form of nihilism, a willful destruction of earthly, including human, values. If some find this ironic, odd, or indeed blasphemous, so be it. It is, as far as we can see, the truth.

Did my own road of moral and philosophic reflection begin, at least in part, in hunting Hennepin's Windblown Bottom? If so, what role does hunting, fishing, or predation in general have in the genesis of civically important philosophic and moral landscapes (worldviews)? Leopold and other Darwinian naturalists, as champions of temporally deep biotic communities, would answer unequivocally: no doubt a great deal, certainly more than urban, human-centered citizens might think. (The religious practices and rituals of traditional, especially hunter and gatherer, societies evidence as much.) The relatively unexplored relations of human predation (an inescapable fact of our existence) to the recognition of our deepest earthly, moral responsibilities is a matter worth further pondering, hopefully informing ever more adequate practical and civic action.

13

Leopold's Wildness

Can Humans and Wolves Be at Home in the Adirondacks?

The proposed reintroduction of wolves into the Adirondack Park and northeastern United States is but a part of a much larger, challenging, and daunting issue: our long-term responsibilities to the region's (and the world's) human communities, natural landscapes, and ecological systems. How, practically and morally, are we going to bring humans and nature together in a viable and ongoing regional, as well as global, future? Humans (individuals and communities) and nature too often and for too long have been kept apart in philosophic and scientific explorations, as well as ethical and social policy deliberations. As a result, theoretically and practically, we are inadequately prepared for the crucial task before us. This is a situation that we must remedy.

This is not the first time that wolves have figured centrally in such questions and explorations. An epiphany occasioned by the shooting and death of a wolf—as recounted in *A Sand County Almanac* (Leopold 1949: 129)—reoriented or converted Aldo Leopold to an evolutionary, ecological, and biotic worldview that includes human communities and fosters long-term responsibilities to the "integrity, stability, and beauty" of the land or the biotic community as a whole, which decidedly includes ourselves (Leopold 1949: 224–25).

Leopold and *A Sand County Almanac* remain directly relevant to the task of fashioning an ethic for the human and natural future. Moreover, we are reminded of an important, but often forgotten, philosophic truth. The meaning and significance of "conservation," "wolves," "wildness," and substantive ethical responsibilities do not exist in a conceptual or intellectual vacuum. They are embedded within a wider and philosophically fundamental view of the world and our place and role in the broader scheme of things. If we honestly wish to embrace and use—or constructively quarrel with—Leopold's land ethic, we must appreciatively and critically understand his fuller worldview. This effort is eminently worthwhile in itself and offers the opportunity of seriously considering whether, from an ethical point of view, we ought to reintroduce wolves into the Adirondacks and northeastern United States. Though we should expect no easy, definitive answers, at least we should better be able to see our serious moral options.

Leopoldian Values, Philosophy, and Ethics

Let us start by considering more closely Leopold and the wolf in the section of *A Sand County Almanac* entitled "Thinking Like a Mountain." Leopold had professionally been involved in game management in the Southwest, specifically the eradication of predators (wolves, bears, cougars) for the sake of increasing deer populations for hunters, if not paving the way for cattle ranching. While on a mountain trip, Leopold and his companions came upon a she-wolf crossing a river to join her grown cubs. Following the dictates of "wise-use" game management and the "trigger itch" of young hunters, the group shot at the wolves, fatally wounding the she-wolf. Leopold found where it had fallen. As he watched the "fierce green fire" dying in the she-wolf's eyes, he was personally and philosophically humbled. The mountain and the wolf knew something that Leopold did not, and what they knew shamed him. Large predators have an ultimate significance and central role to play in evolutionary, ecological, and geological time and the ongoing well-being of ecosystemic nature and the humanly good life. Leopold had previously been thinking, feeling, and acting in a wrong frame of reference. He had been animated by an inadequate and faulty view of the world. He had not taken a long-range biotic, evolutionary, and ecological perspective and did not appreciate the roles that wolves and other large predators play in the overall health of specific ecosystems (keeping prey species at healthy and adequate levels, preventing the overcropping of plant resources, helping the internally complex ecosystemic whole maintain a dynamic stability or equilibrium). Henceforth, Leopold knew better.

What precisely did Leopold now know, think, and feel? What was his new and transformed worldview and moral landscape? Leopold is not as concerned with the universe or cosmos as a whole as he is with our biotic earth. Worldly life is the experiential foothold for his philosophic cosmology, which is decidedly informed by his firsthand experiences of nature and especially the Darwinian sciences of evolutionary biology and ecology. The biotic community (all interacting biological entities, all complex and intermingling food chains, energy circuits, and predator-prey relations) or the Land (all biotic and abiotic entities that together support life on earth) results from historical and still ongoing evolutionary, ecological, biotic processes. In brief, we and all animate things exist amidst and are involved in cosmogonic processes: the genesis or coming-into-being of earthly biotic reality. Life and biotic communities (flora and fauna, interacting individuals, populations, ecosystems, etc.) have literally created, and continue to create, the "land." We humans, immersed as we are in nature and biotic processes and communities, have become increasingly important actors in this ongoing cosmogony, due to our burgeoning uses of natural resources and population pressures.

And again, what does this historical, worldly cosmogony—which decidedly includes humans—mean for Leopold? Practically everything, especially concerning the humanly and naturally good life and our ultimate moral responsibilities. I first want to begin with the meaning and importance of "wild things" for Leopold—mountain ranges, large predators (wolves, bears, cougars), and wild flora and fauna. In their historical interactions, they (along with the abiotic elements) have been world creators, engendering a specific home environment (ecosystems, bioregions, the land) for present and future biotic (evolutionary and ecological) life. Humans are only rather late and problematic actors on this worldly scene. To be in touch with wild things—whether wilderness areas, large predators, birds, or wild flora and fauna as such—is to be in touch with the historical and ongoing cosmogony and our worldly and human origins. "Wildness" here is characterized by, and has the value or emotional valence of, roles played in the cosmogonic, evolutionary-ecological processes, the historical engendering of the diverse forms and capacities of life. This is the wildness of mountains, wolves, bears, cougars, as well as sandhill cranes, grebes, prairie grasses, and more. To be with wild things in their habitats is to be "at home" in a very particular, primordial, and spiritual sense (Naess 2008).

The Darwinian-Leopoldian cosmogony radically transforms our usual sense of "home," "place," and "situation." We ordinarily understand our home, place, or situation to be in the here and now. In a certain sense this is true. Our immediate life is locally embedded in the here and now, in this particular place, time, and region. But Leopold would have us decidedly expand our spatial and temporal horizons. The humans-nature past has generated or built our present selves, communities, and environs—think of organisms' genomes (genetic material) and habitats—and we are in the process of building (creating the ground of) the indefinite future. Thus, given our reality (ontology), our home, place, and situation cannot simply be just here and now. We live in a much larger spatiotemporal, natural, and cultural edifice, with many rooms and passageways, past, present, and future. This way of looking at our home ground should not really surprise us. Our immediate personal lives are dominantly characterized and informed by past memories and future expectations. The world (including the biotic community) merely mirrors in a nonsubjective or nonexperiential way what we subjectively experience. Actually, in all probability we are what we are (bodily subjects experiencing a past, present, and future) because the world is the way it is, that is, a becoming in which past, present, and future are integrally connected (Leopold 1991). Human (and animal) selves arise out of the world and its fundamental (ontological and cosmological) characteristics, not vice versa.

This change of perspective on ourselves and our world is not philosophically and morally innocent. Rather, it is a radically transforming sea change in viewing things, involving numerous "gestalt shifts" in valuation. From the perspective of the becoming, evolving land (our true, final, and primordial home), wolves and other large predators are seen as good (good for the ongoing biota), not bad, and deer and other large herbivores become morally problematic. The former help to uphold the ecological well-being of the mountain land, as well as the rich, reverential, respectful, or fearful liveliness (experience) of us humans. The latter degrade the mountain ranges by overcropping planet resources.

A similar gestalt shift arises when sandhill cranes and grebes are experientially transformed into (interpreted as) the "wildest" and most significant of birds: the great trumpeters and conductors of the orchestra and chorus of the grand evolutionary/ecological symphony (Leopold 1949: 95, 160). They carry us humans back to an aboriginal and immemorial past, to evolutionary origins before we humans arrived on the scene. We are decidedly in their debt for vividly disclosing our home in nature amongst wild things. (We *are* actually at home in nature and the world.)

Moreover, our technological triumphs and our economically good lives (for some of us) become seriously suspect. They tend to make us forget our origins, neglect our worldly home, and threaten the biotic future of the land community. Herein lies the human and ethical importance of Leopold's cosmogonic account, worldview, and moral landscape.

Wolves in the Adirondacks: What Is to Be Done?

In closing, let me turn to several ethical issues that emerge with respect to the proposed reintroduction of wolves into the Adirondack region of New York state (Sharpe, Norton, and Donnelley 2000). These ethical issues involve humans, animals, and nature severally and in their interactions. What can we learn from the foregoing Leopoldian reflections about our ethical options and responsibilities, especially to the human and natural future?

The evolutionary ecology of the Adirondacks. As we have seen, large predators, wolves in particular, have historically played a significant role in the evolutionary and ecological well-being of biotic communities and the land (the long-term well-being of the mountain). Would this be the case for the future ecosystemic well-being of the Adirondack Park, given the presence of humans (including hunters), other predators (coyotes), and likely prey species (deer and beaver)? Would or could wolves be integral to the ongoing health of the Adirondack Land? If so, this would be an especially strong moral argument in favor of their reintroduction.

Wolves and their welfare. Leaving aside the impact on coyotes and prey species, for good or ill, what might be the impact on the wolves themselves? Could they live reasonably natural lives? What if their introduction were successful and their population flourished? We know that wolves are far-ranging, that they would not by themselves keep within the confines of the park. Presumably, wandering wolves would have to be managed—a certain percentage killed or culled. Even if, all things considered, we might morally tolerate this, could we manage wolves in a morally acceptable and humane way? What (if anything) would the culling or killing of individual wolves do to the social structures of wolf packs? For this, we would have to ask wolf ethologists, assuming that they have the answers (there is much that we do not understand about the complex social behavior of wolves).

Humans and their land home. The possible reintroduction of wolves into the Adirondack Park with regard to human values is exceedingly complex, both ethically and ecologically, as we would expect. Many values and responsibilities, some inevitably in conflict, are involved. There are important, if everyday or prosaic, questions of economic impacts on human communities and the safety of livestock and domestic pets, if not humans themselves. However, there are other philosophically interesting and practically important issues as well, particularly relating to our long-term responsibilities to human communities and nature, to our Leopoldian home and all its future inhabitants. Would the reintroduction of wolves spur us to adopt a long-term land ethic, to see the Adirondacks as an important bioregion or ecosystemic complex worthy of protection, scientific study, and "wild" recreational opportunities? Would this fuel a wider and robust global "humans and nature" conservation ethic? If so, bring on the wolves.

Or would the reintroduction and consequent managing of wolves transform the Adirondacks culturally into a Disney-like theme park, experientially cutting humans off from their evolutionary and ecological context, their Leopoldian home and origins so crucial to their spiritual well-being, humanly good life, and sense of ultimate stewardship responsibilities? If this were the likely outcome, might it not be better to expand our horizons to consider our home region to include Canada and Ontario's Algonquin Provincial Park, where we could meet wolves on what is still their own wilder home turf, with freedom to roam north relatively unimpeded and unculled? (The land knows no political and national boundaries—if we are Leopoldian "plain members and citizens" of the land community, why should we limit our vision and our planning to such boundaries?) In the long run, would our journeying north (in thought or reality) serve us better spiritually and ethically than returning wolves to their old Adirondack home, where, due to the history of humans-nature change, they may no longer fit so well, with limited or diminished prospects for the future?

These are the conservation issues that we as a democratic community—emphatically including Adirondackers, but also other legitimately concerned citizens—must squarely face and decide. Note that these issues do not entail merely personal, economic, or political *preferences* (what we just like or dislike). They involve genuine ethical problems or dilemmas. They deal with what is good and bad, right or wrong, with a human and natural reality that is laced with significant values and worth and is vulnerable to harm, ignorant blundering, or willful neglect. Our philosophic worldview here makes all the difference in deciding our moral responsibilities. To ignore or turn our backs on these ethical realities and corresponding imperatives would be morally and politically irresponsible, and certainly no way to treat our evolutionary, ecological, and biotic homes, in the Adirondacks or anywhere else.

14

Leopold's Darwin

Climbing Mountains, Developing Land

Land developers and consumers of natural resources, which directly or indirectly include us all, find themselves in a complex moral predicament. We human beings inescapably and increasingly face long-term moral and civic (often inherently conflicted) responsibilities to both human communities and natural ecosystems and landscapes.

For more than a decade, in collaboration with a distinguished group of scholars, scientists, planners, and policy makers, I have been engaged in work exploring these intertwined obligations in several regions, especially in the Chicago area (roughly southeastern Wisconsin, northeastern Illinois, and northwestern Indiana). My work has aimed at the articulation of a regional (and global) "humans and nature" ethics adequate to our times and the human and natural future (Donnelley 1998b). This research is born out of a sense of regional loss and crisis, plus the lure of future regional opportunities and responsibilities. I think of it as civic research and education involving several conservation, scientific, cultural, and planning organizations trying to grapple with the juggernaut of Chicago's regional sprawl, with its multifaceted, systemic effects from the ecological and natural landscape; to the economic, social, and political; to the cultural, aesthetic, ethical, and spiritual.

During the past twenty-five-year period, the Chicago region's population grew by 4 percent and its land consumption by more than 40 percent, with wildfire platting raging uncontrolled. This should give us a sense of practical moral urgency and intellectual adventure. We need a new civic vision for the region, a new understanding of regional ecological and democratic citizenship, and a practical moral and civic consideration of a full range of human and natural values. We must be deeply concerned with democratic community and social justice, and equally with the region's nature and the other, nonhuman, inhabitants of its checkered, fragmented, in remnants, but still beautiful prairie, farm, savanna, and lake landscapes.

In this work I have been animated by a dominant and complex intellectual, philosophic, moral, and spiritual passion. I am determined to take Darwin's evolutionary and ecological nature seriously. Similarly, I am inspired by the Midwest's conservationist patron saint, Aldo Leopold. We have struggled to bring an updated Darwinian and Leopoldian land ethic to the Chicago region. In short, I believe that we should be philosophically, ethically, and civically committed to thinking humans and nature together. We should envision long-term moral and civic obligations to the region's future by framing a historical humans and nature moral landscape within which regionally concerned citizens can orient themselves. What natural landscapes were here after the last glaciations, some 13,000 years ago? How have humans and nature interacted and mutually transformed one another in the ensuing years? What is the present humans and nature landscape? What are the civic, moral, and natural possibilities for the future? Our questions come down to this: How do we get Darwin's nature into people's minds and hearts, and people living well within the limits of Darwin's nature (in both senses of the phrase)?

Values and spirit—lost, gained, and hanging in the balance—have permeated this work with my colleagues in multidisciplinary explorations and discussions. In my own case, I vividly recall growing up in Libertyville, Illinois, a farm town of 5,000, some forty-five miles from Chicago, with 500 kids (both boys and girls) in baseball uniforms—bicycling on unpaved gravel roads, playing on prairie baseball fields, fishing for bullheads in the muddy Des Plaines River, our region's answer to the mighty Mississippi. At eight years old, I came face to face with nature, red tooth and claw. I confronted a giant snapping turtle eating its way up the body of a recently caught bullhead, thrown back into the Des Plaines on a stringer. The turtle broke off, and I rode my bike back home. I hayed in the summer heat and hunted for doves with my Labrador, Si, in dry creek beds in the cooling evenings of the fall. I only now begin to realize vividly that these were all deeply spiritual or spirited experiences, laced with multiple values stemming from the interfusion and interaction of the emerging human me and my home landscape.

Libertyville now is a Chicago suburb of 30,000 or more people, paved roads and endless traffic replacing gravel bike routes. We must struggle to save what land and farmscape values are left.

For me, not all has been lost. There have been some definite gains in the ensuing fifty years. Darwin and Leopold, among many philosophic, scientific, and artistic others, have entered my mind and animated my body. Like Leopold and others, I too ponder flora and fauna—wild flowers, birds, trout, salmon, bullheads, and snapping turtles—which experientially carry me back to our immemorial worldly origins. I too become overwhelmed with awe, gratitude, guilt, and a sense of responsibility to the world's past, present, and future.

Actually, the regional civic work of reconciling humans and nature has only just begun. We are only beginning to realize that spirit, the spirited, or the spiritual—pick your favorite word—is a mansion of many rooms: that perhaps there are as many forms of spirit, the spirited, or the spiritual as there are values, good and bad, human and natural. The complex historical interfusions and interactions of humans and nature are a rich mine that awaits further, adventurous, human exploration. There is more than enough food for thought about the good and the bad in nature and humanity.

For the remainder of this essay, I want further to explicate and add depth to this ongoing work of building regional communities of conservation by revisiting Aldo Leopold and *A Sand County Almanac,* and by reflecting upon the ethical and civic implications of Leopold's thought.

Climbing Leopold's Mountain

Aldo Leopold is the Alexander Pushkin of American environmental and conservation ethics. All Russian literature must trace its roots back to Pushkin and *Eugene Onegin.* American environmentalists must find their origins in Leopold and *A Sand County Almanac.* As a guiding spirit of modern conservation, Leopold is by now well-covered ground. Yet there remain ongoing, good reasons for reconsidering *A Sand County Almanac.* First of all, Leopold, his work, and his "land ethic," however genuinely seminal, still are largely unknown to the general public, educators, and policy makers, public and private. Whatever can help spread Leopold's word and spirit is all to the good.

Further, there are important philosophical and ethical reasons to revisit Leopold. Trained formally as a forester and scientific ecologist, not as a philosopher or ethicist, Leopold nevertheless was a pioneer explorer in a terra incognita of practical ethics: our long-term moral responsibilities to humans and nature in our post-Darwin era, perhaps the looming issue of our times, in Chicago and elsewhere. Indeed it is arguably Leopold's conversion to a full-blooded Darwinian evolutionary and ecological worldview that accounts for his philosophic and ethical originality, subsumed cryptically under the title of "the land ethic," and his claim to our serious and critical attention.

Leopold's natural predilection and intellectual conversion to a naturalist's worldview and ethic take him outside or beyond characteristic modern philosophic and civic sensibilities, habits, and modes of thought. He was intellectually, emotionally, and spiritually attuned to what most American citizens are not: Darwin's revolutionary scientific theory and broader worldview of the historical evolution of all biotic life from a common origin via genetic and behavioral variation and natural selection. Darwinian biology either explicitly holds or strongly implies the following tenets, which find their way into Leopold's philosophy and worldview (Mayr 1991):

- That nature has no pre-established cosmic design or Designer and is not ruled by cosmic teleology (purpose). Nature, biotic and other, creates its own forms in passing.
- That all biotic (if not other) things are multicaused on multiple spatial and temporal scales. There is no strict causal determinism à la Newtonian science, that is, physical (material) antecedents totally and straightforwardly determining (causing) physical or material consequents. Rather, complex historical contexts and contingencies rule the biological scene.
- That there are no "species types" ("dog," "cat," "human being") as espoused by traditional philosophic and theological worldviews, but only particular and diverse individuals living, interacting, and reproducing in particular "species" populations, wider communities of organisms, ecosystems, bioregions, and the biosphere as a whole. In sum, particularity and diversity, as well as biological and behavioral habits shared in common, characterize the historic biotic realm.
- That human individuals, communities, and cultures arise within historical evolutionary and ecological contexts and processes, that is, in dynamic interaction with nature or the wider "biotic community." Humans have not appeared on the scene from an aworldly elsewhere.

Our task here is to explore and understand how Leopold gathered these fundamental Darwinian tenets up into his own distinct, Midwestern naturalist's worldview and land ethic, which has become so suggestive for our times. Leopold's land ethic is famously summarized by his defining the human moral good and bad in terms of our positive or negative contributions to "the integrity, stability, and beauty" of the biotic community or the land.

To bring out the full moral and other human value dimensions of Leopold's conversion to "the integrity, stability, and beauty" of the land, I want briefly to travel far afield and situate Leopold's thought within a central drama of Western culture and philosophy: a fundamental quarrel over the final nature (interpretation) of the true, good, and beautiful of our world. With respect to ultimate value and significance, ever since Plato and his pre-Socratic forebears, there has been a battle raging between philosophic dualists, who claim two levels or realms of reality, and monists, who adhere to one worldly reality (Donnelley 1998a).

On the one side are the dualists, with their interpretation of our world of historical change and becoming as an imperfect imitation or realization of a higher, unchanging, acosmic reality and perfection. We see this vividly in Plato (in some of his moods) and his doctrine of eternal and unchanging "forms," including the final Form of the Good, which are imperfectly reflected in our worldly reality and the source of whatever order, goodness, and beauty are realized. (Plato is one of the crucial forefathers of essentialist, typological thinking.) In the *Seventh Letter,* Plato speaks of the knowledge of "the fifth entities" (the forms) as the highest form of human, philosophic knowledge. In *The Republic,* he relates the Allegory of the Cave with shadows cast upon the cave's back wall (the appearances of the world that we perceive or experience) and the blinding Sun at the mouth of the cave (the Form of the Good), perceived by the philosopher only after turning away from the "worldly" shadows and an arduous, dedicated struggle after final truth. In the *Symposium,* Socrates is instructed in the school of Eros (desire) and led through the various, ascending stages of worldly beauty (the object of Eros's desires)—sexual objects, friendship, political institutions, knowledge, and more—until the Mantinean priestess Diotima reveals to Socrates the final (aworldly) Form of the Beautiful (the Good and the Real), the consummation of Eros's and the Socratic philosopher's strivings.

Searching beyond the world of becoming and change to discover the truly real and the source of all order, beauty, goodness, and perfection did not start with Plato. He had pre-Socratic predecessors. Most notably, the Pythagoreans believed in an ultimate other-worldly, acosmic principle, *Peras* (the "limited," that which provides definition), the perfect and untainted source of worldly harmonies (order, beauty, goodness), which are realized only by *Peras* informing the *Apeiron* (the "unlimited"), which is this-worldly, dynamic, itself formless, and thus deficient. The Pythagorean philosopher's salvation is in pursuing and apprehending *Peras* in all its manifestations and final purity, in becoming assimilated to ultimate and unchanging harmony and order.

This early philosophic and religious dualism did not go unchallenged, and at the most fundamental levels. According to the pre-Socratic contemporary Heraclitus, such Pythagorean speculations are nonsense. In truth, "it is wise to know that all (the world, the cosmos) is one, an Everliving Fire, kindling and extinguishing in measures" (Heraclitus 1991: §30). This dynamic Logos or *Arche* (that out of which all originates and into which all returns) is the true and *internal* cosmic source of all order, goodness, and beauty, which are forever engendered out of worldly struggle and essential interactions among worldly constituents, including ourselves and all other organisms. Being or reality is born out of becoming and strife. War is the father of all. The world of dynamic, ever-changing harmony, beauty, and order is the philosopher's and our final home and salvation, that is, the realization of the good life (Guthrie 1987).

Here, in brief, is Heraclitus's monism, his single world that comprehends all of reality, which he staunchly opposes to Pythagorean and by implication Platonic dualism. The fundamental philosophic and cultural battle, as yet undecided, is joined. Significantly for our purposes, the convictions of Darwin and Leopold are decidedly more akin to the philosophy of Heraclitus than to Plato and the Pythagoreans.

Despite their differences, the philosophic wars between Plato, on the one side, and Heraclitus and Leopold, on the other, should not blind us to deep philosophic commonalities that are a clue to understanding Leopold and his abiding significance. All three thinkers deal directly with ultimate reality (the real) and the true, even if this reality cannot be fully or adequately grasped or articulated in thought or language. Moreover, fundamental reality is inextricably bound up with and expressed in beauty (beautiful objects and realities captured in human aesthetic and spiritual experience), which in turn expresses reality's ontological ("being"), if not also moral goodness—that which anchors and points the way to our deepest ethical responsibilities to the world.

Plato, Heraclitus, and Leopold are one in claiming that most of us humans are philosophically asleep, in a drunken stupor, or ignorant with respect to the real, the beautiful, and the good. Yet, at least for Leopold, if we do not wake up and get converted to the truth—get our heads screwed on right and our hearts in the right place—there is little lasting hope for us. Worldly reality, human and natural, will seriously degrade with respect to its realized and realizable beauty and goodness.

I want to leave the Greeks and attend more directly to Leopold's conception of reality, beauty, and goodness. We are exploring Leopold's worldview as decidedly Darwinian, forsaking atemporal, essential (platonic) forms and norms as philosophic and moral resources. For Leopold, Darwin, and Mayr, reality is thoroughly temporal, historical, changing, becoming, evolving, building and transfiguring itself over time (Leopold 1949: 108). This is our primary and final worldly and natural (evolutionary, ecological, geological), if not cultural, home. Leopold wanders in a crane marsh and marvels at the bugling of the wildest of birds, the sandhill cranes, who over innumerable eons have interacted with their ecological community to build the marsh reality, laying the foundation for present and hopefully future marsh life. The cranes are claimed to have a historically deep beauty and wisdom (whether genetic, phenotypical, or behavioral) that derive directly from their implication in evolutionary and ecological processes (Leopold 1949: 95).

To destroy, undermine, or degrade this historical, time-engendered, and vulnerable reality is to commit an ultimate, cardinal sin. But that is precisely what we humans have been doing and continue to do in our ignorance of nature's engendering of mountains, crane marshes, and more broadly the land, which is the whole system of biotic (flora and fauna) and abiotic elements that together make up evolutionary, ecological reality, the only final reality (Plato and his followers notwithstanding) that we humans with any certainty know. We ignorant blunderers, transfixed by traditional, culturally inherited and inadequate worldviews, aspirations, and commitments, have striven to be the conquerors of nature while setting up our own provincial human enclaves (cultural communities), whereas we should have become by now "plain members and citizens" of the natural community that includes ourselves and is called the land (Leopold 1949: 203, 210).

Reality, Beauty, and Leopoldian Experience

We need further to unpack Leopold's worldview, since it still remains significantly foreign to our modern philosophic, moral, and civic ears. Most of us are unschooled in a full range of primary experiences of nature and in the fundamental conceptions of evolutionary biology and the still newer sciences of modern ecology and ethology. In short, we need to work hard to approach Leopold's original vision, despite the evocative and well-crafted prose of *A Sand County Almanac*.

First of all, we should note that Leopold accepts philosophically, morally, and spiritually a fundamental Darwinian tenet: Human beings have emerged from and within nature, and it is sheer hubris and egoism to think otherwise, despite our special place or "difference" in the natural world—indeed this significant human difference is predicated on our being a part of nature. Honest recognition of our status in nature is a human and cultural boon rather than a scandal or humiliation. Humans have evolved in interaction with other forms of life. We have been, and increasingly continue to be, active agents, as well as "patients," in life's earthly cosmogony (coming into being). We are and forever will remain (directly or indirectly) part of complex food chains (energy flows and circuits) and biotic pyramids (soil and natural elements, flora, fauna, up to large, "crowning" predators). We are involved in ever-revolving rounds of ecological processes and predator-prey relations, despite our concerted (but ultimately futile) efforts to "get out" of nature economically, socially, culturally, and spiritually (Leopold 1949: 214). Leopold refuses to shrink from the full consequences of recognizing our status in nature. He accepts and affirms the hard Darwinian truth that death, destruction, and disease are directly implicated in the creation of life's historical reality, beauty, and goodness (Leopold 1949: 73). Predation is only a primary example. "The only certain truth is that its (the prairie's) creatures must suck hard, live fast, and die often, lest its losses exceed its gains" (Leopold 1949: 107). The unwearied grebe reminds us that "if all are to survive, each must ceaselessly feed and fight, breed and die" (Leopold 1949: 107).

Unambivalent acceptance of our natural status in evolutionary, ecological nature accounts for Leopold's particular originality and the seeming paradoxes of his thought. On one hand, Leopold feels all flora and fauna to be his communal brethren and neighbors—pine trees, wildflowers, chickadees, woodcocks, dogs, wolves, grizzly bears, and more. (We all inhabit the same tree of life and share a common origin.) Yet Leopold also accepts hunting and fishing for sport: human predation as an essentially atavistic, aesthetic, and spiritual experience, pursued under appropriate ethical constraints (Leopold 1949: 165). He is passionately concerned with preserving rapidly vanishing wilderness areas, wild flora and fauna, and human wilderness experiences (solitude, canoe and horseback-pack trips). Yet he also accepts and advocates active, enlightened management of the land.

The key to understanding (if not resolving) these paradoxes and the key to his aesthetics and ethics is Leopold's particular philosophic appropriation of Darwinian evolutionary biology, ecology, and ethology. In this appropriation we find the admixture of science and his particular brand of human spirituality. The practical ethics of the *scientific* Leopold is concerned with the long-term well-being and health of ecosystems and evolutionary processes, and this at times allows, if not demands, active human management of the land—for example, managing farmland in such a way as concurrently to foster native flora and fauna: wild flowers and prairie grasses, game and other animals (Leopold 1949: 165, 177). Here is Leopold's scientifically informed stewardship or conservation ethics.

Leopold's "humanly spirited" ethic grows out of and beyond his scientifically informed ethic. Ecosystems ("the land") have a deep evolutionary history within which Leopold the conservation actor and philosophic explorer dwells. This is ultimate reality. To be directly in touch with cranes, grebes, wolves, cougars, and other fauna and flora within their natural habitats is to be directly in touch with historically evolved reality and natural and human origins—an ultimately spiritual or religious experience, laced with deep emotional and aesthetic valences, including a vivid sense of tragedy and loss. A mountain with its top predators—wolves, grizzly bears, or mountain lions—is the real thing, deeply felt as such, fearfully, respectfully, or reverentially. A mountain without its wolves; a marsh without its cranes; fields or wetlands without their grebes, plovers, partridge, quail, or historical and characteristic wild flowers, grasses, or trees are denuded and dispirited landscapes, both ecologically and humanly—a loss felt keenly by those who "know" (the naturalist, the evolutionary biologist, the ecologist, the ethologist, the "plain citizen" of the land). Here is the human experience of the ultimate real, beautiful, and good—or its absence.

There are definite and interesting Platonic and Heraclitean themes to all this. There are various levels of participation in the good, the beautiful, and the real, from an unknowing, immediate engagement with its own sensuous, emotional, and spiritual textures, to a knowing, wide-awake, spiritually appreciative participation, an ultimate form of human existence, and a pinnacle of the humanly good life. For Plato, it is awareness of the varying participation of all things in the eternal forms and the final Form of the Good. For Heraclitus, it is keen and knowing awareness of the Everliving Fire (the Logos) that underlies and informs all worldly becoming and achievement, including the "fiery," knowing philosopher him or herself. For Leopold, it is the aesthetic and spiritual appreciation of natural reality, decidedly deepened by the knowledge gained from scientific evolutionary biology, ecology, and ethology and by the active, responsible stewardship that this experience and knowledge foster (Leopold 1949: 165 ff.). This is the cultural, aesthetic, and spiritual harvest to be gained from nature, as augmented by our exploring, questing minds and science's objectivity (concern with facts and empirical truth). Here is humans' specific difference within nature. Only we can know (however imperfectly) and explicitly appreciate the fact of evolution, its history, and our active participation, for better or for worse, in the world's becoming. Only we can actively mourn evolution's historical losses (the extinction of species and ecosystemic life) and our ignorant plundering participation in reality's degradation, for example, the passing of the passenger pigeon and more (Leopold 1949: 108).

The Leopoldian "Upshot"

On one crucial point, Leopold breaks from Plato and Heraclitus. Though each interprets or claims a different reality within which we humans participate, Leopold's *A Sand County Almanac* and his land ethic, by his own admission, are not the final word. They do not carry the authoritative, dogmatic flavor of Heraclitus and (on occasion) Plato. As Leopold was keenly aware, evolutionary biology and especially ecology and ethology were (and are) in their infancy. We are largely ignorant of nature's complex facts and ways. There remains much room for further exploration and cultural harvest. In particular, understanding the "integrity, stability, and beauty" of the land needs ongoing reinterpretation in light of what we further learn about the dynamism of evolutionary, ecological, ethological nature—how much of nature's interactions is dynamic equilibrium and balance and how much is radical ecological and ecosystemic change. Upon this determination importantly rests the norms or criteria for pragmatically and morally judging the good, true, and beautiful of the land—its ongoing integrity, stability, and beauty. Ethically and ecologically we still see through a glass darkly.

Yet despite this and more unfinished business, Leopold's pioneering efforts are of seminal worth. Leopold has given us a realistic moral purchase for critically questioning our cultural, economic, and technological progress, enterprises, and ongoing aspirations. What will they do in the long run to the health and integrity, organic and spiritual, of the land and ourselves? What will be the ongoing natural and cultural harvest? Are we, our human works, and a humanly transfigured nature sustainable or headed for disaster?

Moreover, Leopold has importantly helped to wean us from extra-worldly moral and scientific norms. Leopold the naturalist, scientist, and cultural harvester delights in the spring mating flights and dances of wood-cocks. Leopold the hunter is admonished to leave enough woodcocks in the fall so that there will be plenty of dancers in the next and following springs (Leopold 1949: 30). This is characteristically good conservation ethics, a land ethic that both rings true and allows for multiple human activities and values—various participations in the really real of evolutionary and humanly cultural life. Here is an ethics that is historically and contextually sensitive and deep and that stands in decided contrast to dominant, "pre-Darwinian" forms of normative ethics, utilitarian or Kantian, consequentialist or deontological, which largely leave time and historical becoming out of account. Leopold's norms are creatively (interpretively) drawn from human and natural life as they have evolved and as they variously express biotic, including human, reality's beauty, goodness, and significance. What other ultimate philosophic and ethical resource can we have or need in this age of post-Darwinian "enlightenment"? As Leopold justly claims, the cultural harvest from humans and nature is superabundantly there and sufficient for all who can see, hear, and think. We only have actively to appreciate and fulfill our land responsibilities (Donnelley 2000).

Leopold claimed that no important change in ethics comes about without an internal change in our intellectual emphases, loyalties, affections, and convictions. He was convinced that we needed a sea change in our current human and ethical valuations—new ethical contents, rights and wrongs, obligations, and sacrifices. In trying to capture this sea change in values, I have largely aimed at revealing Leopold's new evolutionary, ecological worldview and its philosophic and ethical implications.

I only want to add a few further speculative reflections on the fundamental philosophic and moral importance of our being human biological organisms—speculations that, if embraced, would further Leopold's enterprise. Our organic mode of being, our fundamental status in reality, is our physical and experiential ticket into the great evolutionary and ecological drama of worldly life. We know life (and its opposite) and other living organisms only because we are instances of biological, animate life ourselves. Life provides us with the epistemic arsenal (tools of knowing) by which we judge the quick from the dead, as well as the various capacities and performances of life. Further, it is only because we humans are mortal, finite, and vulnerable—fundamental characteristics of organic life per se—that we can comprehend life's ways: its tragedies and triumphs, its beauty and goodness. All this is to say that we enjoy Leopold's "human difference" only because we are living organisms. We participate in a worldly realm of value (beauty, goodness, significance, and their opposites) only in virtue of our being complexly organized instances of life ourselves. Only life can know, appreciate, and value life in and for itself. Organic life is fundamentally (ontologically) deeper or more comprehensive than mind or disembodied spirit. Our human souls are decidedly rooted in nature.

Philosophically and ethically these reflections only tighten the Darwinian evolutionary and ecological knot. Perhaps Leopold's final brilliance is in sending us off down the right path, in moving us into a Darwinian philosophic framework of thought that bridges organic life, spirit, and ethics. Yet, even if this is true, we are far from arriving home. The path of understanding ourselves and nature is long, perhaps unending.

One final critical question or reflection does remain. Beyond Leopold's philosophic and scientific (Darwinian) strengths, the conservation philosophy and ethic of *A Sand County Almanac* seem particularly well suited to middle-America, at home in a prairie and plains landscape. Is this a good fit for all regions? Would or does he have the same pull for the citizens of the Hudson River, the Adirondacks, and New York City, or Charleston and South Carolina's coastal Lowcountry? Does each region require its own philosopher-ethicist-scientist to move its citizens to their practical, long-term responsibilities to humans and nature? In the end, how universal is, or can be, Leopold's appeal? Does *A Sand County Almanac* have a requisite cosmopolitan flavor, or is it in the end "provincial," which paradoxically may account for its particular strength? Diversity and particularity, as we are coming increasingly to realize, are the spice, or rather the warp and woof, of life.

Managing Development and Land-Use Responsibilities

Leopold has set us off along the path of fundamental, perhaps unending, philosophic and ethical exploration. This is all to the good. Yet, practical and urgent land-use decisions cannot await endless quests, no matter how legitimate. Practice, by necessity, rears its often ugly head. We must decide upon an interim ethic, à la Leopold, at least as a rough guide for making crucial, perhaps fateful, present decisions.

One important guidance comes from our tendency to commit the fallacy of misplaced concreteness. Alfred North Whitehead ([1925] 1948: 52) coined the term, and Leopold tirelessly pointed out examples of it. Roughly, the idea that underlies the fallacy is that we humans live in a very richly complex world. Whether in science, philosophy, the arts, or practical life, we invariably are ruled by specific human interests, passions, and purposes. We abstract, "take out," or fasten upon specific features of the world's full concrete complexity. This is necessary and perfectly legitimate as long as we remember what we are doing. Mostly we do not. We mistake our abstractions, partial aspects of things for the entire reality of the thing, thus leading to distorted visions of the experienced world and ourselves. Historically, this fateful misstep has led to all sorts of theoretical and practical human misadventures.

This can help us to conceive an interim ethics for land developers and natural resource users (all of us). Briefly, the reasoning goes as follows. To see the problem with misplaced concreteness is to see that we human beings are variously situated within the world—as biological naturalists, economic entrepreneurs, political activists, artists of all stripes, recreationists, sportsmen, spiritual explorers, and more. Each such "worldly situated and interested" actor calls forth a particular potential or capacity of the naturally and culturally engendered human self. Each "takes account of" and values the (cultural and natural) world in a particular way without capturing or exhausting the world's complex, if vulnerable, concrete character. This is our endemic human situation and need not unduly plague us unless we forget ourselves, which, as we have seen, we characteristically, but not inevitably, do.

In short, we know that all our humanly cultural activities—whether economic, social, political, scientific, technological, recreational, artistic, or other—take place within particular and ongoing regional (and global) natural contexts and processes (evolutionary, ecological, and ethological). We must remember and never forget this fundamental fact while pursuing our multifarious situations within the world—our "takings" and valuations. We must respectfully and practically attune our human activities to nature's dynamic historical ways. No doubt our various human takings and valuings spawn conflicts among themselves and with what is the ongoing natural good. "Out of the crooked timber of humanity (and nature), nothing straight ever will be made," to paraphrase Immanuel Kant.

No doubt this is true. This inherent limitation or finitude means that we require an "all things considered" ethics, an art of ethical and civic judgment that recognizes concrete situations of "moral ecology": that many things human and natural demand moral attention, that all important values (human and natural) require promotion, but that, given particular concrete situations, priorities must be established and judicious trade-off decisions must be made, perhaps to be reconsidered at a later date. Such priorities and decisional compromises must seriously take into account the needs and goodness of historical evolutionary, ecological, and ethological nature as well as human beings and their ongoing cultural communities.

For developers and natural resource managers and users, what kind of an ethic is this? It is an ethic for the Leopoldian perplexed. With genuine effort and humility, we can endeavor to address concrete moral situations with our eyes (relatively) wide open, not blinded by special and parochial human interests. We can attempt to be guided by the complex, if conflicting, demands of our own humanity and our historical natural home, especially our obligations to the long-range human and natural future. We can be moved by broad, generous, and nuanced senses of moral care, fairness, and respect for the various forms and capacities of life. Leopold asked for no more—and no less—than such moral art and judgment.

IV

Recovering a Philosophy of Nature

15

What Philosophic Cosmology Can Teach Us

I

Though cosmologies or worldviews are to be judged by their rational coherence and adequacy in interpreting the full reaches of human experience, we do not have to race to take sides. Philosophy is not—or should not be—a heavyweight boxing match from which one contender must emerge victorious. Indeed, given our limited powers of knowing, it may be impossible to declare a final victor. In the nature of things, we find ourselves on the path of self-aware ignorance, unknowing, but knowingly so.

The philosophic cosmology we need today is an unfinished, open-ended worldview. I believe, with Alfred North Whitehead, that certainty is a ruse, an ill-begotten child of Western metaphysics running from Plato to Descartes to our own technological and technocratic orientation. We should especially remain philosophically enticed and puzzled by the ultimate creative restlessness of the universe, the ground of organic life (including our own); orchestral causation; and emergence, including worldly emergent individuals or selves. Such aspects of being can only be glimpsed by our most rigorous and diligent efforts at systems thinking. Worldly interconnections and interactions, especially those of the organic and humanly organic realms, are manifestly mortal, finite, vulnerable to harm, and, thus, matters of ultimate concern.

I have spent much of my professional life on reading thinkers—Spinoza, Darwin, Whitehead, Ernst Mayr, and Hans Jonas—who have provided powerful, ecological alternatives to the dominant contemporary legacy of Cartesian dualism and mechanistic materialism. Now, I would like to lure us one step farther down the path of enlightened ignorance opened up by these thinkers and pull together the threads of my own considered perspective on why an ecological philosophical cosmology or worldview is so important and why an ethic of civic, ecological responsibility consonant with that worldview is fundamental to our future prospects.

Each of these philosophers has his own mode of systems thinking, based on correlative notions of orchestral causation, emergence, and evolving worldly order. Each has his notion of natural (and cultural) upward and downward causation—inclusive wholes influencing included parts, included parts influencing inclusive wholes—a worldly hierarchy of entities characteristically changing at different rates, the "inclusive" more slowly, the "included" more rapidly (cf. Mayr 1997: 16–23; Whitehead [1929] 1978: 48–98). This dynamic, systemic becoming historically and contingently (nondeterministically) realizes novel forms of worldly order and value, including those realized in earthly nature and its resident human communities and cultures. Moreover, worldly, earthly, and human becoming can fare for better or for worse. Ultimate ethical responsibilities are thrust on us, whether we like it or not.

But what are our ethical, earthly responsibilities, especially given that we are confined to paths of enlightened ignorance, that is, given that we in principle do not have, and cannot have, final and certain moral truths, dogmatically fixed moral stars to guide us? Does this situation resign us to moral nihilism or, at best, aimless moral relativism, an "I'm OK, you're OK" syndrome?

No. Manifestly, this is not the inevitable outcome of the path of enlightened ignorance. Quite the opposite. By renouncing the quest for certainty and correlative dreams of perfection, we become, or ought to become, more and more wedded to the finite and vulnerable realized goodness of earthly life—all earthly life. Given what we can discern "through a glass darkly," our moral responsibilities are systemic: to earthly processes, structures, and communities of life, as well as to life's interconnected individuals. Moral responsibility is naturally ecosystemic as well as humanly communal and relational.

In this regard, my own work in philosophic cosmology has turned me in the direction of someone who was not a systematic philosopher but who belongs in this company nonetheless, namely, Aldo Leopold. Spinoza, Darwin, Whitehead, Mayr, and Jonas each would have readily recognized and appreciated Leopold's morally significant "biotic communities" as a genuine conceptual contribution to the adventure of ideas. Indeed, Mayr was explicit about such Leopoldian concerns (Mayr 1997: 268). Leopold's work has been important to me in my life for intellectual and philosophical reasons, but not only for those. As we have seen repeatedly, the intellect does not stand alone or outside the experiential and the relational, and it is in my lived encounters with nature and its abundant forms of life, as much or more than in my reading, that I have heard Leopold's voice.

The philosophical cosmologists are steadfast champions of the goodness of earthly life in all its historical plurality, biological and cultural diversity, and inherent contingency. Each is keenly aware of the evils of worldly life and becoming. But this recognition seems only to have steeled their scientific, philosophic, and moral resolve as the champions of worldly life. They call us to the way of earthly responsibility, however imperfectly understood. Moreover, they have unambiguously shown us the decided preference of paths of adventurous, enlightened ignorance over assorted proud quests for certainty and final perfection.

A nagging problem remains, however. The essence of the problem is, if evolutionary, ecological nature is such an amoral, historically chancy affair, governed by a Blind Tinkerer rather than a Cosmic Designer, how can we arrive at any abiding and stable conceptions of the morally good (or evil) to define our moral responsibilities and guide our moral actions toward nature and our humanly cultural selves? Are we left to cultural conversations among our human selves, with no possible appeals to "objective" standards of the good or the bad that are independent of mere human, subjective preferences (the modern legacy of the original Cartesian split of body and mind)? In short, how can Darwinian naturalism (a form of critical realism) and a true ethics of moral responsibility go hand in hand and have a coherent connection with one another?

I have never succeeded in treating this problem fully. But I do think that some headway has been made. To begin with, I think we must look at things from within Darwinian naturalism, not from within pre-Darwinian essentialist or anti-Darwinian, anti-naturalist perspectives, which defeat the enterprise from the start.

The chanciness and radical contingency of evolutionary and ecological process can be overplayed. Take the evolutionary two-step. Variation (genetic, somatic, or behavioral) may be random, but selection, natural and perhaps sexual, is a nonrandom process, even if carried out amidst historical contingencies. Adaptational processes—adaptation to worldly environments—are not the mere work of chance. Moreover, amidst much becoming and change, there are, as emphasized by Mayr, conservative or conserving factors at work in nature. There are historically engendered and more or less cohesive genomes; fundamental and enduring Bauplans (body types or programs); ongoing adaptations tracking changing environments; and the engendering of biological and cultural diversity. In short, over evolutionary history and time, organic forms and capacities and ecological functions and processes emerge, with more or less robust staying power. Evolutionary, ecological, geologic time is not the hustle and bustle of everyday human life.

These forms, capacities, functions, and processes are not human creations. We can recognize that they have come into being without our creative interventions. Moreover, thanks to our having arisen from the same earthly history, we have decided stakes in this natural, historical drama. Given the natural and cultural capacities that have emerged in us through worldly history, we can recognize the achievements of historical "biocultural diversities" and, however imperfectly, their goodness, including their conduciveness to ongoing life and its flourishing.

If God could create the world in six days and see (declare) that his creation was good, we—differently situated in the historical, creative becoming of nature and culture—can analogously see (understand) that natural and cultural creation is good and explore in an ongoing way what is conducive to natural and cultural well-being. Both natural and cultural forms, capacities, and interconnections stun us aesthetically, spiritually, and morally, both positively and negatively.

We are what we seem. Philosophically, this means taking the inner testimony of our subjective life seriously. This specifically entails recognizing the circumscribed potency of subjectivity and crediting the reality of efficacious purposes in determining autonomous trains of thought and bodily activities.

Our moral worldviews, reflections, and judgments are rooted in, if not rationally derived from, the natural and cultural world. They are rooted in worldly realities (the gift of our being natural organisms living in the world) and are not merely aworldly, cultural conventions. Moral responsibilities to humans and nature are real and historically engendered, they are the abiding interests of humankind. I think that the philosophic cosmologists and other moral naturalists would concur with social and political philosophers like Isaiah Berlin who espouse moral pluralism (innumerable real, objective values, such as freedom, justice, equality, and more) as against moral relativism (mere subjective preferences or tastes, with no essential reference to the real world).

The morally good and bad, right and wrong—natural and cultural—may in truth be a moving target, rather than an atemporal stasis, but its movements, especially its more abiding features, are real and relatively glacial. This must serve as the standard for the moral naturalist, in lieu of an eternal, essentialist form of the morally good. I am not sure that moral naturalism can give more reasons or more of an ultimate answer than this.

II

As I shall argue more fully later, a type of cosmology offered by Spinoza, with its fundamental conception of conative modal existence that intricately ties together the basic themes of organic individuality and world relatedness, has decided philosophic advantages over a Cartesian, multiple substance metaphysics. The gain is on ontological and epistemological grounds and in lending a rational intelligibility to pervasive features of our experience of ourselves and the world. But what relation does such a cosmology have to ethics and in particular ethical responsibilities to the human, animal, and natural future?

The question is complex, but a first point is to understand what modern philosophic cosmology is and what it is not. Descartes and Spinoza notwithstanding, it is *not* the attempt logically to prove the existence and the nature of the world according to some mathematically inspired, deductive mode of reasoning. Philosophy is not geometric proof from rationally unassailable or self-evident first principles or premises. Rather, philosophic cosmology is the speculative attempt to elucidate and further penetrate pre-philosophic human experience in a systematic way: to call to emphatic attention and to lend rational intelligibility and meaning to the fundamental features of the experience that we humans recurrently live through.

The relation of philosophic cosmology to ethics similarly is not one of rational, logical deduction, with ethical theorems derived from ontological premises. The ethical "ought" is not *logically* derived from the ontological "is." Concrete ethical obligations and responsibilities originate from and within real worldly situations and not from rational, conceptual arguments. Yet there is a fundamental and substantive relation between what we conceive ontologically to be and what we consider ethically ought to be that can be spelled out by philosophic cosmology. This holds if "what is" is primarily experienced and subsequently conceived as harboring its own values or goodness and, further, is understood to be vulnerable to (freely determined) human individual or collective action. If such is the case, ethical theory and action ought to cohere with our experiences and rational conceptions of the ontological good. It is the business of philosophy to spell out the possibilities of this coherence and to incorporate ethical experience and perceived responsibilities into its overall cosmological vision.

In short, powerful and persuasive philosophic perspectives focus our attention upon and further elucidate concrete ethical obligations that hold (perhaps implicitly) within our worldly existence prior to rational and systematic reflection. Philosophy does not logically *prove* ethical obligations or oughts, but it brings them more emphatically and sharply into focus. It argues why the obligations are intelligible, rational, and important. This is how we should pragmatically test the ethical relevance and adequacy of a Spinozistic type of cosmology: on how well it articulates the moral or ethical landscape with respect to human, animal, and natural existence. To fasten upon one particular (and for us particularly interesting) example, such understanding must be the basis of an ethical scrutiny of animal biotechnology.

A first task of philosophic cosmology is to interpret and make rationally intelligible the very possibility of our being moral (and immoral) beings. Here the interpretation rests on the notion of conative individuality, as lived out on a complex, human level. As with all organisms, we primordially endeavor to persevere in our own being, as necessarily implicated in the wider, dynamic world. Unlike other organisms, we become acutely and consciously aware of our own "conatus" and the conative implication of all animate entities in the one world. By nature and by culture this experience develops into a twin and interlaced concern for self and others: for the valuable or good whole, which includes naturally assertive individual selves. To be mutually concerned with self and other is the stuff, the warp and the woof, of ethical life. To be concerned disproportionately with oneself (or one's group) amidst a necessary and wider worldly relatedness is the "conative fall" into immorality or irresponsibility.

We need to explicate further the ethical import of the fundamental, twin themes of organic, conative individuality and essential dynamic relatedness to the world. Conative individuality, in virtue of its vulnerability to harm and its realized "natural goodness" (characterized by individual existential effort conjoined with and realized through complex capacities, activities, and physical forms of organic being), is a primary locus of value and ethical concern. Natural or worldly communities, in virtue of being dynamically constituted by, essentially affecting, and themselves vulnerable to conative individuals, are an equally primary locus of value and ethical concern. Thanks to universal dynamic interdependence, conative individuals and worldly communities mutually engender, evolve, and require one another, as within the wider natural universe. (This is a primary meaning of "internal relation or relatedness.") An ethical obligation or responsibility to uphold the ongoing, mutual, interdependent, and vulnerable goodness of conative individuality and worldly community sets the fundamental terms of the moral landscape.

Secondly, conative individuals, and the concrete communities that they foster, are characterized by varying levels of richness and complexity with respect to the realization of natural goodness or value. In the primordial obligation to uphold natural goodness and to prevent significant and irreparable harm to the animate and conative realm, there is a certain differentiation and relative weighting of substantive ethical responsibilities.

With this second feature of the moral landscape we should note the relation of concrete values and natural goodness to worldly becoming and the rigor of animate existence: its "evil" or amoral harshness. The naturally "good" (the definite forms and active powers of individual and communal animate existence) and the naturally "evil" (the infliction or suffering of pain, death, or destruction of realized order) cannot be disjoined. Both symbiosis (cooperation and coordination) and competition (strife) are at the heart of organisms' metabolic mode of existence, natural evolutionary and ecological processes, and the interdependence of all things natural. It is not for naught that Heraclitus long ago declared that (ontologically) "War is father of all." This necessary connection of the darker side of existence and nature's goodness is an essential and inescapable given for ethical reflection and decision making.

The third feature of the moral landscape follows from the first and second. The precariousness and immediate demands of conative life require that one primarily take care of one's own: oneself, one's family, one's local community (human and natural), nation, species, etc. This is a pre-moral, or existential, as well as moral injunction. But the fact that all animate beings instance varying levels of natural goodness and are dynamically and internally related means that the primary, more immediate conative concerns ought ethically to be tempered by wider, less proximate obligations—for example, to spatially or temporally distant individuals or communities, human and natural.

So far we have offered no hard and fast, bright-line principles to decide rationally particular cases of conflicting ethical obligations in a clear-cut and straightforward fashion. Nor may we legitimately expect to arrive at such final rational principles and avoid reliance on fallible moral wisdom and judgment. The real world is too bewilderingly complex and its values too many and diverse to be readily subdued by ethical rationality or reasoning. We need to learn an art of "moral ecology," in which conflicting obligations or responsibilities play themselves against one another in particular and concrete contexts, mutually determining each other's relative weight or strength, until we arrive at a morally satisfactory (if imperfect) judgment, all things considered. Yet we can discern substantive and important general ethical directions or guides, expressible in ethical injunctions. Uphold the ongoing and variously rich animate realm as a whole. Prevent or address significant harms before hazarding improvements upon the presently realized good. (Though vulnerable to human harm, the conative realm takes care of itself prior to human, "ameliorating" interventions.) In particular, beware the ethically harmful systemic effects of particular and necessarily limited corporate human purposes and actions. Give primary ethical attention to the integrity or intactness of conative individuals and worldly communities in their dynamic and temporal interconnections.

Such ethical imperatives and the philosophic cosmologies that underscore them concentrate our ethical attention and propose on what we ethically ought to take into account: again, the fundamental, though varying, significance of organic individuals (human and other) and worldly communities human, animal, and ecosystemic, specifically their worldly needs and integrity or intactness into the indefinite worldly future.

For example, consider the link between philosophical cosmology and ethics in the arena of contemporary biotechnology and genetics. From a naturalistic perspective, biotechnological intervention per se (genetic or otherwise) is not the primary locus of ethical concern. The naturally conative realm, irrespective of human interventions, is continually, dynamically, and internally changing its genetic and phenotypic forms, and the methods of this change seem prima facie morally insignificant. Nor does the change or mixing of individual organisms' genetic material seem ethically important, for genes are not the point, the end, or the final good of the animate realm. (All organisms share genetic material in any case.) What manifestly is ethically significant is the effect or consequences of biotechnological manipulations and interventions on the organic, conative integrity and complexity (richness) of individuals, communities, and ecosystems. "Integrity" and "impoverishment," in their many dimensions, are the key ethical issues. For example, we should be ethically chary of biotechnological interventions that might undermine integrated and complex human capacities of experience, thought, and action and threaten the fundamental terms of individual and communal worldly existence for human beings and other species. Similarly, we should be ethically wary of introducing organisms, biotechnologically engendered or not, into new or foreign environments, with possible systemic and seriously disruptive effects on the well-being of ecosystems, animal populations, and the naturally evolved, conative capacities and behavior of individual organisms.

Moreover, there is a crucial aspect of biotechnology that easily escapes notice or is brushed aside and is ethically difficult to assess. This is the moral effect of biotechnology on the systems of symbolic meaning in human life; that is, on aesthetic, religious, and ethical values and on the experience of the world that these meanings and values sustain.

Consider a seemingly noncontroversial form of biotechnology that is already in widespread use and has been for some time, namely, the practice of introducing transgenic or pen-raised hatchery fish, such as trout or salmon, into wild streams for the sake of sport fishing. Our best evidence suggests that this is ecologically problematic, to say the least. But, in order to make the point that interests me here, let's assume that introducing such specimens into the wild has no adverse effects on the aquatic ecosystems and native populations of species life. Would this kind of biotechnological intervention still make any ethical difference to human life?

I maintain that it would. Purpose-bred or genetically engineered animals become dominantly characterized for us by their instrumental purpose, as does a hammer. Here the purpose might be the trout's or salmon's size, fighting ability, or eagerness in taking an angler's lure. Whichever, the fish have been initially and intentionally removed from a natural and historically deep context of ethological, evolutionary, and ecological processes and humanly impounded, isolated, and manipulated. In our experience, they are domesticated and suffer a symbolic reduction to their humanly conceived "purpose." They no longer have the meaning or significance of a wild trout or salmon. When they are reintroduced into a natural setting, they tend to undermine its wild symbolic valence for humans, if not also devastate the aquatic ecosystem itself.

The wild and the natural in ecosystems are a fecund source of multiple values and valuations. Most primordially, there are the protean, self-renewing, form-engendering, albeit vulnerable and fragile, powers of nature itself. And these forms most beautiful are expressible and expressed in innumerable symbolic forms, no less complex and beautiful in their own realm. This is "nature" in an enduring cosmological and ethical sense, for us still wondrous (if not also awesome and terrifying). It is not ours to remake or improve, although, as a matter of ethical responsibility, it is ours to respect and preserve. Also it is a source to which we characteristically and recurrently return to refresh, recreate, and reeducate ourselves. In a way that no biotechnology can, wild fish in wild streams open up to us the vast, spatiotemporally deep universe that creatively engenders streams, fish, and humans alike. This is "nature creative" (Spinoza's *natura naturans*) to which we all ultimately owe our very being.

Modern urban and technological civilization, and biotechnology in particular, remorselessly if unobtrusively threatens to overtake not only nature but also the multivalenced natural symbols and naturally ingrained values by which we live and humanly sustain ourselves. Nature, once evidenced and symbolized by wild and richly populated trout streams and salmon rivers, now becomes a farm pond of engineered and stocked fish frequented by humans with only practical, provincial, recreational, or status-oriented things in mind. This would be the further demise, begun in earnest in the seventeenth century, of nature as "significant cosmos," as prehumanly and inherently valuable and alive. It should be the business of philosophic cosmologies, in their defense of the full range of human and natural values, to counter such threats and to resist such loss.

It is good to have Mayr and Jonas, with their singular and differing visions, to help us explore, articulate, and act upon these responsibilities. Sometimes it will be Mayr's naturalist's vision of *becoming* that will better help us to see our duties and moral failures. Sometimes it will be Jonas's ethics of natural and moral *being* that may better move us into doing what we know, however imperfectly, is right. We need all the help we can get, from whatever quarter.

16

Nature Alive in Spinoza and Whitehead

Philosophers have long struggled with conceptual dead-ends and blind spots that block or distort insight and a penetrating interpretation of reality and of human experience. Exploring these philosophic struggles—examining dramatic moments in the history of Western philosophy—hopefully will shed light on our current problems and open up a better conceptual or philosophic road to the future.

In this chapter I want to examine one such ongoing struggle that began in the seventeenth century and is still being waged today, although not always explicitly and self-consciously. This is a struggle within what I shall call the domain of "philosophic cosmology." It pits a mechanistic, reductionistic worldview that sets human being apart from the rest of being, and mind or cognition apart from the rest of natural reality, on the one side, against a worldview that aims at ontological monism and the relational being of humans and nature, on the other.

One way to define the terms of this struggle is to compare the philosophies of René Descartes (1596–1650) with those of Baruch Spinoza (1632–1677) and Alfred North Whitehead (1861–1947), who in the twentieth century advanced the development of philosophic cosmology. The thought of both Spinoza and Whitehead moved the focus toward a philosophy of living nature and hence paved the way for an additional important development that took place in the nineteenth century with the growth of evolutionary biology and the fundamental work of Darwin. In the twentieth century, the relational and "ecological" philosophic cosmology has been carried forward by many philosophers deeply engaged with biological and evolutionary questions, foremost among them Ernst Mayr and Hans Jonas. It is through a sustained engagement with their thought that I have endeavored to develop my own and to recover a philosophy of nature for our time and for the future.

To set a contemporary context for discussing the philosophic struggle between Descartes and Spinoza (and, later, Whitehead), I want to raise explicitly the issue of our ethical and civic duties to the future of humans, animals, and nature. Beyond issues of human and animal sentience (pain, suffering, individual life goals or plans), philosophy and ethics must address more elusive questions about the moral significance of the biological and behavioral integrity of individual organisms (including animals) and the integrity and flourishing of natural populations or communities of organisms, particular ecosystems, and the evolutionary process itself. Such systematic considerations are necessary for finally deciding what we ought and ought not to do with respect to the use of animals and nature (biotechnology, land use, biodiversity conservation) for human purposes. Here is a pointed instance where fundamental and contested philosophic issues concerning being or reality (ontology), knowledge (epistemology), and values (axiology) are essentially involved. Spinoza contra Descartes is particularly instructive. It helps to reveal the philosophic stage upon which contemporary dilemmas are played out.

Descartes: Dividing Reality in Two

I start with Descartes's philosophic assertions of the ontological primacy of "substance" and of a multiplicity of substances. Descartes fatefully defines a substance as "that which needs nothing else in order to exist" (Descartes 1969: 323). This definition ultimately resigns all substances, whether of the same or different natures, to merely *external interactions*. Such substances do not, and ontologically cannot, essentially affect or matter to one another. They are what they are independent of each other. Whatever relations might hold between them (however these relations might be characterized or explained) must be adventitious, contingent, and have no bearing on their very being or essence.

Descartes recognizes three types of substance, each with its own unsharable attribute: God, mental substance, and physical substance, the latter two types requiring God for their initial creation and ongoing continuance in existence. Whatever the relation of the other two types of substance to God, *res cogitans* and *res extensa* are independent of each other and have radically different attributes or characters.

This is Descartes's famous metaphysical dualism, which banished all subjective activity and agency from the natural realm and left nature free for the mechanistic causal explanations of the new physics, which was primarily concerned with inorganic nature and mechanics. Yet this metaphysical service to emerging scientific materialism was bought at a heavy philosophic price—a price particularly germane to our ethical interests in humans, animals, and nature. Most fundamentally Cartesian cosmology excludes life (animate, organic life) and mind from nature (Whitehead [1938] 1968: 149). Nature is conceptually reduced to permanent "bits of matter" passively supporting qualities or characters (for example, sensa) in an empty, geometric (three-dimensional) space. Locomotion, change of place, is the sole or dominant mode of change (Whitehead [1938] 1968: 132). Cartesian nature is reduced to "billiard-balls-in-motion." All such material things are simply or singly located. They just are where they are. Nature exists in the instant, that is, atemporally, with no essential reference to time. There are no fundamental relations of individual things to other individual things at other times and places.

Relationships

First is the problem of relationship or connectedness. Minds (*res cogitans*) and bodies (*res extensa*) share absolutely nothing in common, and it is philosophically unintelligible and inexplicable how there can be any direct connection, relation, or communication between the two realms of substance, notwithstanding the mysterious machinations Descartes posited for the pineal gland. Against the primary evidence of our experience, it becomes impossible to comprehend how a thinking subject can direct bodily action and can be introduced to, know, and think about the external, radically other realm of nature. Descartes's own doctrine of innate ideas about external reality or nature strikes contemporary philosophers and scientists as an epistemological deus ex machina. In fact, with Cartesian dualism, God must recurrently be pressed into philosophical service to mediate between the two dimensions of worldly reality—subjectivity and physicality—that have radically been rent asunder. Like Humpty Dumpty, ontology after the fall can never adequately be put back together again.

Nor is the relational problem merely between the two realms of mind and matter. Each realm itself is infected with philosophic unintelligibility. If we suppose, along with Descartes, a plurality of mental substances or human minds, how do they communicate with one another without some use of the radically other physical realm as a medium of communication (for example, written symbol or sound)? How can they break out of a splendid, isolated independence and an egocentric, solipsistic predicament? How do they influence one another's subjective life, or even be assured of each other's existence? Leibniz's philosophically artful ploy, his doctrine of world-experiencing but causally unrelated and windowless monads (old Cartesian substances in new dress) seems an artificial, unhappy solution, and we wince at philosophers who naively tackle the theory-induced conundrum of proving the existence of other minds. Here is a dead end of philosophy's own making.

On the physical side of the metaphysical divide, we encounter similar problems. We may opt for nature as a single physical, extended substance and avoid the problem of external relations to other physical entities altogether. But then, within the mechanistically, blindly determined plenum, what accounts for the systematically related, internal articulations of nature? Most pointedly, what accounts for the existence of complexly organized, bodily organisms and the communities and ecosystems that these organisms together fashion?

If we opt for the atomistic route and an indefinite multiplicity of extended substances, we are no better off. For each extended atom or concatenation of atoms does not require any other physical entities in order to exist. Each atom could exist alone in a universal vacuum. Nor will their physical characteristics, singly or in aggregate, essentially require or be related to one another. Again, all natural order would be radically contingent. Blindly running, externally related billiard balls, in the push and pull of jostling physical existence, would have to foot the explanatory bill for the historically or temporally evolved, internally articulated order of nature, including the terrestrial realm of animate life.

But all this is ontologically implausible. The price of philosophic unintelligibility is just too high. Descartes proposes a philosophy of spiritual, intellectually angelic minds and dead, inorganic, mechanistic nature in which biological organisms and the realm of animate life do not fit. For it is precisely with biological organisms, including our human bodily selves, that there can be no radical split between the realms of mind and organic body. The organic subject or self acts in the world with and through its body, and the living subject is aboriginally introduced to the world via the body's sensory functionings. Further, the particular definite character and capacities of the living organism—physical, physiological, behavioral, and psychic—are coordinated and teleologically or teleonomically structured for the sake of the lively existence of the integral organism itself. Still further, these characters and capacities speak for or reflect the fundamental features of the natural world out of which the organism has evolved. In short, there is a dynamic, if imperfect, fit between organism and environing world. In all dimensions of organic, particularly animal existence, worldly relatedness and dynamic communicative interaction are as essential as psychophysical individuality or selfhood. All this is lost in Descartes's dualistic substance philosophy.

Value and Nature

Relationships aside—what are the value implications of Descartes's philosophic picture? By metaphysical fiat, all subjective agency and purpose are written out of nature, leaving a realm of blind, causally efficient forces. This by definition is a valueless realm, since nothing of worth can be internally aimed at and achieved, and nothing can be benefited or harmed. Nature at best can only have a pragmatic or "instrumental" value for an external, observing, thinking subject. (How thoroughly contemporary culture has embraced this conception of intrinsically valueless nature!) But even this value is philosophically problematic, for the thinking subject has essentially nothing to do with nature existentially or practically and is thus only inexplicably and unintelligibly related to it. Its business is to think and will and perhaps seek agreement among like-minded entities about how to use nature.

In short, Cartesian valuation, whether ethical, aesthetic, or religious, cannot be directed at the living integrity of individual organisms or complex forms, nor toward the concrete activities found in and between living organisms, for they have no inherent value. All is purposeless causal necessity. All organisms, plant and animal, and the ecosystems that they together constitute are but natural mechanisms, contingently arrived at or fashioned by God, to be used as human prudence dictates. Logically, Cartesian eyes are—and must be—blind to natural values. There can be no authentic Cartesian ethics of the natural animate world.

Spinoza: Healing Reality

With respect to organic and humanly organic life, Cartesian modes of thought leave us in a philosophic cul de sac. A chief stumbling block is the conception of "substance" as "that which needs nothing other in order to exist." With such a definition, organisms logically and ontologically *cannot* be substances, for by their fundamental mode of metabolic existence, they essentially require something outside themselves in order to exist. For organisms, individuality (understood as one mode of relatedness to the world) must emerge out of a primordial striving. Organisms must win, and continue to win, their own individuality, integrity, and independence in and through their interaction with the natural world outside themselves.

To conceive philosophically these fundamental and interconnected themes of "individuality" and "relatedness," it is necessary to move beyond Cartesian modes of thought. This was clearly seen by Spinoza. For both logical and ontological reasons, Spinoza abandoned Descartes's dualism and his assertion of multiple substances in favor of a radical monism. There can be only one being or entity that requires "nothing else in order to exist" and that is *causa sui* (cause of itself). This is God or Nature (*Deus sive Natura*) as a whole, acting out of the necessity of its own purely active and dynamic being, characterized by an infinity of attributes of which we humans know only thought and extension.

With this move to a one-substance cosmology, Spinoza philosophically allows for a fundamental reconceptualization of organic life, including human life. Biological organisms and human beings are no longer ontologically separate: animals are not merely natural mechanisms and humans are not essentially detached minds above and outside the natural and material world. Rather, both are considered finite modifications or internal articulations of the unbounded active being of Nature (God), with a "modal" rather than "substantial" existence.

It is with the conception of modal existence that Spinoza philosophically combines the themes of individuality and relatedness. The essence or fundamental character of each finite mode or being (each concrete natural entity) is an *endeavor to persevere in its own individual being*. This is its "conatus," the ontological basis of its individuality, which necessarily implies dynamism, activity, and recurrent effort. Since by ontological necessity all finite modes are causally interconnected and directly or indirectly interactive in the one infinite system or realm of Nature, conative existence can be pursued only in relation to other worldly entities. Concrete individuality must be an ongoing, dynamic affair, won *within* a relatedness to the world. In short, an organism's particular and individual existence is *internally related* to the world.

This conception systematically opens up new and important possibilities for philosophic explanation and intelligibility. For example, Spinoza conceives all organisms, including humans, as ontologically unified or "one." And this oneness is comprehensible both cognitively and materially, under the attributes of both thought and extension. This is an ontological monism, conjoined with conceptual or intellectual pluralism. This is Spinoza's famous "psychophysical parallelism." What is conceived to happen causally under the attribute of extension ("body") also and correlatively happens causally under the attribute of thought ("idea of body") and vice versa. For ontologically they are one and the same happening. The intellectual distinction between mind and body involves no real or ontologically meaningful difference.

Whatever may be the limits of Spinoza's account of this modal psychophysical parallelism, we should not ignore its general and heuristic strengths. In place of Spinoza's deterministic view of a strict ontological necessity to mind and world, one might develop a neo-Darwinian account that is more historically contingent and evolutionary. In either case, organisms are understood to be naturally organized for worldly action and perception that essentially serve the fundamental conative endeavors of the organic individual. Organisms are so constituted as to take account of and to act within the world. This must mean that real potentialities for organic individuality, activity, and experience are woven into the very fabric of nature. For Spinoza, all of nature, both organic and inorganic, is more or less animated or alive. Moreover, there can be varying, naturally constituted levels of organic complexity and organization, yielding conative individuals (human and animal) with varying capacities for worldly activity and experience, for the twin powers of acting upon and "undergoing" or "suffering" the world.

We can now philosophically understand why humans and all other organisms are necessarily worldly actors and sufferers, with psychic and bodily capacities attuned to the world. We must be such in order to be at all. Furthermore, all organisms, most emphatically ourselves, have been forged in the crucible of worldly, natural, dynamic existence. Without divine guarantees of certain knowledge, our perceptual and sensory capacities reveal more or less adequately the realized order of the world. The objective or worldly outer importantly determines the subjective or individual and psychic inner, for nature's finite conative entities mutually and interactively determine one another's character, physical and mental, and the overall realized order of nature. Radical skepticism and the

threat of solipsism are thus a ruse, born of bad metaphysics. Analytic philosophers still talk about what they call the problem of "other minds." But
other minds are no philosophic problem. Rather, they are the most natural
things in the animate world and a basic ingredient of our everyday worldly
experience and interactions.

In short, by natural (ontological/cosmological) necessity, we, in our
own particular and finite human way, are attuned to the natural world—
bodily, perceptually, and actively. In pursuing our own conative and metabolic mode of existence, we perceive in our limited and imperfect human
fashion the order of the world and the interactions among its constituents, and we in turn bodily act upon or with them. We are complex organisms that take account of or know the world, including its own natural
values and goodness. These "natural values" of the world primarily are
nature's organisms themselves: the various concrete forms and instances
of dynamic, conative, and active existence that are interdependently fashioned in the system of nature.

It is within this wider animate and worldly context of existence that
we creatively fashion our peculiarly human world and the complex cultural realms of humanly significant, meaningful, symbolic existence and
activity. These human endeavors include our political, intellectual, artistic, religious, and ethical creations. Yet it is important to keep in mind that
the decidedly human world (our "difference" from the rest of nature) is
itself possible only on the basis of our natural status as organic, conative
creatures within the world. The human world is parasitic upon the natural, animate world in complex ways. The concrete, definite, and dynamic
order of the natural world must be there prior to our taking account of and
creatively acting upon it. Higher human faculties of imagination, thought,
purpose, and controlled bodily action presuppose the capacity for abstraction—of lifting forms out of their specific manifestations and concrete
contexts.

This capacity depends on human language, but it also fundamentally
depends both on the bodily organism's perceptual capacities and on an
independent order within the natural world, no matter how freely we may
vary these abstracted forms in consequent mental activity. Humans ontologically *cannot* be divorced from nature. Moreover, for these abstracted
and freely varied forms to become genuine symbols, carrying their own
weight of human significance and meaning in all their infinite variation,
aboriginally depends on our being conative creatures within a dynamic

and efficacious world. Things can have felt meaning or significance for us primarily because of the dynamic and complex interrelatedness that makes our own efforts and the world existentially matter. Upon ourselves and the world coequally depend our very individual existence. In conative being, naturally organic and cultural or symbolic existence meet and intricately interweave, and perhaps not exclusively on a human level. Other forms of organic, animal life seemingly have their own capacities of abstraction and live their conscious lives also within a world of forms of significance.

Whitehead: Reconciling Nature and Life

Whitehead constitutes another antidote to the failed Cartesian tradition, and he was perhaps the most important philosopher of the twentieth century. However, Whitehead's philosophic cosmology or philosophy of organism is a major philosophic mountain, difficult to ascend and even more difficult to descend, that is, to explain to others.* Characteristically, it is avoided by most philosophers, whether because of its difficulty or because of its being out of contemporary fashion. But what are these philosophers and the rest of us missing? Who is truly out of step and style? And why?

Thanks to recurrent critical discussion of Whitehead's speculative philosophy (especially *Process and Reality* [(1929) 1978]) over the past half century, the fundamental Whiteheadian notion of "actual entity" has become reasonably intelligible (Christian 1967; Leclerc 1965). The notion of actual entity, which refers both to God and to finite, episodic "actual occasions," is Whitehead's reformation of the traditional notion of substance. Actual entities are the "final, really real things" of Whitehead's cosmos. They are its concrete real individuals, world-experiencing, self-creative, self-functioning, working together in constituting the creative advance that is the evolving cosmos, realizing among themselves that emergent order and those novel, concrete values which give the cosmos ongoing significance. So much is reasonably clear. But does this doctrine make sense—real, ontological sense? Can there be real individuals such as conceived by Whitehead? This is a question that demands further critical discussion. It is a question not only about the coherence of Whitehead's system but also about its adequacy as a philosophy of life and a worldview adequate to actual experience.

This question has a specific importance relative to Whitehead's central aims. Above all else, Whitehead wishes rationally to understand our status as living and valuing creatures, to understand our true significance and that of the natural universe, to understand the meaning of civilization and to promote certain future directions of civilized effort. No doubt, these are noble and important aims. And in fulfilling these aims, the philosophic notion of actual entity holds a privileged position. The actual entity (or actual occasion) is the grand home of reconciliation—that concrete entity in which the dominant persuasions of modern science concerning nature (for example, compulsion, lawfulness, necessity) and the dominant persuasions of civilized man concerning life (for example, freedom, effective teleological activity, aims at the realizations of novel values) meet and are reconciled. Nature and life are seen in their mutual requirements, as factors of a concrete individual. The phenomena of life and value, the activities of living and valuing, are saved, spared from the omnipotent grimace of an ironclad, natural necessity impervious to free, selfdetermined functionings and realizations of value. We need not fear being written out of the universe, explained away. Our lively selves, with all the significance and meaning that attend life's necessary freedom, can, and do, peacefully coexist with the natural universe—ontologically, if not practically. Yet, despite the nobility of Whitehead's saving aim, can we accept this home of reconciliation, the Whiteheadian doctrine of actual entity?

I wish to examine a specific critical question. Can there be real individuality—in the sense of a real *concretum* involving self-constituting creative activity, aiming at and realizing some particular value for itself and for others (Whiteheadian criteria)—apart from biological organisms (at least some, if not all, organisms)? If not, Whitehead's speculative philosophy, in all its phases, is undermined (on ontological grounds). His prespeculative assertions are in doubt; his conceptual scheme is thrown in jeopardy, and his interpretation of life and our value experiences are suspect. We are no longer philosophically saved—at least not by Whitehead's system. However, the door may be opened upon a new, more secure philosophic salvation.

Nature Lifeless, Nature Alive

Whitehead's philosophic vision is highly original and is best approached with some care. At his most systematic in *Process and Reality,* Whitehead offers a general scheme of fundamental ideas in terms of which to interpret

or understand the full range of human experience. He considers such philosophy our birthright, the romance of rational thought, the speculative
attempt to make sense of ourselves and our world, including the many-
leveled values and importance of earthly existence. Whitehead's endeavor
is crucially animated by an underlying faith: that the world or cosmos is
coherent; that things hang together, make sense, have their own significance, and can be rendered more or less intelligible.

Whitehead's method of philosophy involves both an empirical, critical exploration of human experience and an exercise of rational imagination. There are rigorous demands of coherence and consistency (rational
demands) that must be checked against our experience of ourselves and the
world (empirical demands). Yet, even at philosophy's best, there is, Whitehead claims, no guarantee of success or certainty. Philosophy and our
explorations of human experience are a never-ending adventure, a critical
and continuing revolt against all cultural, intellectual, and metaphysical
pretension and dogmatism. (Here, at the outset, note Whitehead's contention of the fundamental limitations in all ways of knowing. Certainty
is a ruse. Certain knowledge is beyond our human, intellectual powers,
logic and mathematics notwithstanding.) Yet he further claims that a philosophic worldview, formal or informal, is the necessary background of all
human thought, experience, and action. There is no escaping fundamental
frameworks of thought and feeling. I believe that Whitehead is profoundly
right that fundamental philosophic worldviews or cosmologies, our basic
interpretative schemes of thought, no matter how "finally" uncertain and
open for revision, really matter (positively or negatively) with respect both
to thinking and to practical action. In the end, how we think, so we act.

Thus, philosophy (and ethics) and the way of uncertainty or enlightened ignorance must always learn to travel hand in hand with a never-ending openness to the world (Whitehead [1938] 1968: 152; [1929] 1978: 3–4).
This is Whitehead's neoclassical, grand-style approach to philosophy,
minus the traditional quest for certainty and final truth. As such, it cuts
against the grain of modern positivist sensibilities, which mean to stick to
indubitable facts and avoid all metaphysical nonsense or speculation, resolutely ignoring all that is dubious (Whitehead [1938] 1968: 153 ff.).

Indeed, Whitehead contends that this ascetic, if not arrogant, act of
positivist self-deception is precisely the problem. To make his point, he
undertakes a critical survey of modern science and philosophy begun
in earnest in the sixteenth and seventeenth centuries (Whitehead [1938]

1968: 130 ff.). Whitehead is specifically interested in the reigning, dominant worldview that he terms Common Sense or Sense Perception Nature. This modern science and philosophy of nature rests on a particular theory of knowledge (epistemology): a reliance on sense perception, especially "clear-sighted" vision, as the sole legitimate mode of experience or observation (Whitehead [1938] 1968: 128 ff.). Such a conception of nature does endeavor to be intimately connected in everyday, pre-philosophic human experiential and practically important truth. But, beyond its limited scope, it generates a complete muddle that philosophically acquiesces in the unintelligible, the incoherent, and the meaningless. It thereby undermines civilized thought and action, morally practical and humane. This is Whitehead's core, radical indictment of our modern culture.

Whitehead responds to this pervasive doctrine by underscoring the inadequacy, limitations, and relative superficiality of sense perception: mere sensa (colors, sounds, tastes, touches), spatially or temporally distributed, that tell no tales of themselves, their origins, or their changes. In our experience, sensa are just immediately present in consciousness. End of story. Whitehead further notes the curious hybrid character of sense perception: its twin origination in the physiological functionings of the organic body and our extensive, geometric, spatiotemporal implication in the evolving world. The world is "extensively" arrayed before our experiencing selves (Whitehead [1938] 1968: 132). Moreover, we do not need professional philosophers to point out the occasional and recurrent illusions of sense perception, for example, puddles of water on shimmering summer highways. That sense perception is the *terra firma* of modern science and philosophic cosmology strikes Whitehead as curiously and decidedly odd.

Why would the modern philosophic tradition place such a heavy reliance on sense perception? There are good historical reasons. For one, it closely aligns with positivism, which seeks uncontestable experiential facts as the basis of all empirical, worldly knowledge and its quest for certainty. Whitehead corners his quarry, his *bête noire*, and mounts a counterattack. Positivism acquiesces in ultimate irrationality and incoherence in the name of the observationally and conceptually indubitable: unquestionable, clearly observed, hardheaded facts and correlative ideas. The modern philosophic forbearer of this mood and doctrine is Descartes, with his clear and distinct ideas, guaranteed as certain and true by God and his goodness. From Whitehead's critical perspective, positivism fails resolutely to press for connections (relations) among things and, thus, for any serious philosophic intelligibility. (For Whitehead, making connections between things or ideas is the heart or essence of rational thought, not the narrow string of deductions of logic or mathematical proof.) Specifically, positivism glaringly fails to link nature, life, mentality, and value, which we emphatically feel to be intimately connected in everyday, pre-philosophic human experience. This is nature as dominantly disclosed in and by sense perception, especially vision.

Nature-as-disclosed-by-sense-perception straightaway yields philosophic puzzles or quandaries. These puzzles go beyond the fundamental incoherence introduced by Descartes's mind-body dualism: the radical split of mind (*res cogitans*) and matter (*res extensa*), which have no real, essential, or ontological relations to one another. As noted by Whitehead, such a split-world doctrine leaves no room for recognizing and understanding organic life. Organisms are decidedly not just bodiless minds or "bits of matter," physical automatons, or subtle natural machines. Moreover, in the modern era, transmission theories of light and sound led straightaway to the subjectification of sensa, which we humans naively or straightforwardly experience to inhere in nature—the colors, sounds, tastes, smells, and tactile qualities of things (Whitehead [1938] 1968: 132). Nature is denuded and devalued. All secondary (nongeometric or nonextensive), aesthetic, sensory qualities are banished from nature to the Cartesian mind, leaving nature poets unknowingly, quips Whitehead, singing hosannas only to themselves. In sum, sense perception and its relations to the world abroad become highly problematic, if not unintelligible, in this conception of nature.

On the physical, material side of the dualistic divide, there seems to be no intelligible reason for the gravitational stresses among Isaac Newton's spatially distributed, temporally located, bits of matter. True, we have mathematical formulas about nature's ways, but in themselves such formulas give no philosophic reasons (Whitehead [1938] 1968: 134–35, 154). Why the world's geometric extensiveness? Why the messiness of matter? Why the gravitational stresses? For Sense Perception Nature and its animating positivist spirit, these are mere brute facts with no intelligible connections or compresence.

Intellectual progress since the seventeenth century has effected the scientific demise of the Common Sense or Sense Perception conception of nature, with its empty space, permanent bits of matter, and the later (eighteenth to nineteenth century) halfway house of a jellylike ether that accommodates all sorts of intracosmic stresses and strains. Scientifically, there has been the complete denial of nature as simply located and existing at the instant (White-

head [1938] 1968: 136 ff.). In its place has emerged Nature energetic, enduring, and becoming on all scales (cosmic or regional) dynamic and historical.
This constitutes a fundamental sea change in thought. Nature is one grand
theater of incessant activity with both enduring and changing patterns and
habits of behavior among "group agitations" (the old bits of matter). There are
cosmic epochs of energetic activity with different cosmological characters,
for example, geometric patterns and electromagnetism. However, the characteristics carry no mark of absolute necessity, as claimed by old ironclad laws
of nature. (Unchanging "laws of nature" nicely go hand in hand with belief
in a temporal [unchanging], certain truth.) But, Whitehead asks, why? Why
the activity? What is getting effected? Is this a cosmic theater of the absurd—
a meaningless sound and fury signifying nothing? Has physics been reduced,
or has it reduced itself, to a "mystical chant over an unintelligible universe"
(Whitehead [1938] 1968: 136)?

Here, according to Whitehead, is the fateful philosophic result of a Dead
Nature that yields and can yield no reasons (Whitehead [1938] 1968: 135).
Whitehead boldly breaks from the pack and recoils from such a flat, lifeless, unintelligible conception of nature. Having critically and historically
exposed the emperor's clothes—the philosophic bankruptcy of positivism—
Whitehead opts for a speculative conception of Nature Alive. Indeed, Whitehead considered the status of life in (positivist, physicalist) nature to be the
modern problem of philosophy and science. "The very meaning of life is in
doubt" (Whitehead [1938] 1968: 148). This indeed is a radical charge. If life
is in doubt, then we are in doubt as to our meaning and status, for, first and
foremost, we are human organisms living in the world. We may add, some
seventy years later, that the practical status of life in nature is perhaps the
long-term problem of the political and civic world. Consider the present and
ongoing biodiversity crisis, as connected with habitat destruction and climate
change or global warming. The theoretical and practical problems are not
unrelated.

Enter Whitehead, the modern classical speculative philosopher who refuses to accept ultimate irrationality, absurdity, and meaninglessness. In particular, he rejects the disconnection of fundamental and abiding details of
our human experience of nature, life, mind, and value. He does so by philosophically and resolutely fusing nature and life. Interestingly, it is here that
Whitehead himself most explicitly and directly turns to a path of enlightened
ignorance. He turns his attention to life, living nature, at the cost of any pretension to final philosophic certainty.

Whitehead questions afresh the taken-for-granted aspects of human experience, including the putative clarity and importance of sense perception. Again, note the pervasive, though often silent, reference of sense perception to the organic body and its sense organs—eyes, ears, fingers, nose, and tongue. Don't be seduced by the intermittently clear sensa and the conceptual abstractions that we build on them and call reality. This is to commit the fallacy of misplaced concreteness, focusing on the partial, abstract idea and overlooking the concrete reality in its full complexity (Whitehead [1938] 1968: 138; [1925] 1948: 51, 55). Attend instead to the more fundamental, imperative, vague, and incessant feelings of the organic body. There you will find the immediacy of life, emotional and active, and our personal, intimate human implication in our bodies and the world abroad—nature, life, and mental functionings experienced together. For Whitehead, these are the fundamental facts or deliverances of experience that philosophy ought to connect and render intelligible, rescuing the meaning, value, and significance of nature, life, and ourselves by speculatively interpreting their interconnections, their status vis-à-vis one another, the reasons for their compresence. Giving such reasons is not the same as claiming certain truth.

Herein lies Whitehead's originality and speculative boldness, his decisive break from modern tradition. He stares down Descartes, Hume, Newton, Kant, and other typically skeptical moderns, all in the name of philosophic sanity and civilized practical and moral activity, again with no claim to dogmatic final certainty, which no discipline enjoys, whether mathematics, physics, philosophy, theology, ethics, or some other. The way of enlightened ignorance, fallible knowledge and ignorance intermingled, is an adventure of ideas, undertaken with a combination of boldness and humility.

Whitehead digs deep into personal bodily life and experience (Whitehead [1938] 1968: 150 ff.). Here he finds a certain *absoluteness of self-enjoyment,* an emotional appropriation of the antecedent functionings of the organic body and the physical universe (nature) on the part of an immediate, subjectively alive "occasion of experience." Here he finds an episode of *creative activity,* which is precisely this appropriation, with its mating of the actual or the already realized and the potential, the never before realized, in a new pattern of individual, emotional, value-laden world experience. Here he finds the *efficacy of aim,* involving mental functions more or less effective and dominant, which guides the process of appropriation and self-creation, always with one eye on the past and the other on the impending future. Whitehead philosophically generalizes from this personal, human, concrete bodily experience of the world. (As an integral part of the world ourselves, we are clues to the universe abroad.) Here are nature, life, value, individuality, and mentality together in the final, really real things (actualities) of the world, including their creative implications in the advancing natural universe (Whitehead [1938] 1968: 151 ff.). The natural world is decidedly more than the "sheer or mere activities" studied by the reductive physical sciences, with their abstractions from the naturally concrete. The more concrete or comprehensive perspective of speculative philosophic cosmology unearths Nature Alive, either immediate or past, the scene of multiple values, novel emerging order, and intensities of experience and existence aimed at, realized, or frustrated. Here is a worldview that is a far cry from the lifeless, bloodless, and unintelligible universe of Nature Dead and the corresponding private fantasies of aworldly and anatural human minds, the legacy of Descartes and the seventeenth century, which still fatefully haunts us. We are philosophically reintroduced to the world in which we live.

Whitehead's bold speculations may be a romance of rational philosophic thought. But they are not idle musings. Though renouncing any claim to final truth (we, as noted, are finally *Ignoramus*), Whitehead presses hard for philosophic intelligibility and for giving the world and our human selves their experiential due. Whitehead fuses nature, life, and mentality in interconnected, worldly episodes of subjective experience and existence. (These episodes of experience arise and perish in constituting the creative advance of the universe.) In so doing, he philosophically explains or interprets what the worldview of Common Sense or Sense Perception Nature cannot. Whitehead intelligibly interprets the experienced factors of our world, such as real causation or causal efficacy (both efficient and final or goal directed) and memory (the past effective in the present). Why must definitely charactered things and occasions of experience arise where and when they do (dynamic, historical spatiotemporal contexts as fundamental)? He shows why Instant Nature is an obfuscating fiction, perhaps mirroring an eternal and unchanging transcendent reality, itself suspect; and why endurance, becoming, and change—interconnections of process and reality—are fundamental aspects of ourselves and the world within which we live. He explains why value experience and existence, human and nonhuman, are fundamental and widely shared and are pervasively experienced as such, solipsistic philosophies and philosophers notwithstanding (Whitehead [1938] 1968: 165). Whitehead claims that our fundamental experience of the world is "have care, here is something important." Moreover, for the sake of fundamental philosophic intelligibility,

Whitehead speculatively posits an "Ultimate," *Creativity*, which ongoingly gathers the many occasions of experience of the past into novel, immediately alive occasions of experience, thus giving Nature Alive its fundamental character of an ever-becoming, creative advance into novelty (Whitehead [1938] 1968: 151; [1929] 1978: 16–17).

For those who dwell and toil in the vineyards of everyday life and take worldly responsibilities seriously, there is one central doctrine of Whitehead's Nature Alive that particularly provokes interest: his notion of identity and "mutual immanence." This is his interpretation of the fundamental togetherness or interconnectedness of the world's individuals or final "really real" things, his decisive and important move beyond atomistic cosmologies or worldviews (Whitehead [1938] 1968: 159 ff.).

Starting from our immediate human selves, Whitehead notes several claims to unity and identity based on inescapable feelings of derivation and continuity. The identity and unity of ourselves with our emotional, living bodies. The identity and unity of ourselves with our past stream of personal experiences and existence. The identity and continuity of our living bodies with the rest of dynamically functioning and evolving nature. (In the end, all things are connected.) These various identities and continuities merge and interweave in our immediate human selves; they make us who we are now, more or less active and creative, with real ties to the past and future of our personal lives, our own bodies, and the wider world, humanly cultural and natural. We always and fundamentally find a double sense of inclusion. The enduring self, the body, and the world are experientially found to be in—within—our present experience, as the dynamic basis of our immediate, lively, and self-creative activity. The world is in the self. Alternatively, we find our immediate selves actively embedded within our enduring personal lives, living bodies, and historically cultural and natural worlds. The self is in the world. Here is Whitehead's doctrine of mutual immanence—the double inclusion of self and world—that is meant to recognize and philosophically interpret a central fact of our experience and existence: the essential togetherness of self and world. The self and the world are internally related; that is, they essentially matter to one another with respect to both existence and character (particular forms and capacities). Interestingly, Whitehead here was probably influenced more by advances in physics than advances in evolutionary biology. In "field theory," energetic parts are in the whole, and the energetic whole is in the parts (Whitehead [1938] 1968: 138).

"Mutual immanence" is the heart and soul of Whitehead's philosophic

cosmology of Nature Alive, a doctrine conspicuously absent from the cosmological interpretation of Nature Lifeless or Dead (physical, material, atomistic
nature). For our purposes, we should explore the import of mutual immanence in shedding light on and interpreting our ethical experiences and
responsibilities to human individuals and communities and wider nature.

For example, which philosophic scheme makes better sense of and elu-
cidates conservation philosophy and ethical imperatives of Aldo Leopold's
A Sand County Almanac? Leopold claims that the good and the bad, right
and wrong, are to be understood in terms of the protection and promotion of
the dynamic and historical integrity, stability, and beauty of biotic communities and ecosystems (interrelated flora, fauna, and abiotic elements, from
the regional to the global), which emphatically include our human selves. Is
Leopold better interpreted by the doctrine of the mutual immanence of ourselves and the natural world of Nature Alive or by the mutual exclusions,
alienations, and unintelligible connections of our human selves and Nature
Lifeless or Dead? Which helps us better face a bewilderingly complex, forever
changing but deeply value-laden world, natural and cultural?

We ought to turn these critical remarks and questions to good use. We
should further press Whitehead into philosophic service, aimed at our and
nature's future. As we have seen, Whitehead claims no final truth or certainty for his speculative philosophy and interpretation of the world. Even if
we have quarrels with aspects or the final adequacy of his philosophy, as he
did himself, it is not thereby rendered useless. Significantly, Whitehead has
reclaimed the philosophic high ground of Nature Alive and forcibly warned
us against fallacies of misplaced concreteness. Beware taking our own conceptual abstractions (scientific, philosophic, and other) for the living world's
complex concreteness. Whitehead gives us a crucial purchase or perspective
for critically engaging all philosophies of nature, including those inspired by
Darwin and Leopold. Here is an ongoing and fundamental moral and philosophic challenge, with no end in sight.

Biological Organisms: Organic Wholeness and Integrity

I propose to take this discussion of the relation of biological organism and real
individuality a step further. Hans Jonas maintains that only biological organisms (most obviously, animal organisms) are real individuals. This carries a
correlative assertion. We can only concretely understand organisms in virtue of their being real individuals. Their self-constituting, internally related

activity is what engenders their concrete wholeness and integrity—that which manifests and expresses their real, dynamic individuality. Such an assertion or conceptual perspective can be used to pose a critical question to Whitehead. How adequately does he philosophically interpret biological organisms, with their particular kind of wholeness and integrity? If his system of interpretation should fail this test of adequacy, this would be an important shortcoming of his theory of actual entities (as the final, concrete individuals of the universe in terms of which all else is to be understood).

At this point, Whitehead's systematic interpretation of biological organisms (including man) is sufficiently clear. Biological organisms are enduring nexūs, internally related groups, of constituent, episodic actual occasions, more or less complex modes of togetherness of Whitehead's fundamental, experiencing entities. More specifically, internally complex organisms (including human beings) are living structured societies, which harbor within their complexly patterned selves sub-nexūs or sub-societies that account for organisms' central control of themselves and for the dominant soul of the human organism. The resident actual occasions constitute and sustain the enduring organic society in virtue of their episodic, creative activity, in virtue of imposing dominant complex characters on the experiencings of one another. The society is sustained and nurtured by this genetic inheritance imposed by its members on themselves (along with, less proximally, requisite, more or less stable impositions from the extra-societal environment). Novel functionings of resident members effectively nurture the whole society in novel ways, but only within the confines of the dominant social order that must be sustained.

It is within this general interpretative context that Whitehead accounts for the diversity of biological organisms and for the diversity of their modes of functioning, more or less complex. All depends on the modes and subtlety of organization (togetherness) and on the opportunities for experiential activities that thereby arise. Correlatively, it is within this general interpretative context that Whitehead must account for organic wholeness, including the integrity of the human organism. The adequacy of this interpretation is my specific concern.

It is not difficult to recognize that an individual actual entity is an organic whole. The one self-constituting subject is involved in each constituent prehension (the subject's active taking account of items of the universe other than itself), mutually adjusting them, integrating them into its final, integral, composite self. The one subject stands over and above its various constituents. It is more than the mere summation of its parts. It is a real (ontological) whole. But can this be said of Whitehead's biological (in particular, animal) organisms? They are complexly composite entities, but seemingly there is no one subject presiding over the composition—a single subject that is more than its organic, "material" parts and that survives their metabolic repair.

Rather, there are millions of centers of life, millions of epochal subjects, coordinating among themselves (Whitehead [1925] 1948). A Whiteheadian biological organism is a natural nation with individual citizens, passingly performing requisite, coordinate functions, forming particular sub-societies—a division of labor essentially serving the national purpose, the integrity of the organic nation in internatural relations (and warfare). But *who* is the natural national purpose for? Seemingly, for no singular who. It is for all the democratic individuals, though a fortunate aristocracy (with animal organisms) seems to enjoy the better of the bargain. Even though they have their own crucial social duties, they get the best (and perhaps the worst) of the national experience. Yet the nation is not theirs, save experientially. No one aristocrat owns the organisms, qua an active becoming subject. The organism as a whole is always "other" for any one experience beyond its own immediacy. Further, the social coordination as a whole importantly depends on the persuasive agency of God (via the initial subjective aims of the constituent actual occasions)—one nation, under God.

If in political philosophy it is dangerous or pernicious to conceive a real nation on the model of a natural organism, so in philosophical biology it may be unfortunate to conceive a real organism as analogous to a national society. There may be certain advantages—for example, explaining the so-called dissociation of personality and the seemingly autonomous functionings of organs ripped out of their organic contexts (Whitehead [1925] 1948: 83–90). Yet, as is becoming increasingly evident, such organs *in situ* do not function in complete autonomy. A yogi can take striking command over his bodily functionings. Does this speak for one organic self, of which conscious activities are but a component tip, and which usually effects its own divisions of labor? Or does it speak for many subjects inheriting from one another?

Here of course we are at the critical, thorny, perhaps irresolvable problem of the integral self—how far it dips down into the body, how enduring it is in time. Is it true that the enduring human self is a society of actualities, epochal real selves, inheriting past members' memorial experience? Do I not *fashion* a personal past, rather than inherit it? Inheritance seemingly connotes gaining possession of something that I did not previously own. But do not I, the same me, own or possess my past—a past that frequently leaps up in my face? And what am I doing when I remember my past? Memory seems different from inheritance, something more personally mine, lurking in the bowels of myself, constituting much of myself. Am I more of an integral "person" than Whitehead's interpretive scheme would allow?

In a similar fashion do I really inherit from my body? I have a body; I *am* my present bodily self. This question involves genetic inheritance, certainly, but it is not limited to genetics. The bodily I perhaps inherit from the outer world, but seemingly not from itself (myself). I seem too close to myself for that. It is not that hand, at the end of that arm, which recoils from the hot radiator and informs me that it has done so. *I,* my whole organism, recoils. In short, the self-centered individual that is the organism exists to the boundary of its body (cf. Jonas 1966: 78). Things are either "inside" (me) or "outside" (the others), with the skin patrolling the frontiers—whether or not these be the cavernous avenues meandering through my body or the more exposed flanks.

With regard to the problem of wholes and parts, following Jonas I find the modern analytic tradition of science and philosophy wanting (Jonas 1966: 200 ff.). We must judge whether Whitehead has successfully overcome this deficiency. In the modern tradition wholes are understood as mere summations of parts, mere aggregates, which are not the (final) cause of the parts' organization. "The aristocracy of form is replaced by the democracy of matter," the higher explained in terms of the lower (Jonas 1966: 201). This is decidedly not the case with a biological organism, where the living form is the reason for the organization of the parts and for their metabolic turnover (Jonas 1966: 78).

Here we uncover a neglected side of Spinoza's philosophy: his theory of complex bodies (mind-bodies). Finite individuals are not substances—this is Spinoza's way of avoiding Cartesian dualism—but are modes of the one substance. The individuality, the distinct, continuous identity, of a finite mode is marked by its continuing form of determinateness, not by its substantiality; a form realized through relation (causal communication) with the modal others, a continuance evidencing the mode's basic conatus (Jonas 1974: 212). Jonas comments on this Spinozian notion: "Form, continuity, and relation are integral to the concept of individual and provide a clue to the meaning of its identity" (Jonas 1974: 212).

Such modes, in Spinoza's theory, may be highly complex, that is, be composed of other individual modes in determinate forms of interaction or communication. This *form* of mutual determination, as long as it continues, speaks for the individuality, the individual conatus, of the complex mode. Constituent individuals may change as long as the complex form survives. Thus, Spinoza accounts for the possibility (which may be a necessity) of the metabolic activity of the *one* individual (Jonas 1974: 212). The whole, the determinate pattern, is more than its parts. The pattern lasts; the parts pass. And it is the business of the mode to continue its formal pattern and replace its passing parts.

Further, modal determinations are won on the basis of interactions or causal, communicative relations with the wider, world environment, and there can be various levels of "acting and sufferings," depending on the kind of body involved (Jonas 1974: 212). "Since the individual is a *form of union,* there are qualitative grades of individuality, depending on the degree of differentiated order" (Jonas 1974: 215). With highly complex biological organisms, this means that articulated and differentiated communicative interaction with the world allows the enduring individual to flourish, even as the communicative order reproduces itself and endures via its manifestations in the activity of individuals. Sophisticated abilities of suffering (sensitive reaction) and of activity strictly parallel one another, and are correlative to the uniquely appropriate body.

The decisive point is that such complex organisms are themselves modal wholes. As real individuals, *they* continue "their conative life" in virtue of metabolic activity, of interchange with the larger environment, productive as much as produced, as much "natura naturans" as "natura naturata" (Jonas 1974: 216).

The question remains, do Whitehead's biological, animal organisms pass such tests of organic wholeness? As we know, he claims no total, enduring, embodied subject for such organisms. Their organic wholeness cannot be accounted for by (a single) subjectivity. Within his conceptual scheme, a form of definiteness (a complex character), as *severally* enjoyed (experientially) by each constituent actuality, and as imposed on one another, must foot the bill. Seemingly, this must mean that there is a feeling *for,* a feeling *of,* the bodily integrity (the society) in each constituent occasion, more or less dominant in its experience (Leclerc 1965: 219). Bodily integrity would be a realization of a form of definiteness in the subject's objective datum, provoking subjective response. The whole is in the part, and the part in the whole. This is a necessary part of the occasion's world experience. Other (intra-bodily) social functions are conformed to this form of definiteness, realized by the past members of the society and as a project for new members.

Yet is this satisfactory? There (always) is *only* an experience of the whole, of objectivity, either as settled in the past or as a project for the future. And this is only from a limited perspective within the body. Further, contemporary bodily occasions are atomic. Though tied to a common past and a more or less common future, they are (according to Whitehead) discontinuous relative to one another. Among themselves, they do not even form a society but only, as it were, a loose confederation. If a nation is an ideal entity, existing only in the minds of its citizens, so too seems an organism to be, considered as a lively, immediate whole. Whitehead does not give us the concepts to understand an organism as a real individual, with *its own*, self-constituted integrity. The organism never really is, qua a subject formally speaking.

Whitehead has interpreted biological organisms on the basis of his doctrine of actual occasions, his final, concrete experiential entities, experiencing the experience of former experiencers. Experiencing implies mental functioning, no matter how minimal or "unconscious." With such a scheme of interpretation, has Whitehead really, successfully overcome the subjective bias of modern philosophy? Can experience be all that there really is? Seemingly, we experience because we are bodily organisms, because it is necessary to our mode of material existence (of which experiencing is a partial function), to our maintaining individual integrity by metabolic regeneration. Most likely, we are not organisms because the Creative Advance, spurred by God, wishes to stage particular intensities of experience for Its own enjoyment. The only applause we can safely bank on (and that is not assured) is from other living organisms—because they are lives like ourselves, swimming in the soup of organic existence, needful of one another. Primarily, we experience to live, not live to experience. What we want is our liveliness touched, enhanced, and secured, not the mere, unending accumulation of more and more experiences.

Whitehead wavers on this point. Practically, he keenly appreciates the practical and erotic demands of organic life. Theoretically, he occasionally seems to lose his practical sense. For example, metabolism, which is a phenomenon that seriously concerns the philosophic reflections of Jonas, gains only a passing glance from Whitehead. The reason that there are metabolic entities is that the universe has staged concatenations of actual occasions enjoying the unconscious conceptual activity of reversion (conceptual entertainment of novel forms of definiteness relevant to the subject's worldly situation), which disturbs the equilibrium of their immediate environment (Whitehead [1925] 1948: 100–105). In the name of continuing social order (of the organism), they must repair the damage. They are (in the last analysis) spurred to reversion by the primordial nature of God, by his subjective aim after intensity of experience. Thereby, the organism's robbery of the external environment, including its feasting upon other organisms, is cosmically, if not ethically, justified—all in the name of self-justifying experience. Little is said about the organism being resigned to robbery by its very mode of existence, willing experiencer or no. The chill is taken off organic existence, the necessity of metabolic activity.

In sum, a philosophic understanding of the organic wholeness, integrity, and individuality of an organism—the adequate understanding of our organic natures and existence—may be only one sacrifice at the altar of a philosophy of organism that is too much of a "philosophy of experience"—of a philosophy that commits itself (in pre-speculative assertions) to the fundamental assumption that there is nothing ultimately real or actual but experience and experiencers.

Conclusions

Telling in its critique of Cartesianism, and developing the legacy of Spinoza in important ways, Whitehead's philosophic cosmology nonetheless fails on two counts. First, Whitehead fails to account adequately for real individuals since he fails to see that real individuality is necessarily tied to organic (biological) existence. And he fails adequately to interpret biological (at the very least, animal) organisms because he fails to see that they *are* real individuals, that they are more radically one, qua self-functioning subjects, than he allows. Biological existence and real individuality (in their correlative, infinite shades of complexity and intensity) go hand in hand. If this mutual implication is correct, this is telling evidence against Whitehead's doctrine of actual entities and the scheme of interpretation built on its basis.

I shall return to these issues in a more detailed discussion of Jonas in chapters 17 and 18. Now I wish to close by taking note of the nobility or dignity of Whitehead's philosophic aims, and indeed those of Spinoza and the tradition of philosophical cosmology generally. These aims are nothing less than to understand our status as living and valuing creatures; to understand the meaning and significance of ourselves and our universe; to understand our ultimate worth and duties.

Like Spinoza before him, Whitehead, amidst much darkness and doubt, endeavored to take ourselves as living, natural organisms and our cosmic setting seriously, endeavored to recognize their true contribution and value in the lives we realize. And he forged an impressive conceptual scheme to do so. If we can possibly view individuality and organisms more adequately than Whitehead, this is only because he has helped to clear the way and we can stand on his shoulders. If we are critical, it is only to take his project further—to take the mutual implication of life, organism, and real individuality even more seriously. Herein may be the fulfillment of his aims: to understand the human organism as a knowing, valuing, acting creature; to understand knowledge, valuation, and action as the natural performance of that real individual which is the integral human organism; and finally, to understand the human organism, in its lively integrity, as a religious, ethical, and aesthetic animal, with organic life coming fully to itself in its religious, ethical, and aesthetic dimensions. But this fulfillment awaits a philosophic imagination equal to, or even greater than, Whitehead's.

Note

*Author's Note: The exposition of Whitehead's thought relies heavily on the classic essays "Nature Lifeless" and "Nature Alive" from part 3 ("Nature and Life") of his *Modes of Thought* ([1938] 1968). The essays present the most accessible summary of Whitehead's mature critical and speculative thought. The reader could then consider *Science and the Modern World* ([1925] 1948), *Adventures of Ideas* (1933), and then, finally, *Process and Reality* ([1929] 1978). The latter is admittedly challenging but well worth the effort for those willing to stay the course. For overall interpretations, see Christian (1967) and Leclerc (1965).

17

Neo-Darwinian Cosmologies

Mayr and Jonas

Darwinian Cosmology: Ernst Mayr

Ernst Mayr considers the Darwinian revolution in biology—the theory of the evolution of all life by common descent, behavioral and genetic variation, and natural selection—so profound and far-reaching that it moves beyond scientific theory and constitutes a shift in philosophic and moral outlook, a new worldview—whether or not most of us have made this shift or adequately fleshed out its implications.

In Mayr's interpretation of Darwinian thought, evolution is an eminently natural process, marked by historical dynamism, causal contexts, and contingencies, as well as by the particularity and uniqueness of biological entities. The first philosophic pillar of Western tradition to fall is the vision of *cosmic teleology*, nature conceived as the Grand Design of a Grand Designer (Mayr 1991: 50). In its place, Darwinism holds that nature in passing engenders its own forms of organic order—genetic, organismal, populational, communal, ecosystemic, bioregional, and biospheric. There is an ever-recurring, evolutionary two-step, genetic variation (accomplished by genetic mutation and sexual recombination) and natural selection (as well as sexual selection), which favors those who can survive to reproduce (Mayr 1991: 46, 68 ff.). The evolutionary two-step directly challenges central Judeo-Christian traditions and theologies in which creation of the world is intelligently and purposively directed.

The world of modern Galilean-Cartesian-Newtonian science is a world of reductive analyses and explanations in terms of material efficient causes; nature, in short, consists of particles in motion obeying deterministic laws. Darwinism also challenges this *cosmic determinism* (Mayr 1991: 40, 48). According to Mayr, the biological realm is a much more complex, historically contingent, probabilistic, and stochastic affair than Cartesian science can comprehend. In animate nature, there are always multiple causes at work on multiple spatial and temporal scales—a hierarchy of causes or influences only to be recognized by a systems thinking that transcends mere linear strands of efficient causation. Moreover, and equally as telling, Darwinian biologists confront a material unrecognized by old-time physicalist scientists—DNA, with its programmatic (informational) instructions for organisms' phenotypic development and life, somatic (bodily) and behavioral (Mayr 1991: 108 ff., 132 ff.). Mayr claims that this curious, historically engendered material breaks the bounds of traditional materialist and deterministic science. There are not only the traditional "proximate" causes, amenable to reductive analysis in terms of physical and chemical reactions. There are also "ultimate" causes, here understood as the historical evolution—the coming into being—of particular genomes, the ongoing interplay of genetic and phenotypic variation and environmental pressures (Mayr 1991: 52). The form-giving or -directing potentialities of historically engendered DNA are an enigma to classical materialist science, which in principle cannot capture, let alone rigorously predict, the complex and concrete interactions of organisms and their environments.

Mayr points to a third philosophic pillar of the Western tradition that is brought down: *cosmic essentialism* or typological thinking. Its demise is perhaps the most crucial of all (Mayr 1991: 40). The time-honored species types "dog," "cat," "rose," "human being"—with all individuals considered essentially the same and plagued only by accidental variations—are creatures of outmoded biological, philosophical, and theological conceptions and worldviews. Enter *populational* thinking at the core of evolutionary biology's explanations and explorations (Mayr 1991: 41 ff.). With rare exceptions, all organisms are genetically and phenotypically unique, different from all others. Species of organisms are now commonly understood as potentially or actually interbreeding populations of these organic individuals. The populations themselves are also considered to be concrete historical individuals, constituted by their individual organisms. Contra essentialist modes of thought, the variation among organisms is the very warp and woof of animate life on earth. Without genetic and phenotypical variation, there would be nothing for natural selection to select. Life could not adaptively evolve. What was peripheral to traditional worldviews is at the core of Mayr's new Darwinian worldview—a crucial shift in worldview perspective (Mayr 1991: 26 ff.).

Individual and World

The biological conception of an individual as a "populational being" initiates a sea change in philosophic thinking. An essentialist conception of an individual—that is, thinking of an individual either as an instance of a species type or as a being with its own unique and unchanging essence or character—easily lends itself to atomistic thinking. The individual is conceived as essentially unrelated to the world, alone by itself, in need of no other. (This is Descartes's definition of a substance.) Not so with a populational individual, an organism, which is fundamentally and necessarily tied to the historical world and a life carried out among others. There is a history behind the individual's nature, its life in the world, and its genome, which must interact with its environment if its nature is to emerge. Moreover, an individual must wade into the world to sustain itself and to reproduce.

Mayr's own philosophic worldview and commitments here come to the fore. Mayr is enamored with the diversity of life on individual, population, species, ecosystemic, and bioregional levels, and in life's history, present, and future. In biological explanation, philosophic interpretation, and moral reflection, he characteristically keeps a focused eye on particular, unique, individual organisms, always enmeshed within interacting populations and wider communities of life. He is fascinated by the plural and diverse ways that "tinkering" with animate nature purposelessly pulls off its evolutionary twists and turns. He celebrates life's particularities, contingencies, messiness, and openness to unplanned novelty.

In all this, Mayr remains a naturalist, materialist, empiricist, and pragmatist. He will accept only naturalist (and historical) explanations, no matter how conjectural or open-ended. He holds philosophic and theological rationalists—all who reason a priori—at bay. They are at bottom cosmic essentialists, believers in eternal and unchanging forms of reality, ill-begotten children of Plato. Yet he equally staves off old-time crude reductionists, physicalists, and determinists (for whom nature is at bottom nothing but the billiard-balls-in-motion) and insists on the central and ongoing importance of scientific and philosophic speculation—hypothesis making—held ever open to empirical refutation.

Finally, he insists on the importance of conceptual clarification in exploring the complex, fundamental facts of worldly life. For example, he draws a sharp distinction between cosmic teleology and "teleonomy," the informational programs of DNA that play a crucial role in organic development and behavior (Mayr 1991: 67). These genetic programs can be either closed (hard-wired) or open-ended (amenable to modification through environmental interactions). Mayr thereby repudiates cosmic goal-directedness while leaving open the possibility, if not necessarily the empirical reality, of a naturally circumscribed goal-directedness—potential free will and responsibility—for individual human beings (Mayr 1991: 154 ff.).

This is not to say that Mayr's evolutionary perspective escapes all philosophic riddles. How to reconcile material reality and human freedom has always plagued philosophers, prompting speculative flights that Mayr dismisses. Here remains a genuine philosophic sticking point. Can Mayr's new informational matter, DNA, and the natural world of which it is a part support a genuine if circumscribed human freedom as traditionally conceived? This is a question we should leave open. But at least Mayr has jogged our minds and refocused the terms of the argument and the framework of thinking from which we can retackle the issue. This is the philosophic bequest of Mayr's interpretation of the Darwinian revolution. With the philosophic demise of cosmic teleology, classical determinism, and essentialism, and in its stead the emergence of populational, evolutionary, and ecological thinking, we are offered an opportunity for approaching anew the perennial question of human freedom and responsibility, a question directly germane to our concrete worldly obligations to humans and nature.

The Evolutionary Orchestra

The novel implications of Mayr's philosophic worldview are crucial. Consider his claim of the autonomy of the biological sciences and evolutionary biology, ecology, and ethology in particular (Mayr 1997: xiii, 30). Mayr's nature is a dynamic realm from the molecular level of DNA all the way up, a world of Heraclitean flux and change. This newly conceived nature involves complex, developmentally and behaviorally related, teleonomic programs that emerge from a 3.8-billion-year evolutionary history. These historical dimensions supplement the atemporal laws and discoveries of the physical and chemical sciences. Biology in this sense transcends physics and chemistry; it is not reducible to them.

Furthermore, the presence of informational matter forces a reconceptualization of our understanding of causation. In Mayr's worldview causation is multileveled, comprising both proximate, physical-chemical and ultimate, informational-programmatic causes. The billiard-balls-in-motion model of causation—physical antecedents determining physical consequents, with no feedback loops, no overdeterminations, no emergent properties—is out (Mayr 1991: 66 ff.). "Orchestral causation" is in (Mayr 1991: 151–74). Mayr would have us imagine music performed by an orchestra. Who or what is the cause? The individual instruments severally, the interactions of the composer's programmed score, the players, the conductor, the sounds, the acoustics of the concert hall, and much more, including the differing "musical ears" of the audience. No single and singly sufficient causes are to be picked out. The result is unique, its character in principle unpredictable. It is a novel emergence from the interactions. Emergent properties issuing from the systemic interactions of worldly interactors, and the hierarchies of objects and emerging entities that such interactions engender—cells, organs, organisms, communities, and ecosystems—is a key concept for Mayr.

The concept of emergence also signals the break from the old hegemony of physics and chemistry in science. The concept of emergence raises once again the question of the nature of an individual organism or self—a favorite and central topic for Hans Jonas, as we have seen. For Mayr, the individual, the phenotype that we encounter in everyday experience, is apparently an "emergence"—continuously until it dies. It emerges from the interactions of genetic information, the cellular and bodily environment, and the wider ecosystemic, worldly environment (along with the organism's own history, if any). We have come a long way from Descartes's substantial, aworldly, and unchanging soul or mind.

The individual becomes one of the interacting participants in the process of generating the future. But, again, we are enjoined to keep in mind the centrality of "emergence." Organic, including human, individuality and worldly interaction go hand in hand. (Spinoza, in his critique of Descartes's notion of substance, had said as much.) Individuality conjoined with worldly interaction constitutes a gestalt shift, a conceptual reconfiguration, a moving beyond the traditional modes of thought. Again, note the possibility and the reality of ever more complex emerging individuals with open-ended teleonomic programs, up to and including our human selves. Note further that these fundamental themes of interaction and emergence rule out in principle any strict or reductive genetic or environmental "billiard-balls-in-motion" determinism. Conceptual room is left for contingency and chance, as well as for reflective, intentional, and responsible action.

Jonas: The Philosophy of Life

Hans Jonas provides his own neo-Darwinian critique of the Western philosophic and scientific tradition. In *The Phenomenon of Life* (1966), *Philosophical Essays* (1974), *The Imperative of Responsibility* (1984), and elsewhere, Jonas fastens on Descartes's original, rigid ontological dualism of mind and matter, existing in splendid isolation from one another. Cartesian dualism leaves no room for an adequate philosophic interpretation of organic individuals, identity, and bodily liveliness, human or other (Jonas 1966: 56, 58 ff.). It writes out of the picture real, psychophysical individuals who must make their precarious way in the world.

Jonas levels equally searing and telling critiques on the historical derivatives of dualism, idealism (the claim that all reality is essentially experience or mental functioning), and materialism (the counterclaim that all reality is essentially matter or physical functionings). Dismissing idealism as a self-congratulatory, nonserious story of the presence of mind and psychic phenomena in the world, Jonas focuses his critical attention on classical Newtonian materialism and its correlative epiphenomenalist thesis of mind and subjectivity. However, unlike Mayr, Jonas ranges biology with the deterministic sciences (Jonas 1966: 38 ff.). Here might be one reason Mayr considers Jonas wrong. For Mayr, Jonas does not plumb the depths of the Darwinian revolution and the philosophic implications of historical genomes and "ultimate causation."

Jonas's critique of the Cartesian philosophic cosmology is wide-ranging (Jonas 1984: 205 ff.). His basic contention is that scientific materialism, on its own terms, offers an untenable philosophy of nature and correlative philosophy of mind, subjectivity, or consciousness. Materialism's theory explodes in its face.

Yet Jonas further contends that logically scientific thought need never have strayed into this untenable position, which resulted from a radical lack of self-possession. Science confused itself with philosophy or metaphysics. It failed to distinguish its own methodology and quest for ascertainable, positive knowledge from the methods of philosophy and the rational desire to interpret, understand, or comprehend the nature of things, which is inherently a tentative and speculative adventure (Jonas 1984: 164, 242). Science equated what can be scientifically known or empirically tested with what concretely is, and thereby fatefully fell into what Whitehead termed "the fallacy of misplaced concreteness." Abstractions, a partial rendering of the fullness of facts or a simplified edition of reality, are taken for the complexly concrete. In the case of scientific materialism, the fallacy has an ironic result. The domination of the scientific mind over concrete nature leads to the effective cancellation of mind by that very nature, as scientifically or abstractly understood (Jonas 1984: 207, 215). Materialism wipes its feet out from under itself.

At the heart of the classical materialist theory of nature is the thesis of causal determinism, the hegemony of natural, efficient, "physical" causation. Nature is considered a self-sufficient and closed realm. Every real effect arises from antecedent physical causes and in turn plays a causal role in the determination of consequent physical effects (Jonas 1984: 207). Only in this way, it is claimed, are the well-established constancy laws of nature—for example, the conservation of energy—upheld.

This fundamental fact of physical, efficient causation rules materialism, in theory and practice (Jonas 1984: 639). Scientific experiments are set up to test causal hypotheses, generated in accord with the underlying theory. This is methodologically sound, for this is the only way we can come to know things scientifically, which is just this positive knowledge of causes and effects. The problem comes with the claim that this is all that we do know and that, moreover, this is the only way anything real can be. This is to take the materialist thesis into the bedrock of reality, rather than confining it to certain pervasive features of nature. This is the claim that universal physical determinism is at the bottom of all things. It is scientific theory and methodology fatefully turning metaphysical or philosophical. It is here that the materialist is in trouble, his flanks exposed. By the imperious demands of his own theory, the materialist is inexorably led into inconsistency, incoherence, and absurdity (Jonas 1984: 211 ff.). Brooking no anatural influences or realities from outside the physical realm, the materialist must swallow up man, his subjectivity, and his mind in his monistic thesis. Man in one way or another must be accommodated to the hegemony of physical causation and the constancy laws of nature. This leads to the epiphenomenalist theory of mind, subjectivity, or consciousness.

The materialist must confront the evident fact of mind, including his own, and the phenomena of our subjective life. We aboriginally experience the world and ourselves; enjoy worldly interests, emotions, and passions; originate proposals and fashion theories about the world; and entertain purposes felt to be effective in guiding behavior or bodily actions. So much "phenomenal fact" the materialist must accept, but then he turns philosophic interpreter and engenders his epiphenomenalist thesis, guided by his physicalist theory.

For the materialist, mind is the mere expression or "symbolic representation" of physical reality, curiously arising in conjunction with the central nervous system of certain complex biological organisms (Jonas 1984: 209–10). It is conceived as the most minimal of realities, a mere by-product of physical nature, with no efficacy of its own (Jonas 1984: 211). Nature spends no energy on this by-product "effect" of itself and remains unaffected by mind's impotent symbolic representations. Nature carries on its physically determined, dynamic affairs as if there were no such thing as the "shadow reality" of mind. Physical causation and the constancy laws reign untroubled and supreme. It follows that mind is a systematic self-delusion (Jonas 1984: 213). It inveterately convinces itself of its circumscribed freedom from bodily impingements—of its autonomy over its own thought processes and of its efficacy in purposively determining bodily actions, for example, in waving arms to say good-bye. In truth, the mind is wrong. The bodily organism waves the arm, for and with no intention or purpose. The felt experience of efficacious purpose is a ruse, a mere impotent subjective machination.

Moreover, the experienced autonomy of thought, the thinking self's generation of rationally connected ideas, is a similar fiction. The physical body is the non-energy-expending cause of each and every mental effect (Jonas 1984: 213). Flights of rational imagination are really internal, physically determined movements of the body. If in the age of theological dominion all power was attributed to God, in the age of materialistic science all power is attributed to matter or physical energy. In either age, human subjectivity loses its experiential, self-validating credentials and a foothold in efficacious reality. We radically impotent ones are not what we seem.

This is a philosophic nightmare, the issue of science straying ignorantly beyond its own finite bounds. In so doing, materialism violates its own fundamental tenet. Here is a cause (nature) producing an effect (mind) with no causal expenditure, and an impotent effect with no causal implications. In short, materialism cannot really get mind into its nature (Jonas 1984: 212). This is a fundamental theoretical inconsistency. Moreover, nature is scandalized. With no intention and purpose, nature produces a delusion (the potency) of subjectivity and purpose, which serves no purpose. Things continue to run as if there were no such impotent detours from the real course of things. Why then this extraneous superfluity? Conceptually, nature is rendered incoherent and absurd (Jonas 1984: 215).

The materialist himself fares no better than nature. If mind is radically impotent, if it can effect no purposes in bodily action and sustain no independent trains of rational thought, then the materialist undermines any claim to the validity and legitimacy of his own theory (Jonas 1984: 215). He is as dumb and brute as the rest of us. In any case, we are determined subjectively to ape the internal movements of our own bodies, which are not necessarily attuned to his. Here is the performance of self-canceling thought, the disappearance of a philosophic Cheshire cat, leaving only a grin behind.

We are truly at a philosophic midnight. In denying all causal potency to mind or subjectivity, the materialist has actually denied the very ontological possibility of subjectivity or mind. Subjectivity implies, most emphatically on the human level, an individual actor's activities, predicated on efficacious purposes. (An "effective purpose" is a concrete activity determined by something-to-be-realized [a goal] and having real consequences. It involves something either consciously or unconsciously aimed at, striven for, and more or less successfully achieved.) In denying effective purposes, the materialist denies the reality of activity and thus in turn the reality of actors, subjects, or minds, no matter how intimately tied to organic bodies. We have indeed vanished from the materialist's scene. Correlatively, with the demise of all activity, nature is left as a thoroughly vacuous and valueless realm, where nothing gets effected, because nothing can be aimed at, striven for, and achieved (Jonas 1984: 8). There are merely blind concatenations of physical forces, anyone as good as any other, because all are equally worthless. This is an unimaginable "sound and fury signifying nothing," a valueless landscape remote from the world we subjectively and normally enjoy.

We must recall Jonas's claim that all of this is unnecessary, the result of materialism gone metaphysical. It comes from the idealization, under the august model of mathematics, of empirical principles and theory (Jonas 1984: 208). Nature is granted the universal and absolute purity of abstract thought. This is a fundamental, Parmenidean error. However, scientific materialism does not need absolute or metaphysical determinism. Its measurements are finite and held to certain levels of observation. It requires only that the deterministic thesis—physical consequents determined by physical antecedents, engendering further physical consequences—holds

on its level of observation and most specifically that the "empirically discovered" constancy laws of nature not be violated.

Jonas argues that the reality and potency of mind or subjectivity is
not incompatible with "deterministic" science, if the latter is stripped of
its metaphysical pretensions (Jonas 1984: 216 ff.). At least it is not incompatible with modern quantum theory (Jonas 1984: 230). The freedom and
potency of the mind can work on the "micro level," below the admittedly
limited observations of science. The energy of the world can be deflected
through the free functioning of mental intentionality acting as a "trigger
principle," micro-activities with "macrocausal" bodily and worldly results.
Minimal energy expended by nature in engendering or upholding the
mind can be returned via the mind's efficacious direction of bodily processes. Thus the constancy laws of nature need not be violated. The energy
is only momentarily lost to the "physical realm" and to scientific sight
(Jonas 1984: 220–21).

Thus the materialist, as practicing scientist, need not worry about the
reality and efficacy of mental functionings. He or she need not turn philosopher. However, things are not so simple for the rest of us, especially as
this concerns how we are to act responsibly in our technological age. Here,
with respect to ethics, the reality of mind, subjectivity, and true individuality makes all the difference. The speculative gauntlet is thrown. Nature
and mind must be conceived as compatible, if not requiring one another.

Needful Freedom

Jonas credits the self-evidence of subjectivity, individual agency, and effective purpose that we find in ourselves. As against the reductionist methodology of the physical sciences, Jonas employs a philosophic "regressivist"
method in which he starts with human experience and works backward,
journeying down into the full realm of organic being. He accepts Darwin
and the evolutionary story, which places us in lines of common descent
from all sorts of life forms. Rather than blanch, Jonas embraces this fact. If
we are related to all forms of earthly life, and if we find subjectivity, individual agency, and effective purpose within ourselves, then we can legitimately expect to find them in organic, biological others, in other species,
no matter how attenuated. The method underpins his philosophic, phenomenological, and speculative interpretation of organic life (Jonas 1966;
see also Donnelley 1989; 1995).

Starting with the basic phenomenon of metabolism, Jonas interprets organic life and individual organisms in terms that transcend both Cartesian dualism and its derivatives. For Jonas, the metabolic mode of organic existence speaks for a freedom from the world within a wider dependence upon the natural, material world. Organisms enjoy an ontological status that he terms *needful freedom.* An organism and its identity are constituted by a *living form* existing beyond and through its passing material constituents. (This is the aboriginal instance and form of "needful freedom.") An organism's mode of existence requires the being of an active agent, a self-feeling subject, purposively concerned with itself and its very being. The living individual form, the organic self or individual, embodies an active "no to non-being, to the deadness and valuelessness of inorganic nature." According to Jonas, organic life is an ontological revolution in the history of matter, a radical change in matter's mode of being. Life involves an aboriginal introduction of value into the world, the reality of purposive being and the advent of the ontological and cosmological status of needful freedom, which establishes itself with metabolic existence. Our modes of philosophic thinking must register this shift or revolution in reality's being.

Jonas traces various dimensions of needful freedom from unicellular organisms through floral existence to animal being and human cultural existence. Through evolutionary history, ever more complex forms and capacities have emerged, each involving both new independence from and dependence on the world. New capacities of motility, emotion, perception, practical thinking, and theoretical speculation are introduced into worldly being and must then be used to pursue the newly capacitated existence. Organisms on all levels, their necessarily precarious lives, their value achievements and failures—these mortal, finite, and vulnerable ones—are thus given their philosophic due. Animate nature is philosophically rehabilitated, and human beings are naturalized.

Plainly Jonas emphatically accepts Darwinism and uses it for his own philosophic purposes. He is philosophically an organicist and naturalist, though not a scientific organicist. Yet he makes rather sparing use of Darwinian biology, especially of the role of genetic information. Darwin is characteristically in the background, assigned to footnotes, rarely the focus of central philosophic attention. Jonas is relatively uninterested in the grand evolutionary and ecological story, Mayr's natural symphony. Rather, he is attentive to the existential drama, the inner life and worldly adventures of individual organisms.

Here might be both a singular strength and lingering weakness of Jonas's philosophy. Its strength is in giving an internalist, phenomenological account of life—what it is and feels like to be an organism. Such an analysis complements Mayr's scientifically biological, "objective," more externalist account of life. But Jonas may miss or overlook the full sweep, grandeur, and value-laden nuances of the natural and historical drama. He may not sufficiently appreciate that earthly nature's constituents, biotic and abiotic, have coevolved; that life's forms, capacities, and individuals arise in communities interactively—biotic variation, diversity, and selection constantly at work. Jonas may undervalue the significance for ethics of the communal, cooperative, symbiotic, as well as competitive aspects of pre-human, and human, evolutionary and ecosystemic life.

More than critical questions of philosophic adequacy are at stake here. Rival worldviews stand head to head. Jonas is decidedly more the moral existentialist than Mayr. He has the more searching and wary ethical eye, seeking out not only the reprehensible and outrageous but also the laudable and noble. Though he had a connoisseur's appreciation of such philosophers as Heraclitus, Aristotle, and Spinoza, he did not share their serene cosmological, naturalists' exhilaration over the natural world, as Mayr did. Jonas had human historical scores to settle and pressing worldly responsibilities to champion.

Ontological Individuality, Active Being

Jonas holds that individuality implies something more than an entity being stubbornly there, a mere identical "it" firmly ensconced in a spatio-temporal scheme. He wishes to distinguish between real individuality and particular existence as such, which is possessed by all concrete entities. To warrant the title of a real individual, the concrete entity must also be internally related to itself. Individuality must have a hold in the entity itself, be something internally and essentially owned by it (Jonas 1974: 186). Jonas philosophically interprets the nature and origin of characteristics exhibited by individuals—the ascending range of biological organisms, up to, and including, man.

Jonas endeavors to take a stand "within": to understand what it is, and means, to be an individual from the inner perspective of the individual itself. From this exercise of rational imagination (a phenomenological enterprise), he concludes that individuality, as opposed to some mere

identity—individuality in any ontologically significant sense—is the preroga-
tive of a specific mode of existence, a peculiarity clinging to entities which
take up that mode of existing. These entities are biological organisms (Jonas
1974: 186–87). Their mode of existence is organic existence, which essentially
and fundamentally involves metabolic activity. As we shall see, this activity qua an existential necessity is decisive regarding the ultimate ground of
individuality.

To follow Jonas's line of thinking here and to appreciate his originality,
it is necessary to harken back to Whitehead's thought once more. To support
his conclusions, Jonas proposes initial criteria of individuality. Only entities
whose being is their own doing, their own task, are individual. Such entities
are "delivered up to their being for their being, so that their being is committed to them" (Jonas 1974: 187). So far, Whitehead and Jonas agree, and Whitehead could (from Jonas's perspective) legitimately posit actual entities qua
real individuals for whatever philosophic purpose he wishes—for example, to
account for the ultimate constituents of the world, or to account for ordinary
physical objects and their spatiotemporal interrelations. But then comes the
decisive break, a basic ontological divergence. For Jonas, individuals are committed to keep up their being by ever-renewed acts of it. Otherwise, they are
not (truly) individuals. For Whitehead, a real individual has no such opportunity or onus. An actual occasion, *qua a subject,* arises and perishes with its
one, epochal shot at self-existence. Ontologically, this means that a real individual cannot be a biological organism, considered in its full, ongoing integrity, and that an organism cannot be a real individual, with the particular
inner integrity enjoyed by an individual. Organisms are not one-shot deals,
at least not essentially; they propagate life.

In this divergence of philosophic opinion, the whole inner landscape of
an individual changes. For Jonas, the inner being of an individual is irrevo-
cably exposed to the alternative of not-being. It continually constitutes itself
or achieves its being in answer to this constant, potential imminence (Jonas
1974: 187). This means that individuals are entities "that are temporal in their
innermost nature, that have being only by ever becoming, with each moment
posing a new issue in their history" (Jonas 1974: 187).

With this shift in ontological perspective (which initially moves on the
level of "pre-systematic" discourse), essential characteristics of a real individual, as recognized or posited by Whitehead, must be newly understood
and newly interpreted. The real individual remains (through time) an acting
agent primarily, for itself an experience and an actor, not an object experi-

enced (Jonas 1974: 190). The individual's identity undergoes a sea change, qua a philosophic problem. Identity is a protracted effort, the self-creation of a particular integrity through continuous performance (Jonas 1974: 187). If the definiteness of this identity is unique, it is not unique once and for all.

Further, uniqueness of character is not the fundamental issue, as it is for Whitehead. Vital integrity, self-identity through time, is what is at stake for Jonas. Particular individuality, difference from all other reality, is a peculiar existential necessity, rather than a metaphysical obligation (perhaps serving some cosmic purpose). "*Difference* from the *other,* from the rest of things, is not adventitious and indifferent to them [individuals], but a dynamic attribute of their being, in that the tension of this difference is the very medium of each one's maintaining itself in its selfhood by standing off the other and communing with it at the same time" (Jonas 1974: 187). In sum, individuality is an existential achievement, won in the face of a world to which the individual is necessarily committed. Whitehead says as much. But his individuals, though free to be themselves, are metaphysically guaranteed. There is no existential risk involved, no possibility of *their* nonbeing before the term of their original performance. In that integrity is not the challenge of *continuing* integrity, it is not such a nerve-racking, existential issue. This is one of Jonas's explicit complaints against the adequacy of Whitehead's philosophy (Jonas 1966: 95).

However, there remains the initial, outstanding bone of contention. A natural universe filled to the brim with momentary real individuals stands against a natural universe that harbors relatively few, temporally enduring individuals, all else being the seemingly "dead" matter of inorganic nature, involving passive, extrinsic, or external identities—identities that merely happen or come about due to concatenations of blind forces. How are we to choose between these rival philosophic declarations? How are we to recognize real individuals and to distinguish them from pretenders to the throne of individuality?

The issue is complex. For Jonas, we are natively equipped with an epistemic arsenal that, if not conclusively deciding the outcome, nevertheless decisively controls or sets limits to philosophic speculation. We are real individuals, living creatures, ourselves. We know at firsthand the joys and horrors of internal identity, the struggle to maintain bodily (and psychic) integrity. We are our own clues to other individuals. Certain external signs speak for internal identity; others do not. Life recognizes life and its opposite, non-life (Jonas 1966: 81). What these signs are, I leave to later.

Organisms and Internal Identity

According to Jonas, organic identity, which *can* be observed by external signs, is a necessary and sufficient clue to internal identity (which *cannot* directly be observed) and thus to individuality. Anything that exhibits organic identity is an individual. Anything concrete that does not is not an individual, but a mere particular. This is Jonas's contention. As such, he places on himself the philosophic burden of explaining organic identity and all that it implies. By the fact of metabolic regeneration, organic identity must be different from physical identity—an identity of its own kind. During the course of its life, an organism is continuously changing its material constituents, physical identities, while remaining more or less the same (Jonas 1974: 190). As opposed to Whitehead, Jonas accepts in some form the (more) classical conception of physical identity—some concrete thing (energy or matter) continuously adventuring (blindly) through space-time, recognized only by the (greater or lesser) continuity of its spatiotemporal determinations (Jonas 1974: 188).* Whitehead, philosophically determined by the discontinuity demanded by his atomic theory of actualities (and perhaps by the quantum theory of modern physics), explains physical identity (over space-time) in terms of organic identity (Jonas 1974: 189). What remains is an ongoing *nexūs* of episodic actualities physically inheriting from one another, repeating or reaffirming certain forms of definiteness.

Jonas will have none of this inner dimension of experiential inheritance as the foundation of physical identity. He wishes to save such a dimension for organic creatures (Jonas 1966: 81). We have no warrant to attribute organic identity unless the concretum's identity is somehow *threatened*—unless there is a threat to its existence, felt and overcome by the entity, and recognized by us lively observers (Jonas 1974: 189). Molecules and stones, or their ultimate constituents, do not evince such internal threats.

Beyond the demand of epistemic agnosticism, Jonas wishes to reserve the rights of a "dead" nature, so that organisms (and their organic identities) remain the natural curiosities and the profound ontological puzzle they are (Jonas 1966: 95). He further wishes to preserve the fundamental role of death, of the threatening imminence of not-being, in the organism's self-constituting activities—something he feels Whitehead inadequately accounts for (Jonas 1966: 95). He thereby discharges a philosophic debt to Heidegger. This is not to say that, by so defending the uniqueness of the organic realm, Jonas does not bring philosophic difficulties down on his own shoulders. How can there be interaction between organic and inorganic nature (for example, in metabolism, vegetable and even animal)? How can life arise at all? These remain genuine, if unanswerable, philosophic puzzles for Jonas, which Whitehead's doctrine of actual entities and their prehensive relatedness (their "experiential" bonds) were meant to resolve.

Notwithstanding these philosophic perplexities, organic identity does not rest on physical identity, though the organism essentially requires its passing material constituents (Jonas 1974: 191). There is no physical record of its continuing identity. Organic identity is the identity of a *form* (through time), not of matter (Jonas 1966: 81). Further, it is not the continuing identity of a mere form, but of a self-constituting agent who realizes this living form of itself and continually does so (Jonas 1974: 194). Such a living form is ontologically "the whole structural and dynamical order of a manifold" (Jonas 1974: 92). This living form is what remains the same, thanks to the activities of an imminent agent continually replacing the materials of the structural and dynamic manifold.

The temporal continuity of this living form, this halfway house for physical identities, only transiently resident, is the telling sign, observable from some external perspective, of the internal identity of a real individual, a true subject as distinct from a mere object, an it (Jonas 1966: 80–81). We recognize such individuals because we share something in common—*metabolic activity, with all this entails*—of which we have an intimate, inner acquaintance (because we are continually living through it).

Metabolism with all it entails is the crucial foothold for Jonas, a provincial Archimedean point from which to weave an ontology of individuality and of organic life. It is a prelude (perhaps) to a general ontology, an alternative to Whiteheadian cosmology, a more adequate rediscovery of the philosophy of nature and life that was misplaced with Descartes and modern physical science.

Metabolic activity signifies, and originates, the ontological state of needful freedom (Jonas 1966: 80). Organic identity has to do with the relation between form and matter, in which the living form takes a certain priority over matter (Jonas 1966: 79). It has an independence or freedom relative to anyone passing collection of its material. This is the organism's fundamental freedom vis-à-vis the inorganic universe (Jonas 1966: 81). But to realize itself and to continue itself, the living form needs material constituents and their constant refurbishment. Thus this origin of freedom is balanced by the origin of need (Jonas 1974: 191). A certain independence from the material universe speaks likewise for a certain dependence on that universe. The ontological

individual, by virtue of its very self-constituting activity, stands in the relation of needful freedom to its surrounding environment (Jonas 1974: 193).

According to Jonas, this basic freedom of organism, this certain independence of form from its own matter, as realized in metabolic activity, is an
ontological revolution in the history of matter (Jonas 1966: 81). Thereafter,
the development and enhancement of this freedom or independence is "the
principle of progress in the evolution of life, which in its course produces new
[ontological] revolutions—each an additional step in the initial direction,
that is, the opening of a new horizon of freedom" (Jonas 1966: 81). But each
new freedom is a conditioned, or a relative freedom. It is balanced by new
necessities, new needs, by new kinds of dependency on a world from which
the organism never escapes. Freedom is always needful freedom. The very
variety and scope of an organism's needs, generated by its particular mode of
existing, is the mark of its excellence (Jonas 1974: 193).

The identity of the organism must be located in something that exercises and enjoys the freedom of *continuing* living form (Jonas 1974: 194). The
individual, as the originator and reoriginator of the form, requires "*internal
identity as the subject of its existing in actu*" (Jonas 1974: 195). The living,
dynamic form, passingly enmattered, itself must be understood as in service
to the self-related identity (Jonas 1974: 195). Metabolism is the function of
the lively, crisis-ridden organism, not organism the function of metabolism
(Jonas 1966: 78). The organism's existence is its own performance. It accords
its own identity, thanks to an immanent teleology, which marks the residing
and presiding individual (Jonas 1974: 193).

This fundamentally means that a real individual, according to Jonas, must
be a more substantial, lasting creature than Whitehead's epochal actualities.
Further, thanks to its dialectical relations with its own material substratum,
it (in a sense different and more radical than for Whitehead) engenders the
characteristics of its individual self. "This ontological individual, its very existence at any moment, its duration and its identity in duration is, then, essentially its own function, its own concern, its own continuous achievement"
(Jonas 1966: 80). In sum, according to Jonas's lights (in opposition to Whitehead), an individual's unity, potentialities of unique character, and potential
freedom do not arise from God, qua the guarantor of individuality. They arise
primordially in metabolic activity, in the ontologically novel, dialectical relation of form to matter.

Jonas emphatically underscores the essential finite organic nature, the
necessary dynamic relation of an organism to its environment. Need, indi-

gence, and insufficiency are no less unique distinctions of life than its powers (Jonas 1974: 195). This is the ontological message of metabolism.

The Characteristics of a Real Individual

For Jonas the ontological clues of metabolism, the signs of life's insufficiencies and powers, are philosophically decisive. It is with metabolic activity that we gain primordial philosophic explanation of all essential characteristics realized by individuals (Jonas 1966: 82). The characteristics are explained regarding their origins and their necessary mutual requirement. Such an investigation transforms the philosophic enterprise itself, as conceived by Whitehead and others—transforms the landscape of a real individual: both the nature of its fundamental characteristics and their explanation. At the center of this transformed landscape is the demand for temporal, enduring, worldly integrity (identity).

Teleology and Potentiality

As we have seen, metabolism signifies the twin, correlative virtues of life: liberty and existential necessity. An organism's being is suspended in possibility, the possibility to be or not to be (Jonas 1974: 195). This is the origin of potentiality in its most emphatic, ontological sense, as it is enjoyed by real individuals. To actualize the possibility of being, metabolism necessarily requires the use of the external environment. Thus the "world" originates, as a realm of real possibilities, as a counterpoise to existentially necessary activities. The world supplants or overlays the prior existence of a realm of external necessities, a more or less orderly whirlwind of blind forces. Possibility (in its meaningful, human sense), subjective and objective, comes on the scene with organic existence.

The origination of a world as a realm of possibility not only speaks for the advent of an individual in need. It necessarily marks the advent of teleological activity, the ontological answer to the individual's innermost possibility, which itself is a reflection of need. In short, need is the ultimate ground of possibility—entities qua possibilities for subjects, including the subjects themselves. Teleology necessarily implies possibility (in this restricted, important sense)—and vice versa. Thus this means that need and teleological activity originate, or come upon the cosmic scene, together. "*Teleology* comes in where the continuous identity of being is not assured by mere inertial persistence of a substance, but is continually executed by something *done*, and by something which *has* to be done in order to stay on at all" (Jonas 1974: 197). This demand for constant regenerative activity further augurs the ontological birth of the phenomenon of concern (Jonas 1974: 197). And finally, the basic concern and *telos* of an (organic) individual, the fundamental teleology of an individual, which is an answer to its wanting, is of a particular nature. It is "the acting out of the very tension of the polarities that constitute its being and thus the *process* of its existence as such" (Jonas 1974: 197). Here is teleo-logical activity where it really counts—in service of continuing existential performance, the organism necessarily pulling itself up by its own bootstraps, or, rather, by using its world.

The Self and the World

For Jonas, metabolic activity enacts within itself the cardinal polarities that characterize a real individual—not only the polarity of being and not-being, of freedom and necessity, but also the polarity of self and world (Jonas 1974: 196). He wishes to emphasize that "selfness," which is always self-constituting activity, and "worldliness" originate with metabolic activity. This is the cosmological and ontological origination of experience: both the subject who experiences and that which is experienced. Here is the original trans-formation of the mere universe into a world—such transformation always being effected from the side of the organic subjects. The world only exists for subjects.

The introduction of the term "self," unavoidable in any description of the most elementary instance of life, indicates the emergence, with life as such, of internal identity and hence, as one with that emergence, its self-isolation as well from all the rest of reality. Profound singleness and heterogeneity within a universe of homogeneously interrelated existence mark the selfhood of organism. An identity that from moment to moment reasserts itself, achieves itself, and defies the equalizing forces of physical sameness all around is truly pitted against the rest of things. In the hazardous polarization thus ventured upon by emerging life—that which is not "itself" and borders on the realm of internal identity from without assumes at once for the living individual the character of absolute otherness. The challenge of "selfhood" qualifies every-thing beyond the boundaries of the organism as foreign and somehow oppo-site: as "world," within which, by which, and against which it is committed to maintain itself. Without this universal counterpart of "other," there would be no "self" (Jonas 1974: 196).

Whether all organisms—and organisms at all times—feel such existential anxieties is another question. Unfortunate are those organisms which are visited frequently by such Hobbesian (or Gnostic) moods. There are sunny days when the world, and its resident creatures, invite pleasant commerce. Nevertheless, Jonas's philosophic message is clear. Selfhood is foremost a challenge, not a metaphysically guaranteed opportunity—the challenge of winning the bodily self in the face of, and by means of, the external other.

For Jonas, organic individuality presents a paradox. The organic individual exists at any one time in a simultaneous composition of stuff—its necessary physical, or material, basis. Yet it is not identical with this basis, for, while coinciding with it, it is already in the act of passing beyond it (Jonas 1974: 191). The organism lives as a whole through its entire life span, which means living as a whole in the various material compositions through which it passes. It is no classical substance, but a changing subject of change, which fights to keep its integrity through change.

Further, in that an organism is essentially a "moving beyond the given condition," an openness or a horizon is intrinsic to its very existence (Jonas 1974: 197). "Concerned with its being, engaged in the business of it, it must *for the sake* of this being let go of it as it is now so as to lay hold of it as it will be" (Jonas 1974: 197). Such a basic, forward-looking concern necessarily means, most pointedly with the emergence of animal existence, the advent of temporal and spatial horizons—the inner horizon of temporality and the outer horizon of spatiality, both yoked together by the fundamental, active concern. In short, Jonas can give an account of *why* there is world-experience. He need not resort to a category of the ultimate and other supporting metaphysical principles. There are cosmologically provincial, non-metaphysical reasons—that is, creatures living under the onus of metabolic activity.

Unity and the Problem of Wholeness

As expressed above, Jonas feels that, with living organisms, nature has sprung an ontological surprise. Here are systems of matter that are real unities of a manifold, inexplicable by the mere concurrence of the forces which bind their parts together—that is, inexplicable on purely mechanistic, causal terms (Jonas 1966: 79). Wholeness is no mere accident, no mere phenomenal or extrinsic by-product of subterranean machinations. Organisms are real, composite unities "in virtue of themselves, for the sake of themselves, and continually sustained by themselves. Here *wholeness* is self-integrating in active performance, and form for once is the cause rather than the result of the material collections in which it successively subsists. *Unity* here is self-unifying by means of changing multiplicity. *Sameness,* while it lasts, is perpetual self-renewal through process, borne on the shift of otherness" (Jonas 1966: 79; emphasis added).

Such active self-integration is the essence of a real individual and founding for its ontological conception. Jonas emphasizes self-initiated activity in service of continuing a unity, of continuing an integrity. Unity comes out of unity, integrity out of integrity.

What are the advantages of Jonas's philosophic stance? Unity and individuality are active, existential achievements, with no metaphysical guarantees. As such, there are, and can be, greater and lesser degrees of unity and individuality, depending on the grade of the organism involved and *on its particular performances.* "To be an individual means not-to-be-integrated with the world, and the less so, the more it is an individual. Individuality implies discontinuity" (Jonas 1974: 204). This fundamental message of organic existence, already presaged on the metabolic level, lends intelligibility to certain organic developments—and to the world that opens forth on the basis of these developments.

These organic developments basically concern the centralization of organic individuality, as evidenced in animal existence. This augurs the introduction of new needful freedoms, new ways of serving basic metabolic functions—for example, the concomitant development of powers of motility, perception, and emotion (Jonas 1974: 198). Such developments necessarily imply the centeredness of the one self, with its various powers. The existential functions of the (complexly diverse) sensing self, the emotional self, and the motile self must be pooled in, or emanate from, a single center if they are to issue, as coordinated, in informed, controlled action, serving metabolic (and other) needs (Jonas 1974: 190–200).

This centeredness necessarily implies greater individuality, a more fixed internal identity, a more pronounced unity (Jonas 1974: 201–3). An organism enjoying the advantage of a developed centeredness is less dependent upon, and thus less integrated with, its immediate environment. A far-seeing animal with far-reaching, sustained emotions may roam far in pursuit of food— and in avoidance of enemies. That it must do so, once committed to such a mode of self-nurturing, goes without saying. And there can be perceptual, emotional, and motor breakdowns. The animal may find itself longing for the more domestic, less adventurous life of a plant. Nevertheless, during its season of success, the animal enjoys a self-constituted identity and integrity beyond that enjoyed by a plant. The animal may pick the time and place of its foraging, reverse its field, and take time-outs to rest comfortably with itself (Jonas 1974: 201). Thanks to its concentrated centeredness, evidenced by the development of a central nervous system (Jonas 1974: 200), the animal may run around the world—perceptually, emotionally, and physically—without losing its hard-won sameness (Jonas 1974: 203). It is the same animal that whets its appetite by gazing upon prey from a perch on the rock, and finds itself in hot pursuit of its dinner. A plant could not tolerate such up-rootedness, without losing a hold on itself.

Jonas holds that individuality and freedom in organic existence apply fully only on the level of "centered" animal existence (Jonas 1974: 201). The centeredness of animal organization underscores the "indivisibility which lies in the literal meaning of individual" (Jonas 1974: 204). Yet it is the organism as a whole that is centered, that is the central agent controlling its own parts and functions (Jonas 1974: 200). Centeredness does not mean the loss of the organism's full integrity qua an ontological individual. Individuality does not escape into some ethereal center, to preside over a material country alien to itself. The living form, and thus the individual, extends to the frontier of its body—barring some catastrophe, in which case it must pull in its boundaries.

Individuality is always biological individuality. This necessarily means the tension of selfhood and world (Jonas 1974: 205). The accentuation of this tension is the accentuation of life itself. What results is a more pronounced (organic) self standing over and against a more pronounced world (Jonas 1974: 205). The two necessarily go hand in hand, for both result from the self-constituting activities of the one organic individual.

Organic Life, Worldly Interaction, Ethical Responsibility

Mayr and Jonas have moved us beyond the old philosophic cosmology of Descartes, Newton, and their heirs. The new philosophic cosmologies of Mayr and Jonas, meant explicitly to interpret or further the understanding of organic life, are both centrally "interactionist" in character: they emphasize the essential dynamic relatedness of individual organisms and populations of organisms, humans included, to the historical, temporally deep world. This worldly "interactionist" insight also illuminates how Mayr and Jonas arrived at their respective worldviews, and how we may make the best use of them.

In considering any one thinker, there is a mutual interaction between the individual's philosophic worldview, scientific understandings, ethical convictions, and personal engagement with the world. These various dimensions of experience mutually inform one another without being reducible to one another. In particular, when it comes to deeply felt, compelling ethical demands, our primary interactions with the world have the final, if not also the first, word. Our past experiences, including our philosophic, scientific, and ethical training and reflections, no doubt pour into our present selves, out of which all our personal worldly future must proceed. Yet, certain rationalist philosophers notwithstanding, it is in the primary encounters and interactions with the world that we first experience and respond to ethical obligations, no matter how "informed" we are by prior conceptual, intellectual, and cultural adventures. The experience of ethical oughts or obligations, while nurtured and prepared by natural and cultural evolution, is an aboriginal existential, organismal response to the world, characterized by a "moral" emotional hue (the feeling of obligation). We have other, similar, aboriginal existential and organismal responses—aesthetic, religious, and others. These are the emotion-laden value dimensions of our primary encounters with the world. Here is the worldly setting of our human freedom and responsibility.

This interactionist perspective directly confronts the nagging charge that moral and philosophic naturalists commit the "naturalistic fallacy" of trying to derive "ought" from "is"—of trying to get moral obligations from facts about the world. Consider the "interactionist" alternative. Are my philosophic, scientific, and ethical reflections influenced or informed by my experiences of "what is," my ongoing primary experiences or interactions with the world? Most certainly. Are my ethical obligations logically or rationally derived from "what is" (worldly reality) or from what I take to be worldly reality? No. The mutual interactions of philosophy, science, ethics, and primary worldly experience do not seem to be rationally or logically connected in this sense. The process of mutual informing or influencing is not one of logical deduction. New naturalist or organicist worldviews do not bow to the hegemony of deductive mathematical or logical reasoning—a bad model for philosophy, according to Whitehead. (Note how tight logical reasoning of the mind mirrors strict causal determinism of the body in Cartesian-inspired worldviews. Spinoza's *Ethics* is the unsurpassed example.) Wanting our ethical life to be deeply informed by what we take to be worldly reality, its vulnerabilities to harm and its opportunities for realizing multiple goods, is not to commit the rational blunder of the naturalistic fallacy. It is an attempt to be humanly intelligent, realistically coherent, and deeply responsible to what is and what can be.

This squaring of accounts with the philosophic tradition leads immediately back to Mayr and Jonas. Their final philosophic visions may be in tension with one another, and we may consider that one is more scientifically informed than the other. But this does not mean that one or the other speculative philosophic and ethical worldview is less relevant or adequate to our primary encounters with the world. They may fasten upon and articulate different features of primary and interactive worldly experience, which need not be incompatible with one another.

The inexhaustible richness or complexity of the world as experienced by us humans is not to be captured in any one philosophic, scientific, or ethical worldview. (Most of us have already given up this old rationalist dream.) And the fact of theoretical finitude suggests that a plurality of significant, more or less adequate worldviews is a boon, rather than a curse, in helping further disclose the fullness of our ethical responsibilities to the world, to nature, and to ourselves. Mayr is the philosopher and ethical champion of natural and human *becoming*—of natural and cultural processes, systems, and forms in all their glorious, worldly diversity. Mayr would have us ensure that this grand human and natural show flourishes indefinitely.

Jonas is the philosopher and ethical champion of organic and human *being*. He is less stunned by the innumerable material forms and processes of life than by the very fact of life itself and especially organic life's capacity for moral responsibility, evidenced in human beings. That in a vast universe characterized largely by inorganic, dead matter there has emerged animate and moral being as a revolt against death and valuelessness—these are the realities above all that Jonas enjoins us to protect into the indefinite future.

Both Mayr and Jonas not only write about but themselves exemplify the interaction of philosophy, biology, ethics, and primary experience, although the interaction plays out differently for each. Jonas, veteran of twentieth-century wars and witness of their atrocities, stares modern life and technology in the face and calls for new philosophic and ethical reflection and vision: the centrality of ethical responsibility to the long-term human and natural future, backed by corresponding philosophic and metaphysical reflection. He incorporates what evolutionary biology he deems necessary into his philosophy and ethics.

Mayr incorporates those philosophic conceptions that serve his biological explorations and critical reflections. His moral life and commitments are significantly (though not exclusively) informed by his knowledge of and his passion for nature. Whatever the overlap, the accents of the organicist philosopher Jonas and the philosophic biologist Mayr are markedly different, thanks to their primary worldly experiences, interests, and passions.

Responsible Being and Being Responsible

There remains only the question of the locus or the focus of human ethical concern. Given an eternal God or Nature and the necessary vicissitudes of modal existence, Spinoza's *Ethics* marches inexorably to issues of individual human freedom, the humanly good life, and the politically liberal institutions required for such humanly conative existence. The rest of the conative realm is, and could be, left to its own devices given the atemporal and invulnerable eternity of divine/natural activity.

In Darwinian cosmology, the locus of ultimate ethical concern by necessity shifts. Darwin's and our ultimate locus of concern is the historical realm (past, present, and future) of natural and cultural becoming itself. (Here is a realm of being/becoming truly worthy of ultimate, "religious" respect, awe, and gratitude.) In this realm, nothing is assured or can be taken for granted. All life alike and on all levels is finite, mortal, and vulnerable—especially now—to our human misadventures. Thus moral responsibility to the human and natural future must take ethical pride of place. This responsibility must become a chief ingredient of the humanly good life and the exercise of individual freedom.[†]

Notes

*Author's note: Whether all nature is "alive" or, rather, whether we may with epistemic legitimacy speculate about the concrete reality of inorganic nature is perhaps the final, real bone of contention between Whitehead and Jonas from which all else follows—Jonas finding it more judicious to assume an agnostic stance toward "that which we cannot know."

†Editors' note: In his previously published work on Jonas, Donnelley had come to the point of seeing the importance of Jonas's late work on ethical responsibility in the development of a new philosophic cosmology. Hence the discussion in chapter 18 follows along the trajectory of the philosophical revision discussed here in chapter 17.

Life and the Ethics
of Responsibility

Boris Pasternak, in "Translating Shakespeare," speaks of Hamlet as one whom chance has allocated "the role of judge of his own times and servant of the future," the high destiny of "a life devoted . . . to a heroic task" (Pasternak 1959: 131). Hans Jonas was such a judge and can do great service for our future. In *The Imperative of Responsibility: In Search of an Ethics for the Technological Age* (1984), Jonas casts a critical eye upon the unprecedented powers of modern technological civilization. He fears that our age is rapidly moving toward global ecological and human disaster. Nature, specifically the realm of organic life, cannot long withstand the technological assault. Jonas calls upon us to renounce utopian dreams of human mastery over the conditions of life and to exercise a new responsibility commensurate with our novel powers. Our ethical responsibility, and our fateful ontological option, is to do what is necessary to ensure the ongoing, worldly integrity of man and living nature into the indefinite future.

The signaling of ecological and moral crisis is by now commonplace. However, Jonas's recognition that traditional systems of ethics lack the resources to cope with our unprecedented technological powers, and his endeavor to fill the philosophic and practical vacuum with an "ethics of responsibility," are anything but ordinary (Jonas 1984: ix–x, 128). The fashioning of a new ethics of responsibility is Jonas's heroic task, summoning the full resources of his philosophic abilities and originality. We are taken into previously uncharted waters, and it is important to appreciate carefully the nature and force of his argument.

According to Jonas, the very forces that have spawned our new and fateful powers of action, in particular the twin giants of modern science and technology, have significantly undermined philosophy and ethical theory. The modern philosophy of nature and its practical applications, scientific materialism and its technological successes, have conquered our minds. Philosophy and ethics have been set in disarray, just when they are needed the most. At the heart of the conquest is scientific materialism's forcible theoretical denial of the autonomy of thought and the reality of intrinsic values, ethical or otherwise (Jonas 1984: 22–23).

The modern philosophy of nature is the crux of our philosophic problems and the chief obstacle to an adequate theory of ethical obligations. Jonas squarely fastens on this cardinal issue. He held that the initial fateful move came historically amidst the rise of modern science, with Descartes's dualistic partition of the world into *res extensa* and *res cogitans*. All purpose, subjectivity, and value were banished from nature into mind. Nature was left valueless and dead, a mere play of mechanical forces or efficient causation, just as the new mathematical science required. Correlatively, organic life was written out of this philosophic scene altogether. Organisms were reduced to natural mechanisms. Thinking and its valuations, including ethics, reasonably held their own as long as the autonomy of the mind was upheld, as with Descartes and Kant. Yet logically even here all values and valuations had to be decidedly anthropocentric or theocentric. At least, they could not concern the intrinsic worth of nature, for now by metaphysical fiat it had none. Moreover, backed by the successful thrust of scientific materialism, belief or confidence in an extramundane deity and the autonomy of mind or reason was undercut. Even anthropocentric values lost a legitimate home and any philosophic justification. Blind and arational forces of nature reign supreme, in theory if not in practice. Such forces require and can have no philosophic, rational, or ethical justification (Jonas 1984: 22–23).

This is the dominant cultural and philosophic situation that confronts us and that requires such radical measures to overcome—measures needed to save philosophy, ethical theory, and perhaps in the end the very existence of man and organic life. Although *The Imperative of Responsibility* aims foremost at establishing our practical obligations in the face of technological power and potential ecological disaster, Jonas's argument unobtrusively but crucially involves an explicit and damning critique of the philosophy of nature and the philosophy of mind espoused by scientific materialism (Jonas 1984: 205 ff.). Out of the ruins of the discredited philosophic materialism, Jonas speculatively proposes a new theory of nature that philosophically rehabilitates nature, life, mind, and objective values, and that serves as the ontological and justifying ground of the new ethics of responsibility.

Nature Revalued: The Philosophy of Purposive Being

Jonas begins his substantive speculations and the crucial philosophic rehabilitation of nature by returning to human subjectivity its own self-validating credentials (Jonas 1984: 64–65). We are what we seem. Philosophically, this means taking the inner testimony of our subjective life seriously. This specifically entails recognizing the circumscribed potency of subjectivity and crediting the reality of efficacious purposes in determining autonomous trains of thought and bodily activities.

Moreover, in philosophical speculation we must bow before well-established scientific and empirical facts. Minds or subjectivity are nowhere found independent of physical, organic bodies. In fact, we know directly from inner experience that the activities of mind are impossible without our bodies and the surrounding world. The mind lives off the primary objects of its thoughts, the world abroad, and the interests and emotions arising from the worldly involved organism. In short, if we were not biological organisms, we would and could not be efficaciously purposive subjects or minds.

Further, we know and must take seriously the now incontrovertible fact that all organic life has evolved out of and remains within nature. This fact, coupled with the ultimate organic and worldly grounds of all subjective and mental activities, blocks the serious entertainment of dualistic theses and the intrusion of mind, subjectivity, or soul from some anatural elsewhere (Jonas 1984: 66–67). Philosophically we can no longer accept anatural or antinatural ontological principles. We are all, or should be, post-Darwinian, scientists and philosophers alike. In any case, radical Cartesian dualisms and their like have always been hounded by fatal flaws of incoherence or inconsistency, the problem of bringing dual features of reality—for example, mind and body—rationally together. Things fundamentally or substantially dissimilar do not easily fit into a single scheme of things. The urge toward a philosophic "monism" that respects the full diversity and complexity of the real has always been the more rationally attractive option.

Jonas explicitly adheres to this rational desire to weave a coherent story of man and nature. He starts with the self-evident and widely attested fact of man's subjective potency and employs an eminently sensible philosophic method. Whereas science reduces natural phenomena to their underlying physical causes, which "explain" them scientifically (the "reductionist method"), philosophy in its "interpretation" of concrete nature must work regressively (Jonas 1984: 69 ff.). If man is thoroughly a natural and organic being, and if man exhibits the reality of effective purposes, then purposiveness must be a fundamental principle of reality, reigning in various degrees of intensity throughout nature, as intertwined with "physical" or efficient causation. Nature manifestly shows itself in man, and we must "work back" from the evidence of ourselves.

Human interests, aims (purposes), feelings (emotions), thinking, and bodily activities are all intertwined natural principles and as such can be judiciously or critically employed in philosophically interpreting, if not scientifically explaining, the natural realm (Jonas 1984: 71–72).

In sum, these characteristic human features naturally result from and are ongoingly involved in the dynamics of the natural realm. Using the regressive method and brooking no radical leaps or discontinuities in nature (philosophic monism requires such a principle of continuity [Jonas 1984: 69]), we are rationally justified in asserting that effective purposiveness is a fundamental feature of natural being.

This is decisive. This basic assertion underlies Jonas's bold and original speculative philosophy. The philosophic interpretation of the world and ourselves undergoes a systematic sea change.

Most fundamentally, nature is rehabilitated as a significant realm of existence. It is a realm that harbors its own overall value and specific concrete values, its own intrinsic goodness, and its own "ends-in-themselves" (Jonas 1984: 80 ff.). The materialist's nature, we recall, is inherently valueless, a mere dynamic concatenation of blind physical forces, in which there is no true subjectivity or activity. It is merely and contingently there, indifferent to itself. With respect to value, it is indistinguishable from nothingness or nonbeing.

Not so with purposive nature or being. Individual instances of subjective activity and purpose are the concrete self-affirmations of being in the face of the ever-present potential of not-being or nothingness (Jonas 1984: 81). With subjectivity there is an ever-recurrent and active "no-to-nonbeing," a primordial self-assertion that intrinsically matters to being itself. For Jonas, nature is anything but a realm of indifference. With purposiveness, natural reality becomes inherently dramatic. In ontologically staving off nonbeing, it creates its own particular forms, values, and goodness in passing. (A concrete, natural value is the mating of individual purposive activity and definite form.) The primordial value and goodness of "nature active" is precisely this purposive staving off of nothingness and value-lessness. There is an "infinite distance," an incommensurability, between purposive being and nothingness (Jonas 1984: 46). Concrete purposive activities, laden with their own particular values, are emphatic being over against the purposeless nothing, an absolute chasm never "in reality" to be traversed. Thus individual purposive beings are the aboriginal and self-justifying "ends-in-themselves," ontologically harboring intrinsic "value-in-itself" and "goodness-in-itself" (Jonas 1984: 81, 83).

These philosophic reflections and speculations bring us directly to our contemporary cultural and ethical situation. The ontological facts and achieved results of purposive nature and our natural estate determine both the capacity and the need for ethical responsibility (Donnelley 2002). We now urgently require a substantive philosophy to reveal and to clarify our objective obligations. In us, purposive nature has potentially overrun her-self (Jonas 1984: 138). The vulnerability and finitude of nature and our-selves—with the threats to nature's goodness and intrinsic worth that issue from newly empowered, technological man—must be met by our aborigi-nal but circumscribed powers to say no to not-being (Jonas 1984: 139–40).

Nature and Ethics: The Theory of Responsibility

Jonas's theory of ethical responsibility rests on violating two cardinal prin-ciples of modern philosophy: there can be no metaphysical truth, and no "ought" can be derived from what "is." Both tenets hold within a philosophy crucially determined by scientific materialism (Jonas 1984: 44). If scientific, empirically verifiable knowledge is the epistemic benchmark for all that we can know or understand, then metaphysics, which offers a "speculative," conceptual comprehension of reality, must be an idle pursuit (Jonas 1984: 45). If nature or being is, as the materialism takes it to be, an inherently val-ueless physical realm, then indeed no "ought" can be derived from an "is" (Jonas 1984: 130). Valueless being can offer no clues about what would be for the better or for the worse, let alone establish the foundation of ethical obligation. But nature and life are not devoid of inherent ontological value. Over crucial matters, the fundamental ontological facts of selves and the world determine what we ought, and ought not, to do (Jonas 1984: 131 ff.).

This philosophic reintroduction of value into nature has its darker side. In an indifferent nature, nothing can harm, and nothing can be harmed. The opposite holds in purposive nature. Under its own worldly spur, nature evolves concrete purposive individuals, acting subjects, that are by ontological necessity finite, mortal, and vulnerable (Jonas 1984: 5, 81). In their self-constituting self-affirmations, the natural actors do not merely face blank nothingness. Rather, they necessarily face and essentially depend on each other and on dynamically evolving nature as a whole. In its various and recurrent self-affirmations, purposive activity is fundamentally the meeting of natural, biological necessities and the confrontation with worldly others to which the purposive individual is essentially tied (Jonas 1984: 198). This is the fundamental message of the metabolic existence of biological organisms, nature's most elaborate entities. (Metabolic existence and purposiveness go hand in hand.) Organisms can be only by ever becoming and by riding the crest of relation to the worldly other. In this necessary truck with the world abroad, an organism's purposes can be frustrated and its achievements destroyed, most importantly its own active endeavor to be. To gain entrance into the worldly web of purposive existence is to assume a circumscribed potency constantly threatened and eventually overcome. In short, the fundamental value and goodness of nature active and its inherent vulnerability are intrinsically tied together.

To understand critically Jonas's substantive philosophic vision of nature, we must be clear about what he means, and does not mean, by natural purposiveness and his regressive analysis. He does not claim that conscious human subjectivity is diffused throughout nature in more or less minimal forms. Subjective activity does not necessarily imply consciousness, and purposiveness as such presupposes neither (Jonas 1984: 72–73). To gain a coherent picture of dynamically evolving nature, Jonas speculatively posits concrete instances of "psyche," striving, or aim (that is, purposiveness) that are not individual organisms or subjects in the emphatic biological sense (Jonas 1984: 71). These "inorganic" strivings underlie a natural "telos" of the universe to evolve concrete instances of organic life and individual subjects proper (Jonas 1984: 74–75). (The cosmic reality of purposiveness underlies the advent of subjectivity and conscious mentality; subjectivity and mind do not underlie the reality of purposiveness.) Living organisms are concrete intensifications of nature's primordial purposiveness, the means employed to realize the overall general aim of nature, which is to gain an effective natural foothold and empathic intensification of purposiveness itself, being's own effort to be. Thus Jonas speculatively interprets the coming-to-be of organic and human life within the natural universe (Jonas 1984: 75).

This means that, ontologically, intrinsic value, goodness, and "ends-in-themselves" are not inherently tied to human subjectivity or consciousness. In varying degrees, they are spread throughout nature, most emphatically in the organic realm of life and perhaps minimally beyond. This blocks any overweening anthropocentric vision of the world and philosophically establishes the objective status of intrinsic values, the good, and self-justifying natural beings and activities. The realm of value no longer threatens to be swallowed up and lost in an arbitrary human subjectivity or will radically independent of the natural world.

Correlatively, with our anchoring in natural reality, we are enlightened about our status in the scheme of things and about our circumscribed powers and inherent limitations. In Jonas's monistic vision, we are interpreted as purposive nature's most elaborate performance, engendered in its dynamic ongoingness. In us, efficacious purposiveness has become emphatically subjective and individual, conscious and desiring of itself, moving decisively beyond organic others (Jonas 1984: 129). In our interdependence, in our essential relations with nature and our own human past, present, and future, we have become nature's most significant actors. We are purposive nature become cultural, political, scientific, technological, artistic, religious, philosophical, and moral. But all these decidedly human powers and characteristics are circumscribed and limited. They have not flown in from elsewhere, with an adequacy and sufficiency all their own. They are the issue of the slow evolutionary workings of nature, of which we more and more have become an active agent (Jonas 1984: 27).

Powers of sensory discrimination, emotion, thought, and bodily activity have evolved to meet worldly necessities and to take advantage of worldly opportunities. No powers have been greater than the sustained emotional interest, the vivid imagination, and the conceptual thought that are the natural dynamos behind our science and technology. But even here we remain nature's creatures, plagued and perhaps blessed by mortality, finitude, and vulnerability. We are neither gods nor angels. Jonas emphasizes that we are by nature better equipped to perceive error than to discover final truth, to recognize an imposing *malum* than to ascertain clearly the *summum bonum* (Jonas 1984: 27). Life more or less lives straightforwardly until pressed. Scientific, philosophic, and moral insight are born as much from worldly crisis as from indwelling eros and are always "unfinished."

The key to the objective grounding of obligations and the moving of ethics beyond the bounds of the arbitrary subjective will of man is to discover intrinsic value or a final "good-in-itself" within being (Jonas 1984: 49, 77–78, 84). Jonas recognizes this intrinsic goodness in the general purposiveness and the concrete purposive beings of nature (Jonas 1984: 75). Such ultimate value and goodness, constituted by entities actively fending off nonbeing—the struggle within metabolic life between being and nothingness—has a moral claim on human action. It should subsist. It should be preserved. The goodness of the self-affirmation of being, in which being is concerned with itself, is its own justification and is recognized as such by us, thanks to our own aboriginal status as self-affirming, purposive beings (Jonas 1984: 80).

This primordial "ontological ought" becomes a "moral ought" in the worldly situation in which we find ourselves (Jonas 1984: 80 ff.). Naturally purposive beings, who "ought-to-be" and who are intrinsically finite and vulnerable, come within the reaches of our human power (Jonas 1984: 92 ff.). We can affect them for better or for worse; we can wrong or harm them or benefit and allow them to pursue. Moreover, we are aware of our power and responsibility to do what sustains the good of vulnerable life. In virtue of our native, worldly powers of controlled action, knowing, and circumscribed freedom, the "ought-to-be" of the vulnerable ones becomes the "ought-to-do" of ourselves (Jonas 1984: 89, 93, 129 ff.). Natural being significantly determines human moral action.

The feeling of objective obligations to valuable and vulnerable others is the feeling of responsibility, for which nature has prepared us in the intimate family relation of parent and child (Jonas 1984: 85, 95). The newly born needy one, instinct with purposive life and human capacities to come, ever threatened with nonbeing, addresses those who brought it into existence with the "demand" for care (Jonas 1984: 134). To respond to the insistent demand that issues from the newborn is to act responsibly. Not to do so is to be irresponsible. Over this natural responsibility, there is no choice. Our moral freedom is tied (Jonas 1984: 95). This paradigm of responsibility for our own offspring is the model for the responsibility for the care of all of life and nature.

It is out of such native soil of worldly responsibility that we have creatively evolved as complex moral creatures and philosophically can develop a fleshed-out theory of ethical responsibility (Jonas 1984: 98 ff.).

The substantive content of an ethics of responsibility is determined by the particular ontological facts that pertain to both the objects and the subjects of ethical obligation. This is ethics determined by the concrete, fundamental nature of the constituents of the world, imperatives arising from the abiding character of organic and human life.

To repeat the fundamental facts, organisms, as mortal and vulnerable purposive beings, necessarily live an interdependent existence. Concrete life carries on only by a metabolic mode of existence that requires individual encroachment on the worldly, organic other and the symbiotic balance of the biospheric whole (Jonas 1984: 137). Nestled within this wider realm of life, there have evolved the purposive powers of man, his freedom from nature as within nature. Among these powers is moral responsibility itself, which requires the intertwined capacities of sensory discrimination, emotional feeling, rational insight, will, and bodily activity.

Man's complex, native power of moral responsibility is what the organic realm of life objectively, if silently, addresses. The "cause of the world," the upholding of the already realized manifoldness and intensity of purposive being, objectively binds us to protect and promote the ongoing realization and integrity of man and organic nature into the indefinite future (Jonas 1984: 38 ff.).

In a time of overweening and collective technological power, with its indefinite global and temporal reach, we are ethically enjoined to take care and be cautious (Jonas 1984: 38). Human powers of action dangerously outstrip capacities for knowledge and wisdom. We are to do nothing that would throw evolved man and nature disastrously off balance, threaten their creative being, and thwart their emergent complexity. With respect to man, this specifically means ensuring the continuing potential for morally responsible action—that man's circumscribed but potent capacities for freely taking care of himself and the world be kept intact (Jonas 1984: 99 ff., 117). The concrete ontological essence of man, and whatever we can discern of it in our philosophic "images of man," must find its realization in the indefinite worldly future (Jonas 1984: 43). Given the essential interdependence of all life, this necessarily further entails protecting the ongoing integrity of the organic realm, whose intrinsic goodness and decided significance for the humanly good life already lay objective obligations on us, independent of narrow self-interest (Jonas 1984: 8, 136). The demise of either man or organic nature, but most emphatically of nature's "highest creature," would be an infinite loss. That we, through irresponsible ignorance or indifference, should be responsible for such an infinite loss, such an ultimate sin against the goodness of being, should make us shudder (Jonas 1984: 42 ff.). We should cringe before the possibility of such guilt.

In sum, the objective goodness of things that "ought-to-be" should determine our subjective moral life, our "ought-to-feel," "ought-to-think," and "ought-to-do"—a harmony of objective and subjective being prepared for us, if imperfectly, by nature.

Jonas squarely faces both the goodness of life and the world and our own potentialities for good and evil. He unsentimentally accepts and affirms the metabolic rigors of organic being, that life must use life in order to be itself (Jonas 1984: 131). He recognizes the goodness of finitude and mortality, of purposive being ever beginning anew out of its past achievements (Jonas 1984: 19). He judiciously measures our circumscribed powers and, while clear-eyed about limitations of human powers, calls for their humane, creative, and effective use. We must learn to circumvent inveterate ignorance and unknowing powers of action. We need further to develop native powers of feeling, especially the capacity to fear *malum,* and to exercise vivid and speculative imagination to envisage far-off possibilities of evil, thereby bringing to conscious light the goodness that is already here in actuality and potentiality (Jonas 1984: 27 ff.). All this is to serve, to clarify, and to deepen our objective responsibilities to ourselves and the world, which are most fundamentally to protect ourselves and the world from our own misadventures, practical and theoretical.

Here Jonas shows himself to be the advocate of organic and human life, the world, and their future (Jonas 1984: 125–26). He is the champion of circumscribed purposive freedom ever meeting worldly necessity (Jonas 1984: 135, 198). Thus he sternly judges utopian drifts and dreams—man trying to get out of nature by technologically conquering her, the urge to escape the rigors of worldly life and to get off scot-free (Jonas 1984: 914 ff.).

With all this sober judgment of his own times and his call for us to face objective obligations to the future, Jonas's ethics of responsibility is intrinsically neither ascetic nor grim. It is not a call to abstract or anatural duty, nor to angelic perfection. The required responsibility is for the objective and natural goodness of organic life, the world, and ourselves, in potentiality if not always in fact (Jonas 1984: 201–2). This service to life and call to worldly virtue carries its own inner rewards. The good name thus returned to responsibility is the issue of ethics having gone natural and having realigned itself with the intrinsic and palpable goodness of being.

Primary Experience and the Renewal of Philosophy

Before developing our interpretation of Jonas further, let us pause to contrast once more Mayr and Jonas, this time in terms of their respective accounts of morality and contemporary ethical responsibilities. Both Mayr and Jonas consider themselves enlightened, post-Darwinian anthropocentrists, with responsibilities to humankind foremost, intrinsically conjoined with responsibilities to nature both for its own sake and because of our intricate implication in and dependence on a well-functioning, flourishing nature. However, the two arrive at this destination by decidedly different ethical roads.

Mayr traces the roots of our moral life back to evolutionary processes that include, of course, evolved genetic programs and their interactions with somatic and worldly environments (Mayr 1997: 250 ff.). These genetic programs, Mayr recurrently insists, are often open-ended. We humans, thanks to our time-honed genetic backing, can learn from experience, enter into and creatively evolve human cultures, and decide things for ourselves, freely and responsibly, within worldly (including genetic) constraints and opportunities. There is in Mayr no genetic, environmental, or cultural determinism, bane of the cruder forms of behaviorism and sociobiology. (Mayr is not what Jonas calls an "epiphenomenalist.") The future is open, undecided, in principle unpredictable, and we have become increasingly significant actors in it, often for the worse.

Characteristically, Mayr's ethical interests and reflections are also centrally informed by evolutionary biology and ecology. If we are truly to live up to culturally honored democratic ideals and strive for equal opportunity for all, for example, Mayr insists that we must devise plural modes of education for our citizens, young and old. We do not all have the same capacities or learn in the same way. There is much human biodiversity amidst human commonalties. Mayr's moral pluralism is undergirded by his populational thinking, by his recognition of individual differences.

Further, Mayr is centrally exercised over our biologically ill-informed emphases on individual interests and freedoms at the expense of communal and systemic needs. The latter must be seriously and adequately addressed if we are to flourish in the future. Mayr joins Aldo Leopold and other conservationists in the call to responsibility for nature's future well-being.

Jonas likewise champions our worldly responsibilities for the human and natural future. This is the heart and soul of *The Imperative of Responsibility*. He similarly traces the full reaches of human morality and responsibility back to natural, organic origins—but to the human parent-child relation, to the natural feeling and unchosen responsibility for the utterly needy and vulnerable but intrinsically valuable infant, with all its promise (Jonas 1984: 130 ff.). Jonas does not trace moral capacities back further into natural time, à la Mayr. Rather, he takes a characteristic metaphysical and existentialist turn (Jonas 1984: 46 ff., 79 ff.). The intrinsic or fundamental value of all animate life and organic beings originates in the aboriginal ontological revolution—the purposive "no-to-nonbeing," the active individual assertion of the worldly self, the precarious and ultimately futile staving off of death. The more complexly active and capacitated the effort, the weightier or higher the moral stakes. When life's capacities include moral responsibility itself, as with humankind, we come upon an absolute moral threshold and an ultimate categorical imperative, ontological as well as moral: humankind, and the nature so necessary to humankind and to a morally responsible life, "ought to be." Over this imperative, we have no freedom to choose. Moral responsibility, in potentiality and actuality, harbored in human beings and being human, is for Jonas the ultimate good in itself.

In the main, Mayr would agree with the conclusions, but perhaps not with the philosophy (Donnelley 2002). Though Jonas in *The Imperative of Responsibility* explicitly and critically supersedes Kant's "here and now" categorical imperatives, Jonas's moral arguments retain an unmistakable Kantian ring, a sense of transcendent absoluteness (Jonas 1984: 11). "Humanity and nature ought to be"; "Never put humankind at risk" (Jonas 1984: 38 ff., 43). What are we to make of this Kantian legacy? Has Jonas fully left traditional essentialism behind? Has he adequately superseded Newtonian physicalism and determinism? With his "Nature Purposive," has he fully abandoned cosmic teleology? At one point, Jonas speculatively finds an aboriginal purposive striving (nonconscious and subjectless) behind the advent of organisms and ever more complex organisms or individual subjects. Did Jonas want to join Mayr's naturalist, Darwinian revolution? Indeed, Jonas might not have intended to use philosophic strategies to elaborate a full allegiance to a naturalist's or philosophic evolutionary biological point of view.

Jonas intended his Kantian, absolutist ring, adjusted to the realities he deemed disclosed by evolutionary biology and which he accepted and endorsed. Mayr might retort that, willfully or not, Jonas missed the full import for practical ethical responsibility of the centrality of emergent organic properties, "orchestral causation," and genomes. And in the end, Mayr might be right. Jonas may not have exploited the full philosophic fruits of the Darwinian revolution. Of course, truth be told, we are all more or less in the same boat. We are still largely ignoramuses, peering through a glass darkly, a mystery to ourselves. But recognizing Jonas's possible bias toward the traditional Western philosophical canon does not mean we do not need both Jonas and Mayr in our philosophic arsenal.

Jonas's moral reflections, arguments, and exhortations are timely and compelling. They carry the ring of truth. Yet equally significant is his explicit call to the serious renewal of speculative philosophy or metaphysics, as intimately related to ethics. Jonas's arguments typically move back and forth between ontology, epistemology, scientific fact, and ethics. This is uncharacteristic of our age. Jonas is decidedly out of step with the times. What accounts for Jonas's "going it alone" and whose footsteps should we follow?

The key, I think, is Jonas's fundamental approach to firsthand, immediate experience and his conception of the relation of philosophy and theory to such experience. This is usefully seen in Jonas's quarrel with the scientific materialists and their epiphenomenalist thesis. Beyond all questions of theoretical incoherence, inconsistency, and absurdity, Jonas's fundamental charge is that the epiphenomenalists are not interpreting our experience of ourselves and our world, but are explaining it away in accord with the demands of their theory. But this is the wrong relation of theory to experience. Philosophic theory ought to be generated out of human experience, which in turn it more or less adequately interprets.

This has decided methodological significance. The philosopher must take a first and final stand in the immediate experience of the self and the world and jealously guard this primary, fundamental, and complex evidence against theoretical extravagances. Yet it is precisely theoretical extravagances (bad philosophy or metaphysics) that have taken over our modern minds and made us radically suspicious of immediate experience. We have become "bookish" thinkers, more ruled by theory and great systematizers than by primary worldly evidence. Witness the ease with which the materialists and epiphenomenalists dismiss the reality and efficacy of subjectivity and purpose, a scandal from the perspective of primary experience. Effective purposes are no problem save for a philosophic theory that centrally incorporates the notion of efficient causation as the sole mode of natural efficacy. This is most, if not all, of our modern philosophic theories.

Jonas refuses to be bamboozled by theory and returns to a stand within primary worldly experience. His stance is critical and reflective. He poses questions to, thinks about, and ponders over experience. But he does not belong to what Nietzsche has termed the "Age of Suspicion," commencing with Descartes, which radically doubts the deliverances of experience, whether or not this suspicion be motivated by the theoretical demands of the new science.

Despite Jonas's considerable learning, primary experience is his foothold in the world and the ultimate source and critical check of his philosophizing. This is his Archimedean point, though it is not an epistemologically privileged or secure position. The philosopher is born with no certain ideas or final standards of truths. He has to think his way through things like the rest of us. Moreover, Jonas is chary of philosophic methods, theory driven, which promise a sure way to humanely ascertainable truth—whether these be empiricist reductions to sense data and their connections, Kantian transcendental arguments, Husserlian phenomenological bracketings and reductions, or Wittgensteinian linguistic analyses. All these aim at circumventing the vagaries and pitfalls of concrete experience but threaten to leave important dimensions of experience out of account, for example, the complex reality and efficacy of causation and purpose. Rather, Jonas credits us as thinkers with being natively equipped with limited or circumscribed epistemic and human powers that suffice for speculative philosophy, as long as the latter is critically reflective and renounces any pretension to certain and absolute truth.

Perhaps ironically, this epistemic humility and circumspection are matched by a philosophic boldness uncharacteristic of the more methodically assured "academic" schools. This arises from the strengths that Jonas discovers in primary experience, unsuppressed by theoretical prohibitions. There he finds the reality and efficacy of individual subjects, activity, and purposes. There he finds the ontological goodness of organic being and the self-justification of purposive existence. Finally, there he finds the native feeling of responsibility, our first participation in, if not the origination of, the moral realm. (Note that Jonas argues in terms of *bonum* and *malum,* "good" and "bad," as they are discovered in worldly experience and in terms of the moral responses and principles that these discoveries of goodness engender. He eschews the more abstract, theory-laden language of "interests" and "rights" favored by consequentialists [utilitarians] and deontologists, respectively.) All these "worldly facts" are recognized as there in experience prior to philosophic intervention. They are not created or freely constructed by theoretical imagination. It is the business of human language and theory to gather these fundaments of human reality and experience into explicit, conscious attention and to express their nature and interconnections adequately. This is the task of speculative philosophy. The task is not to create a thought-world prior to and ungrounded in experience.

Critics might charge Jonas with indulging in an unwarranted and delusive "intuitionism." What Jonas has found, he has put there, according to such critics. Philosophy and all theories are artifacts, through and through conventional or cultural constructs. Any connections to experience are thoroughly mediated and transformed by language and prior conceptions.

In my judgment, this charge is both unfair and begs the question of the fundamental philosophic issue at hand, namely, our deep rootedness in experience, organic being, and the world. Jonas can offer no guarantee of his ontological reading of experience and of the final adequacy of his ethical theory. Both are always open to reconsideration and to a philosophic reexamination of experience. Indeed, with his emphasis on "purposiveness" one can ask whether he has downplayed or submerged the ontological and ethical significance of concrete form, wholeness, and integrity, both organic and subjective. But to damn Jonas's enterprise from the start is to take a stand within a rival philosophic position that is itself suspect, most especially if it denies the validity of firsthand experience.

In sum, the ultimate importance of *The Imperative of Responsibility* may be in restoring a circumspect and judicious confidence in the firsthand deliverances, ontological and ethical, of our worldly experience. We should be more on guard against abstract, imperious, and intolerant theories than against the rich texture and complexities of the primary experiential evidence of ourselves and the world. This freedom from the hegemony of theory allows us once again to pursue philosophy seriously.

19

The Philosopher's Poet
Boris Pasternak's Cosmological Vision

Like that of other thinkers in the tradition of philosophic cosmology, Alfred North Whitehead's thinking is marked by a keen sense for aesthetic experience and art. In particular, Whitehead held that philosophy needs poetry to complete it, and philosophers need to have their own poets (Whitehead [1929] 1978: 96). Accordingly, this section concludes with a consideration of a writer who is a strong poet-novelist of philosophic cosmology: Boris Pasternak.

The philosophic dimension of *Doctor Zhivago* is all too often passed over or insufficiently considered. *Doctor Zhivago* is not a mere literary or aesthetic event, but the human document of an artist who himself was early a student of philosophy. Philosophic thought is absolutely central to the novel. Any attempt to appreciate *Doctor Zhivago* without grappling with the philosophy that permeates it is a distorted reading of the book.

Pasternak and the Cosmological Vision

Whitehead wears his speculative cosmology on his sleeve. Pasternak cloaks his philosophy in his art, in his characters and their conversations, and in the imaginative world he creates. Nevertheless, the cosmological character of his vision is no less apparent. All of *Doctor Zhivago*'s major protagonists are infused with a cosmological sensibility. In a culminating meditation over the dead body of Yurii, Lara, aided by the explicit intervention of Pasternak, exclaims:

> Ah, that was just what had united them and had made them so akin! Never, never, even in their moments of richest and wildest happiness, were they unaware of a sublime joy in the total design of the universe,

a feeling that they themselves were a part of that whole, an element in the beauty of the cosmos.

This unity with the whole was the breath of life to them. And the elevation of man above the rest of nature, the modern coddling and worshipping of man, never appealed to them.

The riddle of life, the riddle of death, the enchantment of genius, the enchantment of unadorned beauty—yes, yes, these things were ours [and not the small problems of practical life, like reshaping the planet]. (Pasternak 1958: 417–18)

In an earlier effort to extricate herself from the nightmarish liaison with Komarovsky, Lara turns to the silent, flower-scented, broad expanse of a nature "dearer than her kin, better than a lover, wiser than a book" (Pasternak 1958: 63). She rediscovers the purpose of her life: to grasp the meaning of the earth's wild enchantment, to call each thing by its right name, or to give birth, out of a love for life, to those who could. Nikolai, Yurii's maternal uncle and the novel's resident professional philosopher (Lara and Yurii consider too much philosophizing like a steady diet of horseradish), has his sister's "aristocratic sense of equality with all living creatures and the same gift of taking in everything at a glance" (Pasternak 1958: 11). His speculations on the interconnections of life, religion, art, history, and Christ establish philosophic themes taken up again and again.

Yet it is left to Yurii Zhivago to move decisively beyond cosmological sensibility to more or less sustained cosmological reflection proper, to speculation on the relation of the natural universe to human life in all its facets. The same man who is repeatedly overcome by the sound of waterfalls, the smells of wild cherry and old linden trees, and the color patterns of butterflies undertakes a dual career in art and science, attempting to yoke the two in practice and in theory. Yurii is natively drawn to art and history, has interests in physics and the natural sciences, and chooses medicine as a profession because of its practicality and social usefulness (Pasternak 1958: 57). He has a specialist's knowledge of the eye and writes a paper on the nervous elements of the retina, which he feels is somehow importantly relevant to imagery in art, to the logical structure of ideas, and to artistic creativity (Pasternak 1958: 69). He meditates on the relation of will and purposiveness to the mechanism of natural adaptation, of mimicry to protective coloring, and of the emergence of consciousness to natural selection. He thinks together Darwin and Schelling, the butterfly and modern painting, and envisions the vegetable kingdom as the key to human history and to human life itself (Pasternak 1958: 289, 377). In the dissecting room Yurii is stunned by the beauty of the human body, dead and dismembered, and is overcome by the riddle of life and death and of the fate of individuals. He dreams about writing a culminating book about life, for which his poems are but a preparation (Pasternak 1958: 57).

What are we to make of these catholic interests and tastes and of these bold connections of disparate realms of existence? According to Whitehead, they are endemic to the philosophic spirit. The felt importance of the universe, the world abroad, has many species, provoking a variety of interests irreducible to one another, no one species claiming an ultimate supreme value at the expense of the others. Yet none is alien to the human spirit. We are essentially constituted by our experience of a world of things felt as variously important and by the interests they provoke (Whitehead [1938] 1968: 16).

Amidst these varied interests, the essence of philosophic rationality is connection, seeing patterned connections within and between things, yoking together analogous patterns in disparate realms, thereby discerning their underlying rational relation (Whitehead [1938] 1968). The discovery of general patterns or interconnections uniting seemingly disjoined facts is the cosmological enterprise. Like Yurii, Whitehead thinks together the natural universe and human civilization, living creatures and art, logical and aesthetic experience. Granted that Pasternak is a philosophic cosmologist, what does it all come to? What is at the bottom of this cosmological outlook? The clues have already been given, and they concern not so much the universe in general as man in particular. The core conviction, I believe, is that man is wholly in nature. We are integral members of a natural community that is the cosmos. This seemingly innocuous and ostensibly sensible conviction establishes the cosmological perspective from which all philosophical problems are to be raised and resolved.

Such a perspective carries philosophically fateful consequences. If man is in nature, nature must be so construed as to accommodate man. A status in nature must be found for the life, emotions, mentality, and creativity of man. Correlatively, if human activity is natural activity, then civilized life, ethical and intellectual activity, artistic creativity, aesthetic experience, and religious vision must have an essential relation to this newly construed nature, specifically to organic life.

The essential relation of organic life to all human activity is just what

The Philosopher's Poet   197

we find asserted in both Whitehead and Pasternak. It accounts for the originality of their visions and for their fundamental quarrel with other metaphysical positions.

According to Whitehead, the problem of life, specifically the status of life in nature, is the problem of modern science and philosophy (Whitehead 1968: 202). Our conceptual and practical grasp of life has suffered at the hands of modern thinkers, whose conceptions are importantly traceable to Descartes's deadly dualism of mere mind and mere matter with life—all life—banished to a metaphysical limbo (Whitehead 1968: 204). This banishment of life from a central place in philosophic thought is precisely why philosophies starting with the Cartesian assumptions fail to gain a reasonably coherent and adequate view of the universe and ourselves.

According to Pasternak, life, the opportunity freely to live concrete, individual human lives, is the problem of modern sociopolitical existence. This is central to the tragic vision that is *Doctor Zhivago*. For Whitehead, notwithstanding practical problems, life faces the deadly abstractions of modern science and philosophy. For Pasternak, notwithstanding theoretical problems, life faces the practically fateful, no less deadly abstractions of political rhetoric and ill-informed ideology. The interrelation of the two problems is a fascinating and important topic that we must pass over. Nevertheless, "life and motion" threaten to be lost to our modern civilized existence. Whitehead and Pasternak intend to return them to their rightful places.

This central focus on life, human and nonhuman, rather than on mind or mere matter, seems to make the cosmological perspective philosophically inevitable. For notwithstanding Descartes and his modern followers, life is in nature—how in nature is the fascinating philosophic problem. Life is Whitehead's "nature alive." And, to repeat, if all modes of human activity are modes of life, then nature and human civilization must be brought together rationally. Life is the grand "go-between," the mediator, the concrete link between nature and culture. Culture and civilized life are only further creative elaborations of nature alive, with principles of civilization and human individuality adumbrated in organic life itself. Or so would claim both Whitehead and Pasternak. We find ourselves in nature. We ourselves are concrete instances of life in the cosmos and thus are essential clues to its fundamental character and its natural achievements. We are natively equipped with an epistemic arsenal with which to comprehend reality. We need only to attend to ourselves understandingly. This is the inherent, persuasive logic of the philosophical cosmologist's position, of the thinker who refuses to divorce nature, life, and man.

Given this philosophical persuasion, the fundamental character of life and how concrete instances of "nature alive" are essentially interconnected within the universe become cardinal speculative problems. With these problems in mind, we may approach Pasternak's philosophy proper.

Life and Cosmos in *Doctor Zhivago*

Early in *Doctor Zhivago* Pasternak describes life in rural Russia and the bustle of passengers at a local train station—good Tolstoyan themes (Pasternak 1958: 15). Abruptly, he shifts into philosophical speculation. Taken separately, every motion in the world is calculated and purposeful. People are set in motion by the mechanism of their own personal cares. But taken together, these motions are "spontaneously intoxicated with the general stream of life which united them all." The individual mechanisms of care only work because they are "regulated and governed by a higher sense of an ultimate freedom from care." This sense is derived from the nature of life itself. "This freedom came from the feeling that all human lives were interrelated, a certainty that they flowed into each other—a happy feeling that all events took place not only on the earth, in which the dead are buried, but also in some other region which some called the kingdom of God, others history, and still others by some other name" (Pasternak 1958: 15). The other name of this region is arguably life itself, which, properly understood, comprehends the kingdom of God and history.

Whatever, we are told that all lives are essentially interrelated and flow into one another. And the sense of this interrelation harbors a freedom from care—from a concern over mortality and death. The ongoing general stream of interconnected, individual lives itself is immortally alive. The immortal one is in the many, and the mortal many are in the one. Pasternak delves further into this fundamental theme in Yurii's impromptu lecture at the sickbed of Anna Ivanovna (Pasternak 1958: 59 ff.). Anna is concerned about the immortality of her soul, the survival of her personal consciousness. But, says Yurii, consciousness is a light turned outward, to help us move about in the world. Consciousness is a function of life in its commerce with the world, not an individual, independent substance. (Whitehead agrees.) And what, Yurii continues, do you know of your self? It is always knowledge of an external, active manifestation of yourself in others, in some work of your hands, in your family and friends. "You in others," that is your soul and will be your immortality. The active manifestation of the self in others is the concrete, temporal mechanism interconnecting individual lives. The self essentially matters to the very qualitative liveliness of others. This is the only kind of individual immortality Pasternak will allow. Upon Anna's death, Yurii writes a poem in her memory. This is his active, immortalizing response to her life in him.

This basic mechanism of "life in others," which means that life essentially involves both worldly activity and worldly "suffering" or undergoing, is behind the bewildering interconnections and mutual influences of *Doctor Zhivago*'s characters. The mutual penetration and real connection of lives, each in the other, is the backbone of the novel, undergirding its tragic vision. Lara and Yurii are a real source of life to one another; Komarovsky and Lara essentially influence one another, for worse and for better; Lara, Yurii, and their families cannot escape the savagery of the war, the revolutions, and their champions. Nor can postwar Russia fully escape the persuasive, fateful voice of Yurii's poems. *Doctor Zhivago* is the story of individual, interconnected lives crucifying and resurrecting one another, again and again.

Life "crucified and resurrected" is no mere metaphor but, for Pasternak, a central character of life itself. After denying the traditional religious conception of personal immortality, Yurii tells Anna she should not be concerned. For "all the time, life, one, immense, identical throughout its innumerable combinations and transformations, fills the universe and is continually reborn" (Pasternak 1958: 60). You rose from the dead when you were born and never noticed it. St. John holds the key. There is no death, because life ever renews itself. It resurrects itself out of death, which is the past, the over and done with. Here is adumbrated an important theme that runs throughout *Doctor Zhivago*: death is (ontologically) a friend of life. Life requires death for its own vital regeneration or resurrection. Concrete instances of life spontaneously arise out of the dead, the already become, which provokes life's novel immediacy or activity. (Again, this is good Whitehead—the parallel with the perpetual perishing of actual entities, and their subsequent role as objectively immortal, is too clear to require further elaboration.) Interestingly, this particular conception of life in nature necessarily implies a notion of natural causation that breaks the hegemony of efficient causation, the complete determination of the consequent by the antecedent. For Pasternak, the present is not, or need not be, totally determined by the past. "By nature" there are authentic revolutions, personal and social. These are spontaneous events, breaking right into the middle of things "without cause," wiping away old habits, unjust and just alike (Pasternak 1958: 164). Such events are the backbone of history, which follows the pattern of the vegetable kingdom, spontaneously changing itself without our notice or without our willful interventions (Pasternak 1958: 377). True revolutions, historical change, the vegetable kingdom—all are life aboriginally resurrecting itself out of death, the worldly past. This, in part, is the originality of life.

History, Art, Eros, and Ethics

Life resurrecting itself out of death, the worldly past, and "life in others" are the metaphysical bones of Pasternak's cosmology. On the basis of these conceptions, all else must be interpreted and his singular vision fleshed out. The fundamental theme that runs through his articulated cosmological vision is the central significance of lively individuals in worldly relations. All more specific reflections—on history, art, religious leaders, women, politics, ethics, and so on—are but elaborations of this theme. For the speculative Nikolai, the ultimate importance of individual lives in their immediate, worldly settings was first emphatically recognized by life's consummate genius, Christ. Christ transformed a blinding preoccupation with the old world abstractions of tribes, nations, and overweening sociopolitical projects into a lively concern with the mystery of the individual and of life itself. "The most important thing is that Christ speaks in parables taken from everyday life, that He explains the truth in terms of everyday reality" (Pasternak 1958: 39). The creative elaboration of everyday, concrete reality, an instance of life's vital resurrection, culminates in "the irresistible power of unarmed truth," the inward music that subdues the beast in man and persuasively leads him to goodness by the power of its example.

The idea that underlies this, says Nikolai, is "that the communion between mortals is immortal, and that the whole of life is symbolic because it is meaningful" (Pasternak 1958: 36). Christ natively grasped that life is a primary and ever-recurring ontological drama. It continually carries itself forward by actively renewing itself and its goodness in and through its interrelated, concrete vehicles, worldly individuals.

This idea also underlies Nikolai's conception of history. History is "the centuries of systematic explorations of the riddle of death, with a view to overcoming it. That's why people discover mathematical infinity and electromagnetic waves, that's why they write symphonies" (Pasternak 1958: 13). Human life actively meditates on the given, past world, thereby resurrecting itself. The dead is overcome understandingly or creatively, in science, art, or concrete practice. The past is taken up in an atemporal concept or a newly created form.

Further, this recurrent process is necessarily individual. There are only concrete instances of life, only individual, more or less creative transformations of the given. By the "immortal communion between mortals," "life in others" (ontologically the only way the historical project can be carried out), individual men participate in the creation of ongoing history, influenced and influencing. They do not "die in a ditch like a dog" (Pasternak 1958: 13). History is man's true home in which he creatively springs beyond mere animal life. Yet man's home is in the house of the cosmos, for human history is cosmic life's own creative transformations. History is life endowed with human memory of the past and human aspirations for the future.

For Nikolai, Christ is at the font of truly human history precisely because he emphatically underscores its requisite principles: love of one's neighbor, the supreme form of vital energy (the "immortal communion between mortals"), the idea of free personality (only individuals seek and are persuaded by the truth), and the idea of life as sacrifice, ultimately to life itself (Pasternak 1958: 13).

Christ's genius for life likewise establishes him as the consummate artist, who decisively sets the course for modern art. This is a contribution of primary importance. For Pasternak, art is a crucial ingredient of man's historical project, the overcoming of death and the resurrection of life.

Art, speculates Yurii, is not a category, but a vital principle, a force, a truth realized in its concrete instances. Art is not so much form as a hidden, secret part of content that is always essentially the same. It is "a statement about life so all-embracing that it can't be split up into separate words" (Pasternak 1958: 235). Further, "art always serves beauty, and beauty is delight in form, and form is the key to organic life, since no living thing can exist without it, so that every work of art, including tragedy, expresses the joy of existence" (Pasternak 1958: 378).

Art has its ultimate root in organic life. We are back at our fundamental theme of life, "one, immense, ever-changing, ever the same, concretely renewing itself. Art is a mode of life's vital resurrection. However, an important new note has been sounded that increasingly will occupy us. Life, in art as elsewhere, engenders new forms of itself, out of itself, in its vital resurrection within concrete worldly settings.

Life implies and requires death. Life also implies and requires form. Life, death, and form must philosophically be brought together. This is just what we find in Yurii's further meditations on art.

At Anna Ivanovna's funeral, Yurii notices in a glance peach-colored washing hanging in the monastery yard and how attractive his future wife, Tonia, is in black. In answer to the desolation of others, he is irresistibly drawn into poetic activity, to work out new forms and to create beauty. "More vividly than ever before he realized that art has two constant, two unending concerns: it always meditates on death and thus always creates life. All great, genuine art resembles and continues the revelation of St. John" (Pasternak 1958: 78). Art echoes history, for both are constitutive modes of cosmic life.

The theme of life, death, and form is deepened in Yurii's curious typhus dream. Passing through the crisis of his illness, Yurii dreams of writing a poem about Christ, specifically about the three days of turmoil, the raging earth assailing "the deathless incarnation of love" between His entombment and resurrection (Pasternak 1958: 174). Directly or indirectly, Tonia and Lara are present in the dream, nurturing him back to physical and artistic health. But the dream's most striking feature is the presence of the enigmatic Evgraf, Yurii's half brother, who is helping him write the poem. Yurii recognizes Evgraf as his death. Yurii asks, how could death be useful, a help in creative activity?

Evgraf is the son of Yurii's suicide father, of the unregenerative legacy Yurii explicitly renounced, his "over and done with." Significantly, Evgraf himself is not creative, yet he recurrently pops up in the novel as Yurii's benefactor, temporarily stemming the tide of the havoc wrought by the revolution and civil wars, putting things in order, providing Yurii an opportunity for pursuing his family life and creative talents. Evgraf effectively embodies a vestige of prerevolutionary order and resourcefulness. This is how "death" can finally be a true friend of life, and thus of art. The past world, including the artist's personal past, must have a requisite order if life is humanly to renew itself. Death, the past, must have its definite concrete forms if important and original forms are to merge.

This fundamental insight was originally expressed through and by

Christ. Art's "timeless" history was deflected and deepened by Christ's creative attention to the mystery of the individual and to the importance of everyday life. "Only the familiar transformed by genius is truly great" (Pasternak 1958: 237). Art requires the familiar and ultimately serves everyday life. The great object lesson is Pushkin, who opened the windows and let concrete reality, with its life and motion, storm into the lines of his poetry, "driving out the vaguer parts of speech" (Pasternak 1958: 237). This was more than aesthetic service. Pushkin reaffirmed the sanctity of everyday, "bourgeois" existence—housewives, quiet lives, and big bowls of cabbage soup. With form and content indissoluble, the works of Pushkin (and later Chekov) become irresistible powers of unarmed truth, "like apples picked green, ripening of themselves, mellowing gradually and growing richer in meaning" (Pasternak 1958: 237). They concretely realize the unchanging aim of art: "homecoming, return to one's family, to oneself, to true existence" (Pasternak 1958: 139).

Pushkin performs the same function as Christ. They have the same office and duty: to express the highest native talent, the talent for life, thereby resurrecting a truly human way of life. In some form or other, Christ's passion must be authentically reenacted again and again. We repeatedly must be called back to everyday life and its requisite forms. There will always be a Pushkin, a Yurii, or a Hamlet, whom chance has allotted "the role of judge of his own time and servant of the future," the high destiny of "a life devoted and pre-ordained to a heroic task" (Pasternak 1959: 129). In Pasternak's cosmos, Christ and man are equals, each serving the same master, life itself.

This brings us to a final ingredient of Pasternak's cosmic harmony, without which we cannot fully understand the interrelations of life, death, form, and art. This is eros, love. With love, Pasternak's women emphatically enter the cosmic picture.

The theme of eros and women is explicitly sounded in the eccentric Sima's conversations with Lara, with her original reformation of Nikolai's speculative theses on religion and history. Mary replaces Christ as the inaugurator of modern, truly human history. The everyday girl gives birth to "universal life" by miraculous inspiration (Pasternak 1958: 342). "Universal life," God, becomes man, and henceforth individual lives and the creative elaboration of everyday reality become the life story of God (Pasternak 1958: 343).

Sima ponders why Mary Magdalene is mentioned on the eve of Eas-

ter, as a timely reminder of what life is before the ensuing death and resurrection of "universal life." This reminder is of concrete life, temporal,
sensual, and passionate; crucified and seeking renewal; boldly speaking in
bodily, everyday images. Magdalene embraces Christ in the waves of her
hair, thirsting after his forgiving mercy. Sima exclaims, "What familiar-
ity, what equality between God and life, God and the individual, God and
a woman!" (Pasternak 1958: 345). Sima's Christ is curiously silent. Who
is resurrecting whom? Who is the consummate artist, creatively speaking the truth in terms taken from everyday life? The Magdalene of Yurii's
poems speaks in the same earthly erotic voice, with the same effect. Sima's
speculations suggest that eros, as embodied in individuals, is the true artist, that eros is essential to the renewal of life, to art, and to the origination
of form. For Pasternak, this is indeed so, as we see with Lara.

Lara is crucified by world events, by her womanly erotic impetuousness, and by her sensual embroilment with the "pagan" lawyer Komarovsky. Yet in her worldly involvements, she is a first daughter of the living
cosmos, its natural work of art, and a living example of what Pasternak
envisions human art should be. She is a creature of grace and vital harmony—a dark, husky voice speaking a current of spontaneously flowing
words, commanding by their truthfulness. "She was lovely by virtue of the
matchlessly simple and swift line that the creator had, at a single stroke,
drawn all around her, and in this divine form she had been handed over,
like a child lightly wrapped in a sheet after its birth, into the keeping of
Yurii's soul" (Pasternak 1958: 307).

Lara is eros and form indissoluble.

What precisely did Lara mean to Yurii, to his personal and creative
life? Practically everything. For Yurii, Lara was a deep electric current,
charged with all the femininity in the world; a spring evening punctuated
with the sound of children; vast Russia herself, his incomparable mother,
splendid in all her extravagant contradictions, the blessing of his existence
(Pasternak 1958: 325). Lara was existence itself. "This was exactly what
Lara was. You could not communicate with life and existence, thank them
as one being to another, but she was their representative, their expression,
in her the inarticulate principle of existence became sensitive and capable
of speech" (Pasternak 1958: 325)

Eros is the basal energy of life. Lara is Yurii's gateway to the universe
abroad and his means for understanding everything in the world.

On one side, erotic liveliness is essential to wisdom. Life, for Pasternak, can be intimately and finally known only by true lovers. In "Translating Shakespeare," commenting on *Romeo and Juliet*, Pasternak explicitly asserts that love is an elemental cosmic force, simple and unconditional, wearing a disguise of meekness. It is not a state of mind but the foundation of the universe (Pasternak 1959: 132). For Yurii and Sima, certain individuals, particularly women, are primary embodiments of this universal, sensuous eros, with an instinctive knowledge of life's erotic ways. Final wisdom is understanding the nature of great love: what it requires, what nourishes it, what damns it. This in part is the philosophic significance of Lara and Yurii's relation, of the two who are "by nature" compelled to love. "Most people experience love without becoming aware of the extraordinary nature of this emotion. But to them—and this made them exceptional—the moments when passion visited their doomed human existence like a breath of eternity were moments of revelation, of continually new discoveries about themselves and life" (Pasternak 1958: 328).

Thus we have the "immortal" Platonic dialogues of Yurii and Lara, the modern Socrates and Diotima. Lara, the incarnation of life's universal eros, intuitively comprehends love's need for an orderly, domestic world and for a childlike vision that can grasp life's beauty. She understands that the havoc brought by the war, the overthrow of all old customs and order, the modern reign of untruth and bombastic rhetoric, and the fear of following one's own conscience have destroyed all real love and family life, including her marriage with Pasha (Pasternak 1958: 335). To these reflections, which embody the genius of Nikolai's Christ, Yurii, the "hero of his times," can add little.

Eros, as a fundamental cosmic force, is no less central to art and the creative engendering of form. Yurii's poems are invariably inspired by Lara or other women, by their life in him and his nerve-wracking jealousy over their fateful, suffering involvement in the world. Nevertheless, his poetry is universal and cosmological in tone. The logic is straightforward. Women are particular embodiments of life's universal eros and rekindle the same in Yurii. The fate of his women is importantly the fate of life itself, the final subject of his poems. The universal is in the particular, and it is Yurii's office as a poet to bring the universal forth by transforming the particular (Pasternak 1958: 377).

Most significantly, awakened eros is itself responsible for the poet's creative engendering of new forms. We get a first glance at this in Pasternak's comments on *Romeo and Juliet*. "Being thus basic and primordial,

[love] is the equal of artistic creation. Its dignity is no less, and its expression has no need of art to polish it. The most that an artist can dream of is to over-hear its voice, to catch its ever new, ever unprecedented language. Love has no need of euphony. Truth, not sound, dwells in its heart" (Pasternak 1959: 132).

Romeo and Juliet speak to each other in blank verse. The measure is never stressed nor obvious. There is no declamation. Form never asserts itself at the expense of infinitely discreet content. "This is poetry at its best, and like all such poetry it has the simplicity of prose" (Pasternak 1959: 132).

The theme of eros and the artist's creative engendering of form is fur-ther developed in *Doctor Zhivago*. At Varykino, during what prove to be their last moments together, Lara urges Yurii to return to his poems. Yurii writes "inspired" poetry and speaks of poetic creation. After several stages of nec-essary, preliminary preparation, language takes over the poet and the cre-ative process. "Language, the home and receptacle of beauty and meaning, itself begins to think and speak for man and turns wholly into music, not in terms of sonority but in terms of the impetuousness and power of its inward flow. Then, like the current of a mighty river polishing stones and turning wheels by its very movement, the flow of speech creates in passing, by virtue of its own laws, meter and rhythm and countless other forms and formations, which are even more important" (Pasternak 1958: 363).

This is precisely like the "language of love" that Pasternak finds in *Romeo and Juliet*. Furthermore, the erotic, impetuous, and powerful Lara is the home and receptacle of beauty and meaning. There is no paradox. Language is a mode of cosmic, organic, erotic life, which "creates its own forms in pass-ing." Language is life expressing itself and being expressed, becoming "sensi-tive and capable of speech." Yurii is taken over by "the movement of universal thought and poetry in its present historical stage and the one to come" (Pas-ternak 1958: 364). He assumes his creative role in the historical project that is man's true home. He feels a rare moment of vital peace and blesses his entrance into the incredible, pure realm of existence, which includes the stars, the fields, and Lara and her daughter Katenka in the bed beside him.

The origin of created form in erotic life is finally and most emphatically asserted in the culminating moment of *Doctor Zhivago* mentioned earlier. In Lara's momentary resurrection over Yurii's dead body, she takes leave of him in a spontaneous, original monologue, informed by her instinctive knowl-edge of life, love, and death. She addresses Yurii "in the direct language of everyday life. Her speech, though lively and informal, was not down-to-earth . . . its logic was not rational but emotional. The rhetorical strain in her effortless, spontaneous talk came from her grief . . . [her tears] seemed to hold her words together in a tender, quick whispering like the rustling of silky leaves in a warm, windy rain" (Pasternak 1958: 417).

This seems what Yurii always aimed at, but which cost him so much effort. Here are nature, individual human being, and art merged in a way that makes sense only in a cosmos governed by life, and only if this fundamental cosmic principle is erotic and engenders its own forms. Human creativity, feeling, and thinking are in nature, and nature is alive in man.

This is Pasternak's cosmological vision: Individuals are essentially involved with one another and with the universe abroad. Life renews itself out of death, and human love and creative activity are the truest and fullest expressions of cosmic reality. This vision is founded on Pasternak's deep passion for the particular, the concrete, the truly lively. Only real, individual lives are ultimately important, and these lives always find themselves in particular worldly relations with one another.

Pasternak's cosmology, in all its developments, supports this passion for the individual and for life. Without understanding his passion and the cosmological vision that philosophically justifies it, we cannot appreciate a final aspect of *Doctor Zhivago*. This is the novel's ethical dimension, Pasternak's emphatic indictment of Soviet Russia and our modern world.

Above all else, Pasternak is deeply repelled by social and political "blueprintism," the willful foisting of rigid, unyielding forms on humanly communal life, and by individuals denying their original, native personalities in favor of imitating someone or something else (Pasternak 1958: 147, 418). He is repelled by all those who are unwilling to attend to life's aboriginal ways and who give up on their individually unique lives in favor of grand poses, public or private. He is repelled by those who treat life as a substance to be molded (an attitude that only reveals their profound misunderstanding of life), and by all who delight in marching to deadly, "world-important" causes, the abstract issues of ironfisted, uncreative wills (Pasternak 1958: 208, 248, 282). Life cannot be treated with such impunity without disastrous consequences and without sinning against the very goodness of existence.

V

Postlude

20

Francis of Mepkin

Editors' note: These remarks were delivered at the memorial service for Father Francis Kline, Mepkin Abbey, September 1, 2006.

Father Francis Kline, Abbot, Mepkin Abbey, Moncks Corner, South Carolina. Francis of Mepkin. Francis chose his religious, Cistercian name well, no doubt with great care and deliberation, mindful of Church history.

Let me at the outset say how deeply honored I am for the opportunity to talk briefly about Francis's contribution to conservation and the environment. In six all-too-short years, Francis became a brother to me: a brother in spirit; a brother in exploring the ultimate significance of nature for our human lives; a brother in trying to plumb the depths of our present cultural crisis. We borrowed a Wes Jackson agricultural metaphor: We find ourselves in a shallow-rooted, market-driven, land-destroying, technology-manipulated annuals monoculture of corn, soybeans, and their human correlates. If we are to thrive into the future, we need to live in a deep-valued, deep-rooted perennial polyculture; an analogue of a tall grass prairie, big and little blue stem with their native biota, evolving, adapting, persisting in ecological time and space. Finally, we were brothers in sharing our personal lives and concerns. Francis spoke at my mother's memorial service and officiated at my daughter Naomi's wedding. On both occasions he delivered a spontaneous, profoundly thoughtful riff, leaving us all speechless. I say all this knowing that many of you could tell similar brotherly stories.

Francis's contributions to the cultural and natural conservation of Berkeley County, Charleston and the Lowcountry, and beyond are extraordinary—Strawberry Hill and its chapel; Bonneau Ferry; the recent conservation easement on Mepkin Abbey, among many others. However, I want to talk about Francis's extraordinary, perhaps unique, power and effectiveness as a conservation leader. To do so, I want to steal a trick from the seventeenth-century British metaphysical poet John Donne and play upon a mathematical image. Francis would approve.

Some of you will sufferingly remember the symbolic logician's Venn diagram: three intersecting circles with an overlapping area shared by all three, always the point of interest. Let one circle stand for God, Spirit, or the Ultimate, according to your persuasions and convictions. Let a second circle stand for geological, evolutionary, ecological, ecospheric nature. Let the third circle stand for humanity and its many historical cultures. Francis actively dwelled in the region of the circles' intersection. To dwell solely in, and be solely concerned for, God, Nature, or Humanity is to lead a humanly deficient life. Only where the three realms of existence interweave and interfuse can we live a full, humanly rich life, and only if we continually explore this, for us, terra incognita, which we comprehend only through a glass darkly. Francis claimed as much. He emphatically and explicitly disowned any dogmatic, certain truth. He and his fellow Cistercians are enjoined not to take sacred texts literally, but always to be interpreters: explorers of reality, meaning, significance, beauty, goodness, and truth.

Here, I think, is a key to Francis's persuasive power. He did not argue for cultural and natural conservation in terms of economic expediency, for example, ecosystem services, or biological and ecosystemic necessity, as important as these might be. The conservation of nature and human cultural communities are matters of ultimate concern both for ourselves and to the natural communities and landscapes within which we live. These, at bottom, are matters of moral and spiritual responsibility and should be explicitly recognized as such. Thus Francis's unflagging and passionate moral concern for the future of the Lowcountry's natural landscapes and ecosystems and many human cultural communities, both in their many-leveled, value-laden dimensions. Thus his concern for the past, present, and future of the Cooper River and Berkeley County. Thus his passionate intervention in the Bonneau Ferry saga. Francis forcibly threatened to bring the wrath of God down upon those complicit in its potential development. (To paraphrase an old blues song, "Don't mess around with Mother Nature or Francis. You'll be sorry if you do. We'll rain on your parade and stomp all over you.") Once again Francis rendered his audience speechless and opened the way for the eventual preservation of Bonneau Ferry and some 24,000 to 40,000 historically and naturally significant acres in Berkeley County. As Wes Jackson would say, here was a powerful form of prayer that was heard and answered.

Francis of Mepkin, Agnus Dei, tiger in the cause of humans and nature. There is so much more to say, but I must stop. We have suffered an unimaginable loss. Who can replace Francis? No one. On the other hand, we are blessed with the prospect of an unimaginable gain. Francis, his spirit, his cares and concerns live deep in the bowels of many of us. He has literally become an integral part of our very selves. If we can pool the many Francises in us—if we can stick together—perhaps the sum can equal the departed part, and together we can do many wonderful things. We owe that to both Francis and ourselves.

Editors' Afterword

Strachan Donnelley was working to complete this book at the time of his death in 2008. The manuscript that he left in our care was composed of several essays that had been published in scattered journals and book chapters and of many new essays, previously unpublished, that he had written during a remarkably productive period in the last five years of his life. It fell to us to put the finishing editorial touches on this work and to group the chapters in an order of presentation that we hoped would weave together the two genres at which he excelled—the personal, observational storytelling of an outdoorsman whose copy of *A Sand County Almanac* was never far from his side, and the deeply reflective essay of a professional philosopher with a lifelong engagement in the adventure of ideas. The result, we feel, is a unique kind of book. It offers a new perspective on questions that are at once as old as Western philosophy and of urgent contemporary importance. It displays a remarkable openness to life all around us and to a broad range of powerful minds from the past, thinking deeply. Above all it exemplifies habits of imagination that are crucial today—curiosity, humility, and a deep sense of responsibility for the conservation of "nature alive."

The first section of this afterword is written by Ceara Donnelley, and the second section is by Bruce Jennings.

I

My dad offhandedly suggested that I be his literary executor from a hospital bed at Sloan-Kettering. He had been admitted that morning, or maybe the day before, after a routine pre-chemo checkup with his oncologist revealed an inoperable bowel obstruction. Until that morning my dad, and the rest of us, had been willing ourselves to believe the improbable: that he was tolerating chemo fairly well; that the stomach cancer cells, or "yapping puppies," in my dad's vernacular, were at least staying obediently in place; that he might have more than mere months left. Since his diagnosis six months earlier, my dad had not been concerned with tying up loose ends or saying good-bye—all he wanted was to keep doing what he was doing, living his full, rich life. Indeed, the afternoon of his cancer diagnosis he trooped off to an auction in search of elusive Audubon and Catesby prints. Two weeks later, he was in rare form on the dance floor at my wedding, and not just during our daddy-daughter dance to Mose Allison's "Don't Get Around Much Anymore" (a nostalgic and, it turns out, ironic choice that I suggested as an alternative to his initial request, "Wild Man"). And until that fateful Thursday checkup, just days after we celebrated his sixty-sixth birthday, my dad was determinedly focused on the future—particularly that of the Center for Humans and Nature, a nonprofit he had founded four years earlier, where he was hatching big ideas and hitting his professional stride.

When a young resident suggested that we may be looking at weeks, not months (and certainly not years), that we should line up round-the-clock care and install a hospital bed on the first floor of the brownstone my parents had lived in for almost forty years, my dad confronted the reality of death for the first time. Well, not quite—I don't think he'd ever been afraid of death in the same way many of us are. The news of his impending mortality instead forced him to confront the reality of life, even just weeks of it, without really living. My dad had always lived well, in the best sense of the word. He zealously pursued his passion for fly-fishing, hunting, and the outdoors. He loved music, from Mose Allison to Mozart to Verdi, and spent many Tuesday nights at Carnegie Hall or the Met, often with tears in his eyes (listening to great works was one of the few things that made my dad cry). He used his good fortune to collect and enjoy the things he loved—duck decoys, ancient and Northwest Indian art and artifacts, red wine. With my mom, he created and coveted a "wild and woolly" family: five headstrong daughters, Labradors, and a steady stream of stray cats. Amid and in addition to all of this, he *thought*—he was a philosopher. He eagerly went to work each day, at the Hastings Center and, later, at the Center for Humans and Nature, hungry to explore big ideas and inscrutable questions in thought, conversation, and writing.

In the hospital, when it became clear that many of these fruits of the good life were no longer available to him, my dad spent little time mourning their loss. Instead, he homed in on what he still had—his mind. This book is the product of my dad's last four months, spent, yes, in hospice care, but on his own terms. As long as my dad still had his mind, he refused to allow bodily deterioration to slow the final task he lit upon in that hospital bed: to reread, reflect upon, and assemble into a manuscript the articles and essays he had written over the course of forty-plus years of philosophical work. He did this from his back room on our home's second floor; from his attic office overlooking a field, sometimes filled with wild turkeys, at our country house in Massachusetts; and, remarkably, from his childhood farm in Libertyville, Illinois, where he convened one last conference of colleagues and compatriots to ponder the future of the Center for Humans and Nature and the farm itself. He more than proved that alarmist oncologist wrong. In his last months (not weeks), colostomy bag and eventually oxygen tank in place, my dad not only did stairs but endured three-hour car rides and a cramped seat in American Airline's economy section to live and work in the places he loved, surrounded by the people he loved.

And when he could work no more—when mind finally followed body, the two ever connected—my dad died. One Saturday morning in early July my mom called me and mentioned that something seemed to have shifted. My dad was delirious, his words no longer attaching to reality. I walked down to their house, and my mom said he was upstairs, resting. I went up and sat down beside him on the bed. He seemed to be sleeping, but suddenly his eyes flew open. He looked at me with alarm, sat bolt upright, swung his legs over the side of the bed, and tried to stand. I did what I could to get him to sit down, but he looked at me and said, with such urgency, "I have to get to work." It had been a few days since he'd had the strength to sit in his chair, working on this book, and somewhere in the clouding ether of his brain that reality was finally hitting him. He would not be still. I called to my younger sister, Tegan, to come help me, and we moved my dad to his chair. Clutching his hands, biting back tears, I started reading these essays aloud. I chose "Big Little Snake," my personal favorite, and in moments my dad settled, closed his eyes, and every now and then faintly nodded. He died a week later, even though the hospice nurses warned us that this in-between delirium, and then coma, could last much longer. I think we knew better. When he could think no more, work no more, my dad's body would take its cue and, again in his words, "turf it."

〜

Though this book was compiled in my dad's final few months, it is far more than a testament to his equanimity and resolve in the face of mortality. Rather, it captures the evolution of those big ideas and inscrutable questions that followed and propelled my dad through his good life. At first glance, the book's sections may seem unconventional in that they contain works of academic philosophy alongside essays on natural encounters, literature, political events, and even a close friend. That is fitting—my father was an unconventional man (or, as he came to call himself, a marginalist). When he first assembled these works, he identified two dominant strands: those essays tackling his philosophical "magic mountains" (see his own introduction for an explanation of the term), and those drawing on his encounters in the natural world, or the "living waters" (for such encounters often, though not always, involved fly-fishing). But even he knew that these two categories could not capture the breadth of his writing, and so it was up to us to find the right way to assemble this volume.

The aspects of my dad's mind and intellectual curiosity captured in the sections herein reflect the dominant strands of his intellectual and personal identity: Strachan the Agitator ("A Guide for the Naturally Perplexed"), Strachan the Naturalist ("Variations on Aldo Leopold"), and Strachan the Philosopher ("Recovering a Philosophy of Nature"). They are bookended by meditations on one of the most profound and transformative relationships of my dad's life. Father Francis Kline's friendship revealed to my father a deep spirituality that he might not have otherwise recognized in himself, and it lent language to a critical self-identification my dad had not yet made: Strachan the Marginalist.

Woven throughout the book are common themes, thinkers, and ideas. The modes of thought that my dad practiced fed very much off one another, and though these sections represent an evolution of his thinking and his philosophical and practical concerns, it was a nuanced evolution (isn't it always?), with much circling back to seminal themes, early ideas and notions, first intuited roughly and later honed through thought and experience. Indeed, critical to an understanding of this book, and my dad, is the faith that profound insight and deep truth come in many forms and through wildly diverse experience—so an idea first sparked in grappling with Whitehead as a graduate student may take shape later in a trout stream, or while reading Russian literature, or while listening to a great Verdian opus.

The totality of life is what interested my dad. He wanted to live it, first and foremost; then try to understand it; and then work to use that full life and its contemplation to better this earthly world, its humans and nature alike. Throughout this ambitious endeavor, my dad remained ever humble—he was equally convinced of the need for deep thinking as he was of the fundamental limits of the human capacity to understand the natural (including human) world and its workings. A favorite line of my dad's was "*Ignoramus:* we are ignorant." But that didn't stop him from always trying to learn and understand more about the world in which we live, and nor should it stop us.

I leave the rest to my dad to tell you about, and to his trusted friend and colleague, Bruce Jennings, who ably sketches the contours of my dad's ideas and professional journey. What I hope to have conveyed in these brief words is that in addition to a book about ideas formed through philosophy and fishing and living, broadly speaking, this is also a book about an extraordinary father. Growing up, my sisters and I met my dad's magic mountains around the dinner table, and we waded the living waters with him. We were challenged to think big and beyond ourselves, but always with wisdom, humor, humility, and love. And we were, in the end, blessed by a final gift I'm not sure my dad realized he gave us: the witnessing of a graceful if untimely death, a rare glimpse of the most profound of humans and nature experiences. My hope for this book is that it be an equally powerful gift to those who read it, by provoking contemplation of what it is to lead a good life, by asking big questions about this human and natural world, and, hopefully, by pointing the way to some answers.

II

When Strachan Donnelley was told that he had only a short time left to live, he responded with a fortitude and grace that came as no surprise to those who knew him well. There was much he had to do in those final months, but a high priority for him was to say in print what he had been saying about the human responsibility for the natural world in his founding and leadership of the Center for Humans and Nature, in his lecturing and teaching, in his community service, and in his philanthropy. The key to his vision was the relationship between evolutionary biology, ecology, and ethics; out of a synthesis of those bodies of knowledge would emerge a new sensibility, a new worldview, a recovered and reborn philosophy of nature.

So Donnelley returned to his published work, and to a large body of unpublished essays that he had produced in the last few years, with the intention of expressing the experience that had shaped his life as a naturalist, conservationist, and outdoorsman (what he called his "living waters"). He then intended to express the learning and reflection that had shaped his life as a philosopher, building on significant thinkers and ideas that had influenced him (his "magic mountains"). No less important, he aspired to unite those two modes of knowing, those two poles of his own identity, not so much for personal reasons as in an attempt to heal the wound in our contemporary ways of thinking, feeling, and living, a wound brought about by our mechanistic conception of nature and by our abstract, artificial, denatured conception of the human condition.

I had the privilege of working closely with him during those final months, together with my co-editor, Ceara Donnelley, and several others, to review and organize his wide-ranging work into a form that would be accessible to a broad audience and suitable for posthumous publication. *Frog Pond Philosophy* is a volume that embodies the synthesis of naturalism and philosophy he sought. The essays included here show his mind tacking back and forth between the wisdom of a trout stream, a pond, or a prairie landscape and the wisdom of philosophy and science.

It is my hope that these essays will delight and reinspire those who have read his work before, and that they will introduce new readers to a remarkably nuanced and original thinker. Unlike many in his discipline, Donnelley did not build grand theory, and he did not write as though he were the first to have the ideas he presents and defends. On the contrary, he was deeply aware of the various traditions out of which his thinking grew and was constantly engaged with the work of key thinkers of the past. His method of exposition was largely exegetical and indirect. His originality comes from his reading, but it is an active, purposive reading. In the end his purpose is not scholarship per se. He attends meticulously to what others have thought and said, not as an end in itself, but as a way of understanding what they (and we) *should* think and say. A gifted expositor, Donnelley can summarize and go to the heart of a complex philosophical argument so clearly that the reader does not need to be familiar with the thinker being discussed in order to follow the discussion. Few readers, though, can finish these essays without wanting to go back to the source texts; so those who have not read Spinoza, Charles Darwin, Aldo Leopold, Alfred North Whitehead, Hans Jonas, or Ernst Mayr and company may soon find themselves doing so.

⌒

Strachan Donnelley's abiding purpose was to explore ways of thinking "humans" and "nature" together—to restore a kind of philosophical and ethical practice that can overcome the separation of human being and the rest of natural being that has been created by dominant currents in modern philosophy and modern science. This he called a "philosophy of nature" or "philosophical cosmology." In these terms his goal was to contribute to a new ecologically oriented philosophic cosmology informed by evolutionary biology.

His intellectual career was devoted to the task of revitalizing the philosophy of nature, long eclipsed by post-Cartesian and analytic philosophy and recently rendered suspect by (in his view) a mistaken interpretation of Nietzsche and the postmodernist skepticism and constructivism that it has spawned. The basic tenet of his philosophical cosmology is that human beings are a part of nature—not separate from nature. That is, humans do not stand above the natural world at the top of a hierarchical structure watching nonhuman life from on high. Nor can we humans rightfully stand beside the natural world, sharing biological footing but claiming that our intellect confers special status on our species. Instead, Donnelley held that the natural world consists of humans and all other species, each one part of a vital whole, and that humans have an ethical obligation to conserve, respect, promote, and nurture that complex living whole in all its richness and diversity and out of respect for its sheer evolutionary accomplishment.

In addition, he had the constant aim of informing the important work of conservationism and environmentalism by bringing them back to their philosophical roots and fundamentals. An important part of doing that, he thought, is to always keep in view the evolutionary dimension of nature, as richly and creatively understood by Darwin and as supplemented by the work of neo-Darwinian evolutionary theorists such as Mayr. Put in its simplest, but not simplistic, terms: we must recover a strong understanding of the fact that nature is real and that nature is alive. And we humans, as natural and as a part of nature ourselves, must recover a strong sense of moral responsibility toward the integrity and preservation of nature alive.

Finally, Donnelley's intent is to bring philosophical reflection and personal experience into a creative encounter. In the philosophy of nature he develops here, categorical distinctions—between the human and the natural, between the organic and the inorganic, between reason and feeling, and between the moral and the aesthetic—are subjected to critical scrutiny and are found wanting in significant respects. This philosophy mirrors his own experience, in which the direct encounter with nature alive—in a prairie landscape growing up in Illinois, in a trout stream, sitting in a duck blind or on a turkey shoot—informed his philosophical thinking even as these experiences presented themselves to him in memory as moments of lived experience that is fecund with philosophical insight and meaning.

Donnelley had a deep and abiding respect for systematic philosophy and metaphysics, something to which Americans are allergic, as his mentor Hans Jonas once warned him, and as he became keenly aware over the years. But he was not a system builder. He was an explorer in the terrain of ideas and an essayist in mode of presentation. He admired the stance of those who were "marginalists," such as his good friend, Father Francis Kline, because they creatively questioned received traditions and were willing to depart from the mainstream to explore other currents.

The essay form permitted him to work with the two kinds of material that compose *Frog Pond Philosophy*—the phenomenological and existential encounters with nonhuman nature, and the critical, probing encounters with a number of great philosophical minds. His living waters and his magic mountains. The essays in this book wade in these waters and trek on these slopes. Taken together, I believe they provide a narrative of pushing ahead, getting lost, backtracking, finding a new path, and gradually making headway. Headway toward what? Not final answers or truths, but toward an improved articulation of a number of quandaries, insights, and choices that we all face and that become more significant and more urgent with each passing year.

Donnelley's method was to begin by identifying a problem and then to examine it in its complexity and ambiguity, often through exegesis of a powerful thinker (most often Spinoza, Whitehead, Leopold, Jonas, and Mayr) and through his own gift for critical extrapolation. This he does, not only with wise old thinkers but also with a wise old trout on the line, dancing and contending with him, the two organisms matching wile and cunning. When he does this with philosophers, scientists, and naturalists—minds different from and more broad-ranging than the trout's—he is always trying to unravel their secrets and bring them to bear on the moral, political, and indeed spiritual challenges of a society that, quite literally, has forgotten how to "mind" nature—to care about and to care for nature and to comprehend nature as something alive rather than merely instrumental and objectified, or "dead."

Donnelley was always a philosopher, but he never really pursued a conventional or disciplinary philosophical career. He found his niche among those who have devoted their lives to an engaged kind of activity (or contemplation). Somewhere around the middle of his journey, he met people like Father Francis Kline of Mepkin Abbey in South Carolina and Wes Jackson of the Land Institute in Kansas, whose character and example provided him with a gripping model of the kind of quester, the kind of marginalist, who still accomplished and built lasting things. Earlier than that, he set off toward the destination this book represents under the guidance of his great teacher, Hans Jonas, who supervised his doctoral work at the New School for Social Research on the philosophy of Alfred North Whitehead.

Soon after his doctorate was completed and he had some teaching under his belt, in 1986 he began a new chapter at the Hastings Center, an interdisciplinary research and educational institute, where he worked on bioethical issues such as end-of-life care and the development of bioethics teaching and research in central and eastern Europe. He also created an environmental ethics and philosophy program and developed that during his tenure as the Hastings Center's president from 1997 to 1999, and he continued to direct that program at the Hastings Center until 2003. During that period of his work, he became increasingly interested in those aspects of the life sciences that the field of "bioethics" tended to overlook, such as biodiversity, evolution, animal communities and behavior, and the like.

During the same period, in the 1990s Donnelley began to study Darwin in earnest and to see the significance of the ways in which a Darwinian understanding of evolution and the "entangled bank" of life formed interconnections and intimations with so many philosophers, past and present, who had made their mark on him earlier, but who now seemed to come together in new ways—Heraclitus, Spinoza, Nietzsche, the great Russian novelists, especially Leo Tolstoy and Boris Pasternak, the pluralistic liberal political philosopher Isaiah Berlin, and of course, Whitehead and Jonas. The intellectual excitement of those years was given further impetus and direction by the work of Mayr, who was one of the principal contributors to the New Synthesis of Darwinism—which brought genetics together with evolutionary theory—and, in his later work, who made his mark as a leading historian and philosopher of the biological sciences.

In 2003 Donnelley left the Hastings Center to set up a new organization, the Center for Humans and Nature. After that he became even more deeply involved in the work of cutting-edge conservation groups and ecological and evolutionary thinkers. As he studied the social and policy issues with which the conversation movement grapples today, from wilderness preservation to prairie restoration, from soil erosion and fresh water reclamation to global climate change, he became increasingly convinced that radical new practices are urgent and essential, but they won't come without a fundamental reorientation of our culture at the level of conceptual thought and moral feeling.

In an inaugural letter written for the website of the Center for Humans and Nature, Donnelley wrote: "Organic life baffles our modern minds. The very meaning of life is in doubt. The problem of life is *the* problem of modern philosophy and science—so claimed Alfred North Whitehead more than 75 years ago. Despite the advances in the biological sciences, genetics and biochemistry, but also evolutionary biology and ecology, this situation has changed little. In fact, arguably things have gotten worse. Now life is also *the* practical problem of modern culture, society, politics, and the global economy." He steadfastly insisted that we ask ourselves, how flourishing and resilient, or how degraded and vulnerable, will humankind allow the web of life on the planet to become? Surely this is the sentinel question of the twenty-first century.

Donnelley argued that we have unthinkingly plunged head first into complex environmental, conservation, community, and cultural crises, already here or looming, that threaten ecosystems, species populations (flora and fauna), fertile soils, freshwater resources, and climate, indeed, the future diversity of life itself. The causes of these natural and cultural crises are many and interact with one another: a burgeoning human population (over 7.5 billion and climbing), overuse of natural resources, and economic and other activities that degrade and pollute the earth's nature and the resiliency of its long-term evolutionary, ecological, and humanly cultural processes.

We must explore, articulate, and promote long-term moral and civic responsibility for human communities and the natural ecosystems and landscapes within which they are embedded. Following the insights of evolutionary biology, ecology, and everyday life, we must recognize the bewilderingly complex and inescapable interactions—historical, dynamic, systemic—of humans and nature. This fundamental earthly reality sets the terms of the intellectual, moral, and civic work that lies ahead, and of the work of Donnelley's own writing.

On April 24, 1992, there was a memorial service in the Rockefeller Chapel at the University of Chicago for Gaylord Donnelley, who was an extraordinarily influential figure in the fields of business, education, philanthropy, and conservation. On that occasion Strachan Donnelley memorialized his father, noting the rhythms of his father's life and sensibility in the following way:

> Dad would frequently and regularly leave the public world of Chicago and elsewhere, which he truly relished, and run off to Hennepin to duck hunt, to Coleman Lake to fly-fish, to Ashepoo and South Carolina's coastal salt marshes. . . . These were not mere time-offs from public life for Dad. They were a move into another world about which, in his own way, he was as deeply serious and passionate. This was the extraordinary world of nature. I think it was this moving back and forth between his two worlds, public life and nature, that kept him so enlivened and such a boon to his family and friends. It was why he could be so publicly high-minded and concerned and so fun-loving at the same time. Why he could tackle fundamental, long-range social issues and be personal and down-to-earth.

In this regard, Strachan Donnelley certainly followed in the footsteps of his father. In this book we trace a mind moving back and forth between fundamental ideas of public life, with its philosophical blind spots and its human ethical responsibilities, and the down-to-earth world of nature, with its trout streams, its prairie ball fields, and its Hennepin's wind-blown bottoms.

Donnelley believed that it is essential to nurture and support the work of those daring enough to swing for the fences with Louisville Slugger (a famous brand of baseball bat) ideas; for it is only from the work of philosophical mavericks and marginalists, not from conventional thinking about policy, law, economics, and science, that we will get the reorientation we need. This is not the work of a day. And we are unlikely to have a single dominant mind, like Darwin, who can pull off such a paradigm shift. But the work is urgent, and we do not have forever—nature will not give us unlimited time—to get it done. Many hands can contribute to it.

It is in this spirit that I suggest this book should be read.

III

Overview and Organization of the Book

The book has been arranged in four sections. Uniting them is the quest to reanimate, deepen, and extend the philosophy and ethics of environmental conservation. This quest has three main aspects.

One aspect of this project involves the reclamation of an intellectual tradition of ecological philosophic cosmology. This tradition is a counterpoint to the dominant materialistic or "physicalist" philosophic cosmology that informed the great scientific revolution of the modern era. In Donnelley's view, the foundations of this ecological cosmology can be traced to the pre-Socratic philosopher Heraclitus, but it emerged in the modern era in the works of Spinoza, Darwin, Whitehead, Leopold, Jonas, and Mayr. The chapters in part IV of the book explicate and explore the salient points of conflict between physicalist and ecological philosophic cosmology. These chapters tell the story of the progressive development of the ecological vision as one moves from Spinoza and Whitehead, the great metaphysical exponents of this worldview, to the contemporary neo-Darwinian reinterpretation of the tradition in Mayr and Jonas. Mindful of the fact that this worldview has a richness that lends itself to more than technical philosophical expression, Donnelley also enlarges his interpretation of ecological cosmology through a brief reading of the great Russian novelist Boris Pasternak.

A special aspect of our editorial work should be mentioned in connection with part IV. In the published essays upon which this part of the book is based, Donnelley did not arrange his discussion of the thinkers in this tradition in chronological order. His approach instead was to write a series of essays taking up comparative discussions of earlier and later thinkers, often in groups of two or three. And he would intersperse presentations of his own original views as it were within the interstices of these comparative discussions. To reduce repetition and to provide a more clear exposition of the intellectual development that Donnelley saw in this tradition of philosophical cosmology, we have reorganized the material in these earlier essays to form chapters in this book that present more clearly the argument that Donnelley made about how later philosophers drew upon and departed from earlier thinkers. Thus we have brought several discussions of Descartes, Spinoza, and Whitehead together and juxtaposed them in chapter 16. Something similar has been done with discussions of Mayr and Jonas in chapters 17 and 18. We have reorganized, but we have not rewritten his words. Aside from a few transitional sentences here and there, the chapters in part IV reflect Donnelley's views of the history of philosophic cosmology and its crucial ecological turn under the influence of Jonas, Mayr, and Leopold, and which set the context for his own contribution to that tradition.

Finally, a word about the status of chapter 15. Donnelley frequently closed his essays with a discussion of what he saw as the contemporary, practical, and ethical implications of the theories and concepts (the worldviews) of the thinkers he discussed. However, when these separate conclusions were left at the end of various chapters, the reader was left with the task of synthesizing and connecting them. We have decided, therefore, to bring this material together in a separate chapter in order to capture in a more accessible and direct way the themes and lessons that Donnelley found in the history and critical exposition of philosophic cosmology. The words in this chapter are his own, but he did not develop them in a separate essay as has been done here. We have made every effort not to distort his meaning or intention when we have moved passages out of their original context. We believe that a synthetic statement of this kind is a fitting and useful way to begin part IV of this book.

A second aspect of the project to reanimate a conservation philosophy and ethic is learning to see nature in new ways through reflection on direct experience and encounters with and in it. This is found in part III of the book, which contains an insightful reading of Leopold and an interpretation of his influential land ethic. It also contains a series of vivid short essays occasioned by Donnelley's own experiences as an outdoorsman, a hunter and fisherman, who possessed an acute and often lyric naturalistic imagination. In these essays we find existential encounters with ducks and turkeys, trout and salmon in landscapes as varied as the South Carolina Lowcountry, the lakes of Wisconsin and northern Illinois, and the powerful running waters of Iceland. Invariably these encounters lead to reflections, meditations, prayers almost, on the nature of organic life and metaphoric, meaning-making humanness. Blindness and insight. Losing and finding oneself.

The third aspect of Donnelley's conservation philosophy emerges in various chapters in part II, the unifying theme of which is a resistance to dogmatism and human overconfident illusions of mastery and superiority. For Donnelley these illusions are born out of a failure to recognize our essential interdependence with ecosystems that sustain us, other species and forms of life, and others of our own kind. The alternative to this ethical misprision is a perspective that he calls "moral ecology," a set of ethical duties and responsibilities that are not simply matters of human agreement or convention, but are called forth by the fundamental being and becoming of organic life itself, where ontological individuality and agency is inextricably bound up with connectedness, relationality, and dependency. This is a being and becoming of orchestral rather than mechanistic cause and effect; a world of creativity and emerging new modes of being alive. This alternative forms a bridge between the essays in part II and those in part IV. It also undergirds Donnelley's critical discussions of biotechnology, land use, and agricultural policies destructive of biodiversity, the mindset of economic instrumental values overshadowing all other values and considerations, and efforts to undermine an ecological worldview by attacking the scientific teaching of evolutionary biology in our public schools.

The book begins with an autobiographical prelude tracing the twin passions of the outdoors and fundamental philosophy. It also begins and ends with a tribute to the transforming influence of Father Francis Kline, a Cistercian monk and Abbot of Mepkin Abbey in South Carolina. The prelude on Klein and the postlude provide a glimpse of one of the most intense friendships of Donnelley's life, a friendship cut short by Father Kline's premature death in 2006. Although it left only a few traces in his written work, this friendship opened to Donnelley a dimension not so much of religion as of spirituality that had a surprising depth and worldly engagement he had not fully appreciated before. It did what Donnelley valued above all in the work of others and strove for in his own life and work—it brought together thinking and acting and it compelled, enabled, one to see in new ways. This was the unification of the man of ideas and the man of philanthropy; the philosopher and the fly-fisherman.

Ceara Donnelley

Bruce Jennings

Acknowledgments

The editors gratefully acknowledge permission to draw upon previously published material in the following chapters:

Chapter 5: "At the Center: Kansas on My Mind," *Hastings Center Report* 30, no. 1 (January/February 2000). Reprinted with the permission of The Hastings Center.

Chapter 6: "Scientists' Public Responsibilities," in Joel Cracraft and Francesca T. Grifo, eds., *The Living Planet in Crisis* (New York: Columbia University Press, 1999), 298–300. Reprinted with permission of Columbia University Press.

Chapter 8: "Transgenic Animals and 'Wild' Nature: A Landscape of Moral Ecology," in Jennifer Chesworth, ed., *The Ecology of Health: Identifying Issues and Alternatives* (Thousand Oaks, CA: Sage Publications, 1996), 47–58. Reprinted with permission of Sage Publications.

Chapter 9: "Water Wildness," *The Land Report*, no. 83 (Fall 2005). Reprinted with permission of the Land Institute.

Chapter 13: "Leopold's Wildness: Can Humans and Wolves Be at Home in the Adirondacks?," in Virginia A. Sharpe, Bryan G. Norton, and Strachan Donnelley, eds., *Wolves and Human Communities: Biology, Politics, and Ethics* (Washington, DC: Island Press, 2000), 191–98. © 2001 Island Press. Reprinted with permission of the Island Press, Washington, DC.

Chapter 14: "Leopold's Darwin: Climbing Mountains, Developing Land," in Stephen R. Kellert and Timothy J. Farnham, eds., *The Good in Nature and Humanity* (Washington, DC: Island Press, 2002), 161–74. © 2002 Island Press. Reprinted with permission of The Island Press, Washington, DC.

Chapter 18: "Hans Jonas, the Philosophy of Nature, and the Ethics of Responsibility," *Social Research* 56, no. 3 (1989): 635–57. © 1989 the New School for Social Research. Reprinted with permission of Johns Hopkins University Press.

The grouse "head shot" on the book's cover is taken from a print of a wood engraving by the contemporary artist Ansell Bray, and it serves as the avatar for the Center for Humans and Nature. The engraving was inspired by a nineteenth-century Makah grouse rattle. Connected to the land that is now Washington State, the Makah would have used this rattle during secular tribal ceremonies. Strachan Donnelley chose the image for the center because it expresses the complex interfusion of humans and nature, cultural understandings, and social practices—both past and present.

Bibliography

The Publications of Strachan Donnelley, 1978–2008

"Whitehead and Jonas: On Biological Organisms and Real Individuals." In *Organism, Medicine, and Metaphysics* (*Philosophy and Medicine* 8). Dordrecht: D. Reidel, 1978.

"Whitehead and Jonas: Organism, Causality, and Perception." *International Philosophy Quarterly* (Spring 1982).

"Whitehead and Nietzsche: Overcoming the Evil of Time." *Process Studies* (Spring 1982).

"The Philosopher's Poet: Boris Pasternak, *Dr. Zhivago,* and Whitehead's Cosmological Vision." *Process Studies* (Spring 1984).

"Human Selves, Chronic Illness, and the Ethics of Medicine." *Hastings Center Report* 18, no. 2 (April/May 1988).

"The Heart of the Matter." *Hastings Center Report* 19, no. 1 (January/February 1989).

"Speculative Philosophy, the Troubled Middle, and the Ethics of Animal Experimentation." *Hastings Center Report* 19, no. 2 (March/April 1989).

"Hans Jonas, the Philosophy of Nature, and the Ethics of Responsibility." *Social Research* 56, no. 3 (Autumn 1989).

"Hans Jonas, la Philosophie de la Nature et l'éthique de la Responsabilité." Translated by Robert Brisart. *Etudes Phénoménologique,* November 1989.

"Bioethics and the Use of Animals in Science." In Bruce Jennings, ed., *New Choices, New Responsibilities.* Nutley, NJ: Hoffman-LaRoche, 1990.

"The Economic Costs of End-of-Life Treatments: Should Patients Know?" *Decisions Near the End of Life,* Magazine no. 4. Newton, MA: Education Development Center; and Garrison, NY: Hastings Center, 1990.

"Epistemology, Ethics, and Evolution." *Behavior and Brain Sciences* 13, no. 1 (March 1990).

"Animals in Science: The Justification Issue." Section II in Strachan Donnelley and Kathleen Nolan, eds., "Animals, Science, and Ethics," Special Supplement, *Hastings Center Report* 20, no. 3 (May/June 1990).

"Future Directions." In Strachan Donnelley and Kathleen Nolan, eds., "Animals, Science, and Ethics," Special Supplement, *Hastings Center Report* 20, no. 3 (May/June 1990).

"The Troubled Middle *In Medias Res.*" Introduction to Strachan Donnelley and Kathleen Nolan, eds., "Animals, Science, and Ethics," Special Supplement, *Hastings Center Report* 20, no. 3 (May/June 1990).

"Hastings on the Adriatic." *Hastings Center Report* 20, no. 6 (November/December 1990).

"The Hastings Center Project: The Ethics of Animal Experimentation and Research." *Humane Innovations and Alternatives in Animal Experimentation,* no. 5 (1991).

"Political Sea Changes and Bioethics: Prague 1991." *Hastings Center Report* 21, no. 6 (November/December 1991).

"Homeless Families in Westchester: A Case Study in Individual, Social, and Professional Ethics." With Lillie Shortridge and Bruce Jennings. In Juanita K. Hunter, ed., *Nursing and Health Care for the Homeless.* Albany: State University of New York Press, 1993.

"Morally Good Sense" (Review of Mary Midgley, *Can't We Make Moral Judgments?*). *Hastings Center Report* 23, no. 1 (January/February 1993).

"Exploring Ethical Landscapes." Introduction to Strachan Donnelley, Charles McCarthy, and Rivers Singleton Jr., eds., "The Brave New World of Animal Biotechnology," Special Supplement, *Hastings Center Report* 24, no. 1 (January/February 1994).

"Philosophic and Ethical Challenges of Animal Biotechnology." In Strachan Donnelley, Charles McCarthy, and Rivers Singleton Jr., eds., "The Brave New World of Animal Biotechnology," Special Supplement, *Hastings Center Report* 24, no. 1 (January/February 1994).

"The Tracheostomy Tube—Commentary." *Hastings Center Report* 24, no. 2 (March/April 1994).

"Animals, Fish, and Philosophers." *Angler's Club Bulletin* 71, no. 3 (Spring 1994).

"Animals, Suffering, and Science" (Review of F. B. Orlans, *In the Name of Science*). *SCAW Newsletter* 16, no. 2 (Summer 1994).

"Descartes, Spinoza un Biotechnik mit Tieren." *Scheidewege,* Jahrang 24, 1994/95.

"Biotechnology's Ethical Challenges to IACUCS." In Kathryn A. L. Bayne, Molly Greene, and Ernest D. Prentice, eds., *Current Issues and New Frontiers in Animal Research: Proceedings of a Conference Sponsored by the Scientists Center for Animal Welfare and the University of Texas Health Science Center at San Antonio in San Antonio, Texas on December 8–9, 1994.* Greenbelt, MD: Scientists Center for Animal Welfare, 1995.

"Humans within Nature: Hans Jonas and the *Imperative of Responsibility.*" *Infectious Disease Clinics of North America* 9, no. 2 (June 1995).

"The Art of Moral Ecology." *Ecosystem Health* 1, no. 3 (September 1995).

"At the Center—'Porcine Affairs.'" *Hastings Center Report* 25, no. 5 (September/October 1995).

"Bioethical Troubles: Animal Individuals and Human Organisms." In Strachan Donnelley, ed., "The Legacy of Hans Jonas," Special Issue, *Hastings Center Report* 25, no. 7 (December 1995).

"The Legacy of Hans Jonas." In Strachan Donnelley, ed., "The Legacy of Hans Jonas," Special Issue, *Hastings Center Report* 25, no. 7 (December 1995).

"Transgenic Animals and 'Wild' Nature: A Landscape of Moral Ecology." In Jennifer Chesworth, ed., *The Ecology of Health: Identifying Issues and Alternatives.* Thousand Oaks, CA: Sage, 1996.

"At the Center—The Center of the Inbetween." *Hastings Center Report* 26, no. 5 (September/October 1996).

"Nature as Reality Check." *Hastings Center Report* 26, no. 6 (November/December 1996).

"At the Center: Hastings on Hudson." *Hastings Center Report* 27, no. 6 (November/December 1997).

"Human Nature, Views Of." *Encyclopedia of Applied Ethics.* London: Academic Press, 1998.

"Civic Responsibility and the Future of the Chicago Region." In Strachan Donnelley, ed., "Nature, Polis, Ethics: Chicago Regional Planning," Special Supplement, *Hastings Center Report* 28, no. 6 (November/December 1998).

"How and Why Animals Matter." *ILAR* 40, no. 2 (1999).

"Scientists' Public Responsibilities." In Joel Cracraft and Francesca T. Grifo, eds., *The Living Planet in Crisis.* New York: Columbia University Press, 1999.

"Leopold's Wildness: Can Humans and Wolves Be at Home in the Adirondacks?" In Virginia A. Sharpe, Bryan G. Norton, and Strachan Donnelley, eds., *Wolves and Human Communities: Biology, Politics, and Ethics.* Washington, DC: Island Press, 2000.

At the Center: Kansas on My Mind." *Hastings Center Report* 30, no. 1 (January/February 2000).

"Nature, Freedom, and Responsibility: Ernst Mayr and Isaiah Berlin." *Social Research* 67, no. 4 (Winter 2000).

"Animal Matters." In A. W. Galston and E. G. Shurr, eds., *New Dimensions in Bioethics.* Boston: Kluwer Academic, 2001.

"Human Nature, Views Of." In Ruth Chadwick, ed., *The Concise Encyclopedia Ethics of New Technologies.* London: Academic Press, 2001.

"Leopold's Darwin: Climbing Mountains, Developing Land." In Stephen R. Kellert and Timothy J. Farnham, eds., *The Good in Nature and Humanity.* Washington, DC: Island Press, 2001.

"Philosophy, Evolutionary Biology, and Ethics: Ernst Mayr and Hans Jonas." *Graduate Faculty Philosophy Journal* 23, no. 1 (2001).

"At the Center." *Hastings Center Report* 32, no. 3 (May/June 2002).

"Natural Responsibilities—Philosophy, Biology, and Ethics in Ernst Mayr and Hans Jonas." *Hastings Center Report* 32, no. 4 (July/August 2002).

"Tolstoy Rules." In "Mapping the Moral Landscape," *Brain Injury Source* 6, no. 4 (Summer 2003).

"Chartering the Earth for Life's Odyssey." *Worldviews: Environment, Culture, Religion* 8, no. 1 (2004).

"Water Wildness." *The Land Report,* no. 83 (Fall 2005).

"Ethical Boundaries of Animal Biotechnology: Descartes, Spinoza, and Darwin." In Charles S. Brown and Ted Toadvine, eds., *Nature's Edge: Boundary Explorations in Ecological Theory and Practice.* Albany: SUNY Press, 2007.

"The Path of Enlightened Ignorance: Alfred North Whitehead and Ernst Mayr." In Bill Vitek and Wes Jackson, eds., *The Virtues of Ignorance: Complexity, Sustainability, and the Limits of Knowledge.* Lexington: University Press of Kentucky, 2007.

"Hans Jonas and Ernst Mayr: On Organic Life and Human Responsibility." In Hava Tirosh-Samuelson and Christian Wiese, eds., *The Legacy of Hans Jonas: Judaism and the Phenomena of Life.* Boston: Brill Academic, 2008.

"Minding Nature, Minding Ourselves." *Minding Nature* 1, no. 1 (December 2008).

References

Allen, J. D., and A. S. Flecker. 1993. "Biodiversity Conservation in Running Waters." *BioScience* 43, no. 1: 32–43.

Berlin, I. 1969. *Four Essays on Liberty*. New York: Oxford University Press.

Brennan, A. 1992. "Moral Pluralism and the Environment." *Environmental Values* 1, no. 1: 15–33.

Christian, W. 1967. *An Interpretation of Whitehead's Metaphysics*. New Haven, CT: Yale University Press.

Darwin, C. [1859] 1993. *On the Origin of Species*. New York: Modern Library.

Descartes, R. 1969. *Principles of Philosophy*, Part 1, Section 51. In M. D. Wilson, ed., *The Essential Descartes*. New York: Mentor Books.

Donnelley, S. 1989. "Hans Jonas, the Philosophy of Nature, and the Ethics of Responsibility." *Social Research* 56, no. 3: 635–57.

Donnelley, S. 1995. "Bioethical Troubles: Animal Individuals and Human Organisms." In "The Legacy of Hans Jonas," *Hastings Center Report* 25, no. 7 (December): 21–29.

Donnelley, S. 1998a. "Human Nature, Views Of." In Ruth Chadwick, ed., *Encyclopedia of Applied Ethics*, vol. 2. London: Academic Press.

Donnelley, S., ed. 1998b. "Nature, Polis, Ethics: Chicago Regional Planning." Special Supplement, *Hastings Center Report* 28, no. 6 (November/December): S1–S41.

Donnelley, S. 2000. "Nature, Freedom, Responsibility: Ernst Mayr and Isaiah Berlin." *Social Research* 67, no. 4 (Winter): 1117–35.

Donnelley, S. 2002. "Natural Responsibilities: Philosophy, Biology, and Ethics in Ernst Mayr and Hans Jonas." *Hastings Center Report* 32, no. 4 (July/August): 36–43.

Donnelley, S., and K. Nolan, eds. 1990. "Animals, Science, and Ethics." Special Supplement, *Hastings Center Report* 20, no. 3 (May/June): 1–32.

Dresser, R. 1988. "Ethical and Legal Issues in Patenting New Animal Life." *Jurimetrics Journal* 28, no. 4: 399–435.

Eliade, M. 1985. *Cosmos and History: The Myth of the Eternal Return*. New York: Garland.

Evans, J. W., and A. Hollaender, eds. 1986. *Genetic Engineering of Animals: An Agricultural Perspective*. New York: Plenum.

Guthrie, W. K. C. 1987. *A History of Green Philosophy*, vol. 1 (The Earlier

Presocratics and the Pythagoreans). Cambridge: Cambridge University Press.

Heraclitus. 1991. *Fragments*. Text and translation by T. M. Robinson. Toronto: University of Toronto Press.

Jackson, W. 1980. *New Roots for Agriculture*. Lincoln: University of Nebraska Press.

Jackson, W. 2011. *Consulting the Genius of the Place: An Ecological Approach to a New Agriculture*. Berkeley, CA: Counterpoint.

Jonas, H. 1966. *The Phenomenon of Life: Toward a Philosophical Biology*. New York: Harper and Row.

Jonas, H. 1974. *Philosophical Essays: From Ancient Creed to Technological Man*. Upper Saddle River, NJ: Prentice-Hall.

Jonas, H. 1984. *The Imperative of Responsibility: In Search of an Ethics for the Technological Age*. Chicago: University of Chicago Press.

Klein, R. 2013. "Kansas' New Science Standards Make Evolution and Climate Change Key Part of Curriculum." *Huffington Post*, June 14, 2013. http://www.huffingtonpost.com/2013/06/13/kansas-science-standards-evolution-climate-change_n_3437257.html.

Krimsky, S. 1991. *Bioethics and Society: The Rise of Industrial Genetics*. Upper Saddle River, NJ: Prentice Hall.

Leclerc, I. 1965. *Whitehead's Metaphysic*. London: George Allen and Unwin.

Leopold, A. 1949. *A Sand County Almanac*. Oxford: Oxford University Press.

Leopold, A. 1991. *The River of the Mother of God*. Edited by S. L. Frader and J. B. Callicott. Madison: University of Wisconsin Press.

Mayr, E. 1982. *The Growth of Biological Thought: Diversity, Evolution, and Inheritance*. Cambridge, MA: Harvard University Press.

Mayr, E. 1991. *One Long Argument*. Cambridge, MA: Harvard University Press.

Mayr, E. 1997. *This Is Biology*. Cambridge, MA: Harvard University Press.

Meine, C. 1987. *Aldo Leopold: His Life and Work*. Madison: University of Wisconsin Press.

Midgley, M. 1993. *Can't We Make Moral Judgments?* London: Palgrave Macmillan.

Naess, A. 2008. *The Ecology of Wisdom: Writings of Arne Naess*. Edited by A. Drengson and B. Devall. Berkeley, CA: Counterpoint.

Norton, B. G. 1991. *Toward Unity among Environmentalists*. Oxford: Oxford University Press.

Owen, J. 2005. "Farming Claims Almost Half Earth's Land, New Maps Show." *National Geographic News*, December 9. http://news.nationalgeographic.com/news/2005/12/1209_051209_crops_map.html.

Pasternak, B. 1958. *Doctor Zhivago*. Translated by Max Hayward and Manya Harari. New York: Signet Books, New American Library.

Pasternak, B. 1959. "Translating Shakespeare." In *I Remember,* translated by Manya Harari. New York: Pantheon Books.

Pearce, M. 2012. "Kansas' Evolution Debate Just Keeps Evolving." *Los Angeles Times,* July 30. http://articles.latimes.com/2012/jul/30/nation/la-na-nn-kansas-schools-evolution-debate-20120729.

Ralston, H., III. 1989. *Philosophy Gone Wild.* Buffalo, NY: Prometheus Books.

Sharpe, V. A., B. Norton, and S. Donnelley, eds. 2000. *Wolves and Human Communities: Biology, Politics, and Ethics.* Washington, DC: Island Press.

Spinoza, B. 1951. *The Ethics.* Translated by R. H. M. Elwes. New York: Dover.

Verhoog, H. 1992. "The Concept of Intrinsic Value and Transgenic Animals." *Journal of Agricultural and Environmental Ethics* 5: 47–60.

Whitehead, A. N. [1925] 1948. *Science and the Modern World.* New York: Macmillan.

Whitehead, A. N. [1929] 1978. *Process and Reality.* Corrected edition. Edited by D. R. Griffin and D. W. Sherburne. New York: The Free Press.

Whitehead, A. N. 1933. *Adventures of Ideas.* New York: Mentor Books.

Whitehead, A. N. [1938] 1968. *Modes of Thought.* New York: The Free Press.

Index

death, 168, 199–200, 202
deer, 92–93
Deism, 22–23
Deity: Whitehead's concept of, 37
Descartes, René: "Age of Suspicion"
    and, 192; philosophic struggle with
    Spinoza, 129, 130, 158; substance
    philosophy and the problems of,
    22–23, 130–33. *See also* Cartesian
    dualism; substance philosophy
Des Plaines River, 18, 103
Diotima, 106
Divine intelligence, 24
DNA, 155, 156–57
Doctor Zhivago (Pasternak): history,
    art, eros, and ethics in, 200–207;
    life and cosmos in, 198–200;
    Pasternak's cosmological vision
    and, 194–98
dogmatism: in the debate between
    evolutionary biology and
    creationism, 36–37; the greater
    value of philosophic exploration,
    38–39; Francis Kline on, 8–9
Donnelley, Elliott, 74, 88
Donnelley, Gaylord, 223–24
Donnelley, Inanna, 67
Donnelley, Mimi, 9–10, 90
Donnelley, Naomi, 10
Donnelley, Strachan: accounts of
    the life, career, and philosophic
    pursuits of, 216–18, 219–24;
    essay form and, 221; final illness,
    activities, and death of, 214–16,
    218–19; Francis Kline and, 7–15,
    211–13, 217, 221, 222, 227; major
    influences on, 2, 3, 4, 120–21,
    129–30, 221, 222; memorial speech
    for Gaylord Donnelley, 223–24;
    reflections on childhood and
    baseball, 17–20; reflections on
    childhood in Libertyville, 103;
    reflections on the major concerns

and ideas engaged by, 1–4; study of
    Darwin, 222; study of philosophy,
    20, 222; transitions at age sixty-
    five, 73–77
Donnelley, Tegan, 41, 67, 216
Donnelley, Vivian, 41, 74
double flies, 80
doves, 103
droppers, 80
dualism: Heraclitian monism and,
    107; versus monism, 106–7;
    Platonic, 106–7. *See also* Cartesian
    dualism
duck decoy carvers, 88
ducks: on Fenwick Island, 70–71;
    hunting, 88–90

economic bottom line: critique
    of, 47–51; nature alive as an
    alternative to, 51–53
economic markets: animal
    biotechnology and issues of moral
    plurality, 58–60
ecosystems: Center for Humans and
    Nature meetings on the concept
    of, 78; ethics of biotechnology
    and, 127–28; Leopold's "humanly
    spirited" ethic and, 110–11;
    philosophical questions regarding,
    78–79; Whitehead's doctrine of
    mutual immanence and, 146
Edisto River, 74
efficacy of aim, 143
Elliston, Robert, 88
emergence/emergent properties:
    conservation ethics and, 27–28;
    in Mayr's Darwinian cosmology,
    158; as metaphor, 83; notion of
    biological species and, 25, 26–27;
    notions of individuality and, 158
Enormous Room, The (cummings), 2
environmental ethics: Donnelley's
    philosophic concerns, 220;

importance of Leopold to, 104. *See also* ethics
environmental problems: critique of the economic bottom line-ism approach to, 47–51; nature alive approach to, 51–53
epiphenomenalists, 159, 160–61, 191
epistemological pluralism, 86
eros/Eros: in *Doctor Zhivago*, 203–7; Socrates and, 106
essentialist thinking: concept of the individual, 156; critiqued by Mayr's Darwinian cosmology, 24, 25, 155, 156; evolutionary and ecological thinking as an alternative to, 62–63; overview, 62
ethical responsibility: contrast between Jonas and Mayr, 189–91; explication of Jonas's theory of, 183–89; Jonas's critique of modern technological civilization and, 179–81; Jonas's fundamental approach to philosophy, 191–93; Jonas's philosophy of purposive being and, 181–83. *See also* moral responsibility
ethics: challenges of animal biotechnology, 55–56; implications of wolf reintroduction in Adirondack Park, 95–96, 99–101; Leopold and, 96–99, 104–8, 112–13; Pasternak's indictment of the modern world in *Doctor Zhivago*, 207; philosophic cosmology and, 119–28, 130
Ethics (Spinoza), 3, 176, 178
Eugene Onegin (Pushkin), 104
Everliving Fire, 22, 107, 111
evil: conative individuals and, 125
evolutionary biology and ecology: as an alternative to essentialist thinking, 62–63; chance and conservative forces in, 121–22;

Darwinian cosmology and, 23–29; dogmatic debate with creationists, 36–37, 38–39; metaphor and, 82–83; scientists' public responsibilities, 44–46. *See also* Darwinian biology; Darwinian/neo-Darwinian cosmologies

Fenwick Island, 70–71
field theory, 145
fish: transgenic, 55–56. *See also* salmon; trout
fishing/fly-fishing: human involvement in wildness and, 67–70; human membership in the biotic community and, 87–88, 94, 110; Leopold and, 87–88; on the Little Snake River, 80–81; in Montana, 41; salmon fishing, 43, 68–70; trout fishing, 41, 67–68, 80–81; in Wisconsin, 40, 67–68; in Yellowstone Park, 41
fly-fishing philosophy: Donnelley on, 2; on human involvement in wildness, 67–72; on Kansas, fundamentalism, and the importance of understanding evolutionary biology and ecology, 40–43; on nature, organism, and metaphor, 78–86
Form of the Beautiful, 106
Form of the Good, 106, 111
forms, Platonic, 106
fossil fuels, 16
freedom: centered animal existence and, 175; Jonas's conception of metabolic organisms and, 169–70; Mayr's Darwinian cosmology and, 157
frog pond analogy, 33–35
fundamentalism/creationism, 40–43

genetic engineering: ethics of, 126–28
gestalt shifts, 98